Survey of American Poetry

Volume X
Midcentury to 1984;
General Indexes

Poetry Anthology Press

The World's Best Poetry

Volume   I   Home and Friendship
         II   Love
         III   Sorrow and Consolation
         IV   The Higher Life
         V   Nature
         VI   Fancy and Sentiment
         VII   Descriptive and Narrative
         VIII   National Spirit
         IX   Tragedy and Humor
         X   Poetical Quotations; General Indexes

Supplement   I   Twentieth Century English and American Verse, 1900-1929
         II   Twentieth Century English and American Verse, 1930-1950
         III   Critical Companion

Survey of American Poetry

Volume   I   Colonial Period, 1607-1765
         II   Revolutionary Era, 1766-1799
         III   Early 19th Century, 1800-1829
         IV   First Great Period, 1830-1860
         V   Civil War and Aftermath, 1861-1889
         VI   Twilight Interval, 1890-1912
         VII   Poetic Renaissance, 1913-1919
         VIII   Interval Between World Wars, 1920-1939
         IX   World War II and Aftermath, 1940-1950
         X   Midcentury to 1984; General Indexes

Survey of American Poetry

Volume X
Midcentury to 1984;
General Indexes

Prepared by
The Editorial Board, Roth Publishing, Inc.
(formerly Granger Book Co., Inc.)

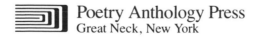 Poetry Anthology Press
Great Neck, New York

The acknowledgments on pages 371-373 constitute a continuation of this copyright notice.

CONTENTS

PREFACE xi
INTRODUCTION xii
EXPLANATORY NOTES xxii
CHARLES OLSON 1
    The Kingfishers 3
    I, Maximus of Gloucester, to You 9
    The Songs of Maximus 12
    Maximus, to Himself 16
    The Ring Of 17
    A Newly Discovered 'Homeric' Hymn 19
    Cole's Island 20
    The Moon Is the Number 18 22
LAWRENCE FERLINGHETTI 24
    He 25
    Constantly Risking Absurdity 29
    The Pennycandystore Beyond the El 30
    Monet's Lilies Shuddering 30
    The Third World 31
    Stone Reality Meditation 33
    An Elegy to Dispel Gloom 33
    Night Light 35
    I Am Waiting 36
DENISE LEVERTOV 40
    Crystal Night, fr. During the Eichmann Trial 41
    Pleasures 42
    Cancion 43
    The Goddess 43
    The Hands 44
    Scenes from the Life of the Peppertrees 45
    Wedding-Ring 46
    The Old Adam 47
    Rain Spirit Passing 49
    Come into Animal Presence 50
    Writing in the Dark 51
LOUIS SIMPSON 52
    American Poetry 53
    A Story About Chicken Soup 53
    Walt Whitman at Bear Mountain 54
    Hot Night on Water Street 56

My Father in the Night Commanding No 57
Chocolates 58
Physical Universe 59
KENNETH KOCH 63
In Bed, sels. 64
Mending Sump 69
Fresh Air 69
You Were Wearing 76
ROBERT CREELEY 79
For You 79
For My Mother: Genevieve Jules Creeley 79
The Name 83
Kore 84
The Language 85
The Rescue 86
A Gift of Great Value 87
The World 87
Fire 89
Time 90
Just Friends 91
For Fear 92
Song 93
ALLEN GINSBERG 94
Ode to Failure 96
Wales Visitation 99
My Sad Self 100
JAMES MERRILL 102
The Broken Home 103
The Mad Scene 106
The Parnassians 107
Last Words 107
An Urban Convalescence 108
The Octopus 110
The Peacock 111
Foliage of Vision 112
FRANK O'HARA 114
Steps 115
Poem ("Lana Turner Has Collapsed!") 116
Ode: Salute to the French Negro Poets 117
Why I Am Not a Painter 119

A True Account of Talking to the Sun at Fire Island 119
Hôtel Transylvanie 121
Les Etiquettes Jaunes 123
For James Dean 123
Poem ("When I Am Feeling Anxious and Sullen") 126
To John Ashbery 127
Autobiographia Literaria 127
W.D. SNODGRASS 128
   Mhtis Outis 129
   At the Park Dance 129
   April Inventory 130
   The Campus on the Hill 132
   Old Apple Trees 133
   Monet: "Les Nympheas" 134
   Inquest 135
   After Experience Taught Me... 137
   The Fuhrer Bunker, sels. 139
JOHN ASHBERY 143
   Endless Variation 144
   The Instruction Manual 145
   Some Trees 148
   Fear of Death 149
   The Tennis Court Oath 150
   A Boy 151
GALWAY KINNELL 153
   The Bear 154
   In Fields of Summer 157
   Cells Breathe in the Emptiness 157
   Vapor Trail Reflected in the Frog Pond 158
   For Robert Frost 160
   The Homecoming of Emma Lazarus 163
   The Comfort of Darkness 165
   Westport 166
W.S. MERWIN 167
   The Drunk in the Furnace 168
   The Asians Dying 169
   Fog-Horn 170
   The Removal 170
   The River of Bees 173
   Footprints on the Glacier 174

Leviathan 175
Lemuel's Blessing 176
Blind William's Song 179
ADRIENNE RICH 181
Diving into the Wreck 182
Planetarium 185
Snapshots of a Daughter-in-law 186
The Stranger 190
Orion 191
Prospective Immigrants Please Note 192
GREGORY CORSO 193
Marriage 194
Zizi's Lament 197
Uccello 198
The Mad Yak 199
The Vestal Lady on Brattle 199
But I Do Not Need Kindness 200
Hello 202
Waterchew! 202
Vision of Rotterdam 203
GARY SNYDER 204
Riprap 205
Milton by Firelight 206
Water 207
Things to Do Around a Lookout 207
Myths & Texts, sels. 208
Affluence 213
Bedrock 214
The Late Snow & Lumber Strike of the
    Summer of Fifty-Four 215
Four Poems for Robin 216
GEORGE STARBUCK 219
Of Late 220
Cora Punctuated with Strawberries 221
Outbreak of Spring 222
On First Looking in on Blodgett's Keats's
    "Chapman's Homer" 223
Bone Thoughts on a Dry Day 223
Unfriendly Witness 224
Communication to the City Fathers of Boston 225

SYLVIA PLATH 228
  Daddy 230
  Nick and the Candlestick 232
  A Birthday Present 234
  The Bee Meeting 236
  The Colossus 238
  Words 239
LEROI JONES ["IMAMU AMIRI BARAKA"] 240
  A Guerrilla Handbook 241
  Ka'Ba 241
  Political Poem 242
  In Memory of Radio 243
  Beautiful Black Women... 244
  Preface to a Twenty Volume Suicide Note 245
  An Agony. As Now. 246
  Goodbye! 247
N. SCOTT MOMADAY 248
  The Gourd Dancer 249
  The Delight Song of Tsoai-Talee 251
  Krasnopresnenskaya Station 252
DIANE WAKOSKI 253
  Patriotic Poem 254
  Sestina from the Home Gardener 256
  An Apology 257
  From a Girl in a Mental Institution 258
  Belly Dancer 260
  Picture of a Girl Drawn in Black and White 261
AL YOUNG 263
  One West Coast 264
  Identities 265
  Sweet Sixteen Lines 266
  Birthday Poem 267
NIKKI GIOVANNI 268
  Nikki-Rosa 269
  Kidnap Poem 270
  They Clapped 270
  Knoxville, Tennessee 272
  The Funeral of Martin Luther King, Jr. 272
  The World Is Not a Pleasant Place to Be 273
  Scrapbooks 273

LOUISE GLUCK 276
   Portrait 277
   The Garden 277
   Gretel in Darkness 280
   World Breaking Apart 281
JAMES TATE 282
   The Eagle Exterminating Company 283
   The Lost Pilot 284
   Pity Ascending with the Fog 285
   Stray Animals 286
   Read the Great Poets 287
   Letting Him Go 288
   Schizophrenic Kiss 289
ALICE WALKER 290
   Facing the Way 291
   Janie Crawford 292
   Now That the Book Is Finished 292
   Good Night Willie Lee, I'll See You in the Morning 293
GREGORY ORR 294
   The Voyages 295
   A Shelf Is a Ledge 295
   Gathering the Bones Together 296
   Making Beasts 299
MARK JARMAN 300
   Writing for Nora 301
   Lullaby for Amy 302
   Greensleeves 303
LORNA DEE CERVANTES 305
   Poem for the Young White Man Who Asked Me How I,
   an Intelligent, Well-Read Person, Could Believe in the War Between
   Races 306
JANICE MIRIKITANI 308
   Sing with Your Body 309
   Breaking Silence 310
GENERAL INDEXES 314

Preface

The publications of **Poetry Anthology Press** constitute a comprehensive conspectus of international verse in English designed to form the core of a library's poetry collection. Covering the entire range of poetic literature, these anthologies encompass all topics and national literatures.

Each collection, published in a multivolume continuing series format, is devoted to a major area of the whole undertaking and contains complete author, title, and first line indexes. Biographical data is also provided.

The World's Best Poetry, with coverage through the 19th century, is topically classified and arranged by subject matter. Supplements keep the 10 volume foundation collection current and complete.

Survey of American Poetry is an anthology of American verse arranged chronologically in 10 volumes. Each volume presents a significant period of American poetic history, from 1607 to 1984.

INTRODUCTION

The United States, during the years 1950 to 1980, experienced substantial and significant changes historically and poetically. During these three decades the country was involved in three foreign wars and endured domestic strife arising from such disparate sources as McCarthyism, the struggle for civil rights, and political scandals. Initially the turmoil caused the new generation of poets to retreat from political and social issues and to focus on exploring their own psyches, thereby creating a very personal poetry which changed the language they used to address all concerns. Many schools of poetry emerged as poets grouped to reevaluate tradition, to reexamine their basic assumptions about the world and about man, and to engage in prolific experimentation. To appreciate what motivated the variety of poetic responses during this period, it is important to understand the historical context in which these poets were writing.

During World War II, the United States and Russia fought together on the side of the Allies. After the war, however, relations between the two countries became confrontational when Russia actively extended its influence over other countries including China and many Eastern European nations. Fear of Communist expansion and the determination to counteract this aggression by defending threatened non-Communist countries became the primary factor in shaping U.S. foreign policy. The U.S. and Russia began building up their defenses; Russia test exploded an atomic bomb in September of 1949, and in January of 1950 Truman had the U.S. Atomic Energy Commission proceed with work on a Hydrogen bomb which would be vastly more powerful than the atomic bombs used in World War II. Despite their uncontrolled build up of arms, the potential of a nuclear war made both sides cautious. This struggle between Russia and the United States became known as the Cold War, a war which consisted only of threats, propaganda, and aid to weak countries rather than fullscale fighting. Both Truman and Eisenhower, the first two Presidents of the Cold War period, gave military support and billions of dollars to any country being threatened by Communism. In the midst of this shaky world situation, the United States soon was drawn into a major regional war against Communist forces in Korea. On June 25, 1950, troops from

Communist North Korea, backed by Russia, invaded South Korea. The United States successfully urged the United Nations Security Council to send military forces to Korea in order to counteract Communist aggression; Truman also sent troops under the command of General MacArthur. The defense of South Korea was initially effective as Communist North Korean forces were pushed north of the 38th parallel. However, this favorable situation was soon reversed as an overwhelming number of Chinese Communist troops compelled U.S. forces to retreat back to their original position below the 38th parallel, where both sides were held in a stalemate. Armistice talks to end the war began in 1951, but it was not until 1953 that the war finally ended.

The continuing spread of Communism sparked fear domestically as well, and the country began focusing on increased charges of Communist infiltration in the government. Two major espionage related trials implicating Americans in the early fifties crystallized these national security concerns. Julius and Ethel Rosenberg were convicted of passing atomic secrets to the Russians and were executed, and Alger Hiss, a former employee of the State Department, was tried for perjury in denying under oath that he delivered classified documents to a confessed Communist agent during the late thirties. He was subsequently convicted in a second trial. Capitalizing upon the furor, Senator Joseph McCarthy claimed that he had a list of people loyal to the Communist Party who were still in the State Department. The Senate Foreign Relations Committee found the charges groundless, but McCarthy caused a national sensation with other charges. He blamed many of the nation's problems on the secret presence of Communists in the government. Entertainers, clergy, journalists, and professors came under suspicion, and some organizations blacklisted people accused of Communist affiliations. McCarthyism began its decline after 1954, and McCarthy was eventually condemned for behavior unbecoming a Senator.

Although Americans were preoccupied with the fear of Communism, economically many were enjoying a postwar period of prosperity. Because military spending during World War II brought the United States out of the Great Depression of the thirties, major industries were able to resume production on a larger scale than before the war, while newer industries such as electronics, plastics, and frozen foods were booming. The shortage of goods during the war was a major factor in creating the huge market that now existed for American products. Between 1950 and 1960 the U.S. population grew by about 28 million, and labor unions became stronger, procuring higher wages and better benefits for their members. This period of prosperity enabled many Americans to enjoy a new type of lifestyle.

After the war, millions of Americans were able to afford new housing, and construction companies began building clusters of housing developments in the suburbs. As more people moved to the suburbs, there was a rise in automobile ownership since most suburbs lacked adequate mass transportation. By 1960 three quarters of all American families owned a car. Increased automobile ownership led to the building of superhighways and increased tourism. Motels, fast food restaurants, and gas stations were built to fill the needs of tourists. Technology changed Americans' lives in other ways. Television, which was experimental before World War II, became a commonplace feature of almost every American home during the 1950's. Television watching became one of the most popular leisure activities, and new appliances such as automatic washers, driers, dishwashers, and garbage disposals made household work much easier.

Though the general prosperity changed many Americans' lives for the better, millions of others continued to live in poverty, especially a large percentage of Blacks. The disparity in wealth distribution throughout the country triggered a period of social protest that has continued to the present. After World War II, many Blacks and whites joined in a common cause to extend civil rights to Blacks. This movement brought about several Supreme Court decisions which attacked racial discrimination, such as the ruling against compulsory segregation in public schools (Brown vs. The Board of Education of Topeka, 1954); however, progress came very slowly. In 1955 Martin Luther King, Jr. organized demonstrations to protest discrimination in employment, housing, education, and other areas, and by the early sixties the Civil Rights Movement became a major domestic issue. This movement was also the precursor of other organized movements in the seventies aimed at gaining equality for minorities such as American Indians, Hispanics, and women. John F. Kennedy, who became President in 1961, urged Congress to pass legislation to outlaw discrimination based on race. When Kennedy was assassinated in 1963 and Vice President Lyndon B. Johnson became President, Johnson persuaded Congress to pass many civil rights laws. In addition, Johnson envisioned a Great Society and created a domestic program called the War on Poverty in which he convinced Congress to provide financial aid for the needy. However, despite such government aid, poverty remained a major problem, particularly in the large cities. Discontent grew, and during the mid sixties riots were staged in the ghettos of Detroit, New York, Los Angeles, Chicago, and other cities. More riots broke out in 1968 when Martin Luther King, Jr. was assassinated.

The Vietnam war was another source of domestic turmoil for the U.S. during the sixties. The war began in 1957 as a battle for control of South Vietnam by Communist and non-Communist governments. During the late fifties and early sixties, Presidents Eisenhower and Kennedy sent military aid and advisors to support the South Vietnamese against Communist aggression. Not long after Johnson became President, the Communists threatened to overthrow the South Vietnamese government. In response to this, Johnson sent hundreds of thousands of American troops and, by the mid sixties, the United States was completely involved in the Vietnam war. The majority of Americans at first supported the war effort, but public opinion shifted sharply by the late sixties. Throughout the country college students and others staged anti-war demonstrations. In 1968 Richard Nixon was elected President partly because he promised to end the United States' involvement in Vietnam, but U.S. troops remained in the war for the rest of the decade. It was not until 1973 that Nixon removed the last American ground troops; two years later South Vietnam fell to the Communists.

One of the few high notes during the troubled sixties was provided by space exploration. On May 5, 1961, Alan B. Shepard, Jr. became the first American in space. During the sixties, the United States and the Soviet Union competed with each other in an effort to land the first person on the moon. The Americans won that distinction on July 20, 1969, as millions of people watched Neil Armstrong on television as he first stepped foot on the moon.

With the seventies, however, came more unrest in the form of political scandals. Though there were many cases of corruption on the local and the state level, the most notorious instances were on the federal level. In 1973 Spiro Agnew, Nixon's Vice President, came under criminal investigation. The investigation covered the time that he held office in Maryland and the time he was Vice President. A federal grand jury heard charges that he was involved in widespread extortion in Maryland, and on October 10, 1973, he resigned from the Vice Presidency. Within eleven months Nixon's resignation would follow. In 1972 campaign workers for Nixon's reelection committee committed burglary at the Democratic Political Headquarters in the Watergate building complex in Washington D.C. Nixon was later charged with covering up the burglary and other illegal activities. In July of 1974 articles of impeachment were voted against him. As incriminating evidence mounted, and it became clear that the Senate would remove him from office, Nixon became the first U.S. President to resign from office. Gerald Ford, who was appointed Vice President upon Agnew's resignation, became President and pardoned Nixon for all federal crimes he might have committed during his term in office.

In 1976 James ("Jimmy") Carter was elected President. He worked to improve America's relationship with China and Russia, continuing the work that Nixon had begun in the early seventies. In 1979, the U.S. and China established diplomatic relations. Later that year, Carter and Leonid Brezhnev, the leader of the Soviet Communist Party, signed a treaty limiting the use of nuclear arms between the two nations. However, when the Soviets invaded Afghanistan in late 1979, U.S. and Soviet relations became strained once again. Troubles in the Middle East, an area extremely important to U.S. security, also posed problems for the U.S. during Carter's presidency. In 1978 Carter arranged meetings at Camp David between President Anwar Sadat of Egypt and President Menachem Begin of Israel, which resulted in the first Arab-Israeli peace agreement. Then in February of 1979 a revolution to overthrow the Shah of Iran broke out. In protest of American aid to the deposed Shah, revolutionaries took over the U.S. Embassy in Teheran in November of the same year. Hostages were taken, and the crisis continued into 1981.

Domestically, America's population and industry continued to grow during the seventies and with it so did environmental pollution. Wastes and smoke from factories and fumes from cars filled the nation's air and rivers. Though the government passed many anti-pollution laws in response to national protests, the problem remained severe. Industries, cars, and households also placed a drain on the national energy supply. In 1973 and 1979 oil shortages caused by turmoil in the Middle East curtailed power for industry, heat for homes, and gasoline for motor vehicles. Fuel shortage was just one problem that America faced as the postwar economic boom lapsed into a recession that would continue into the eighties.

American poets at the midcentury point continued to be influenced by the devastating effects of World War II (the development of nuclear weaponry and the possibility of species-wide genocide), as well as by

McCarthyism, the Cold War tension, and the Korean War. The ongoing state of world strife prompted the new generation of poets to focus, almost exclusively, on the individual. Poets turned to man's inner world as their prime source of material, experimenting with new verse forms in an effort to develop their individual style and their personal response to the world. Poets explored their flaws, needs, and violent impulses in a more open fashion than ever before and became interested in myth, dreams, and the unconscious.

Poets such as Galway Kinnell and W.S. Merwin explored the subconscious workings of the mind through literary and psychological archtype. The writings of Freud and Jung held great interest for these poets. However, the style of their poetry was still entrenched in complex rhyme schemes and utilized such literary devices as irony and paradox which caused it to be classed with the academic verse popular in the forties. Another group of introspective poets, belonging to the Confessional School, moved radically away from rhetorical devices in their poetry, using their autobiography in addition to literary allusions and substituting their own voices for dramatic personae. Because of the personal nature of the subject matter, poets such as W.D. Snodgrass and Sylvia Plath seem to be revealing themselves completely to their readers as the typical Confessional themes of inadequacy, loss, sickness, and insanity would suggest. However, in order to create art out of these experiences, the poet has to manipulate his original emotions to fit his artistic design. The result is a critical reworking of the poet's experience and, ironically, not the spontaneous feelings that initially prompted the poem. Nevertheless, this school is responsible for a more candid expression of subject matters, such as sexuality and suicide, which had previously been approached indirectly through allusion, metaphor, and other figures of speech, if at all.

The personal trend in poetry is also exemplified by the highly subjective poetry of the New York school. Rather than use plot, character or symbol, these poets created their verse with randomly placed perceptions, similar to stream of consciousness writing. However, in poetry after the midcentury, there was no guarantee of an underlying layer of meaning with which to make sense of the confusing outward distortions. John Ashbery, Kenneth Koch, Frank O'Hara, Barbara Guest, and James Schuyler comprised the nucleus of the New York school and are the poets best known for purposely avoiding consistency of meaning while focusing on abstract images and specialized knowledge, especially in the fields of art and music.

Ashbery, Koch, and O'Hara met at Harvard University and were associated with the Poet's Theater, an experimental drama group of the early fifties. Inspired by the paintings of such abstract expressionist artists as Jackson Pollock and Willem de Kooning, the poets moved to New York and immersed themselves in the modern art scene. In New York they met Schuyler and Guest and worked with the Living Theatre, a controversial drama group with a leftist bent. Though some of their poetry is difficult to understand, the collage-like patterns and the experiments with language produced by these poets was an attempt to free the poet's imagination and to revitalize poetry which the new generation of poets felt had settled into stereotyped, traditional forms.

Experimenting with poetic forms has been at the forefront of activity during the modern era, and Charles Olson, through his influential essay, "Projective Verse" (1950), spurred on the third generation of modern poets to continue to try new ways of writing and thinking about poetry. Olson argued for a free form verse where the meter of the line is dictated by the artist's breath and heartbeat rather than by an artificially imposed rhyme scheme, such as iambic pentameter. The form of the line should be tailored to the artist's subject matter and to his biological and emotional state rather than twisted to fit into a traditional mold. It is a poetics designed for and by the individual. Olson believed that a poem should transfer energy from the poet to the reader; therefore, it should be written in the active tense rather than in a passive, descriptive mode. He also felt that experience should be valued for its own sake and not as a symbol of another reality. This antisymbolist stance became widely accepted among the third generation moderns. Olson used Ezra Pound and William Carlos Williams as his models and was one of the first to espouse the importance of those poets to the younger generation.

During the early fifties, Olson, Robert Duncan, and Robert Creeley taught at Black Mountain College in North Carolina, an experimental school which became the meeting ground for a lot of avant-garde talent such as John Cage, Merce Cunningham, and Buckminster Fuller, as well as for poets dissatisfied with conservative, academic verse. The Black Mountain poets were also interested in verse rooted in the American experience and reflecting American speech patterns. The direction that the Black Mountain school was taking poetry held an attraction for many poets such as Denise Levertov, and the school was also instrumental in fostering new talent by publishing them in two journals, the *Black Mountain Review* and *Origin*. The impact of this group spread slowly, but the poets who were published in the journals kept in touch through letters and developed the principles of the movement in this fashion. By the mid sixties, free form verse became the norm and exerted great influence on many poets, such as Louis Simpson who revamped the style in which he wrote, as well as on the New York poets and the Beats of the late fifties and early sixties. The Beat poets, in fact, were showcased in the last issue of the *Black Mountain Review* in which Allen Ginsberg was the contributing editor.

The Beat poets shared the Black Mountain poets' interest in Pound and Williams, who wrote an introduction to Ginsberg's "Howl," and were influenced by free form verse, which they used to create a very personal poetry by tuning into their subconscious and writing from their own inner rhythms. What distinguishes the Beats is their objection to the conservatism of the times on grounds broader than those which motivated the New York and Black Mountain poets. The New York and Black Mountain poets desired only to liberate poetry from the stale bonds of the past. The Beats, however, set themselves in opposition to a whole society which was caught in the grips of Communist hysteria and ultraconservatism.

The Beat movement started in New York, centering around Greenwich Village. The movement grew to Denver and New Orleans, as the Beats made their nonstop trips to these cities; however, it was in San Francisco that they attracted the most attention. Allen Ginsberg, Jack Kerouac, Gregory Corso, and Gary Snyder, among others, congregated there, many giving the type of readings that Lawrence Ferlinghetti was already becoming known for: poetry performances accompanied by music, often jazz, which emphasized the oral aspect of poetry in the tradition of Vachel Lindsay. When the Beats arrived in San Francisco they lent their energy to a poetic renaissance which had already begun. In crowded bookshops and cafes, where intellectuals of all persuasions gathered, poetry was being sold and recited and literature was being discussed and written. The Beats admired the anti-traditionalist stance of such San Francisco poets as Kenneth Patchen, Kenneth Rexroth, and Karl Shapiro, with whom they shared similar lifestyles, friendships, values, and a common rejection of the complacent middle class of the fifties. However, the Beats maintained a distinct identity through their fascination with drugs, mysticism, and meditation as a means to liberate their unconscious mind. Many of the Beats believed that society could be transformed if one's inner self were freed and made to speak for itself. They believed that society was rooted in the individual. Therefore, the Beats went to great lengths to assert their individuality through their lifestyle and through their poetry, many times shocking their audiences with obscenities, blasphemies or disclosures of intimate personal details. The Beats' lifestyle and literature were influenced by the poetry of Whitman and Blake, Black culture, jazz, Mexican peasant culture, and Orientalism.

The Beats were not actively political until they became absorbed into the Hippie movement and the Civil Rights movement of the sixties, but as early as the late fifties a new type of political and angry poetry appeared with the emergence of the Black power movement. This poetry was militant, proud, and had a strong sense of community. Some of the poetry came from the streets, some from literary tradition. Leroi Jones, who associated with the Beats and admired the tenets of projective verse, became a Black Nationalist, worked with other Black artists, and used his poetry to focus his anger on racial issues. During the sixties and the seventies, with the emergence of the Women's Liberation Movement and the Civil Rights Movement, poets such as Adrienne Rich, Alice Walker, N. Scott Momaday, Nikki Giovanni, Janice Mirikitani, and Lorna Dee Cervantes explored their identity and their experience of being part of a minority class—be it Black, female, American Indian, Asian-American or Hispanic—in their poetry.

Although there were many schools of poetry which appeared since midcentury, as poets banded together to experiment and share with each other, there were poets that did not fall solidly into any of the categories discussed. James Merrill continued to write in a traditional verse style, W.S. Merwin began writing in traditional style and then moved on to free form, Diane Wakoski experimented with "deep imagism" in which images are depicted as they are distorted by the unconscious, and many poets, especially the younger ones—James Tate, Al Young, Louise Gluck, Gregory Orr, Mark Jarman—utilize an eclectic approach. They are not readily identified as being part of the established groups; instead, they integrate various influences into their verse. The growth of poetry throughout the fifties, sixties and seventies, in fact, has depended on this process of drawing on and assimilating such sources as romanticism, surrealism, Zen Buddhism, and the numerous literary traditions of world poetry which had been brought to the attention of American poets through the prolific translations of such poets as Merwin and Snyder. Poets of each generation typically find past solutions inadequate to deal with their present situation;

therefore, each generation must create their own response through reinterpretation of the past, an openness to new influences, and experimentation. This was the process of growth contemporary poetry underwent during the fifties, sixties and seventies and how poetry, no doubt, must continue to evolve in the future.

EXPLANATORY NOTES

The present anthology is arranged chronologically. Its aim is (a) to provide the reader with a sense of the development of verse during the historical period and (b) to help place select works within the span of each poet's creative output. Accordingly, it lists the poets in sequence—by date of birth—and, wherever possible, gives the date of individual poems.

Words are spelled as they appear in the original sources; punctuation, capitalization, and usage are treated the same way. No attempt has been made to reconcile resulting inconsistencies. This, however, should not hinder a basic appreciation of the material. In some cases, the poems entered constitute selections; these are chosen to convey to the reader the essence of a major work which is too long to publish in the context of the anthology.

Authors, titles, and first lines are arranged in a single alphabetical listing in the Index. Poet names are in boldface; poem titles are in italics; and poem first lines are enclosed in quotation marks. When a title and first line are identical, only the title is given.

CHARLES OLSON [1910-1970]

Charles Olson was born on December 27 in Worcester, Massachusetts. His father, a postman, was born in Sweden; his mother was Irish-American. Charles was their only son. Although the family lived in Worcester, they summered in Gloucester, a coastal town known primarily for its fishing industry. Their summer house was in a community called Dogtown which is separated from the rest of Gloucester by a channel flowing into the inner harbor. This small community became the ground from which Olson's *magnum opus, The Maximus Poems*, would spring. But that would come much later. In 1928, Olson was just graduating high school where he had been class president, valedictorian and a prize winning orator. He then attended Wesleyan University for five years where he continued to excel in orating, acting, editing a college newspaper, playing goalie on the soccer team, and graduating Phi Beta Kappa. In 1933, he left Wesleyan with a Masters degree. He taught at Clark University for a few years before beginning work on a Ph.D. in a new American studies program at Harvard, where he had also briefly taught. He left Harvard, finished with his courses but without receiving his degree, in 1938 when he was awarded a Guggenheim Fellowship. He used this opportunity to work on a critical study of Melville. Although he amassed four hundred pages on the subject, the result was a slim, but highly original book, *Call Me Ishmael* (1947).

During World War II Olson served in the Office of War Information. Not too long afterwards, he resigned from the O.W.I., annoyed with their ineptitude, and became an advisor and strategist for the Democratic Party during Franklin Roosevelt's campaign for a fourth term. When Roosevelt died, Olson was informally offered a high governmental position under the Truman Administration; however, Olson declined and left politics permanently in order to write. His first poem was published in 1945. In 1946, the *Partisan Review* published Olson's defense of Ezra Pound who was being tried at that time for treason. The article is called, "This Is Yeats Speaking," and it was written after Olson had spent many hours speaking with Pound. Olson acted as reporter for the *Review* in order to be admitted into Pound's first arraignment.

In 1948 Olson took a teaching job, vacated by his close friend Edward Dahlberg, at Black Mountain College. Black Mountain had been founded in 1933 to provide an alternative to traditional methods of education and had already attracted the philosopher John Dewey and the artist Willem de Kooning. Olson became the rector of the college in 1951. He received a grant from the Wenner-Gren Foundation in 1952 to study Mayan hieroglyphics in Yucatan. Both *Mayan Letters* and the essay "Human Universe" were written during that period. When Black Mountain College closed in 1956, Olson returned to Gloucester to work on *The Maximus Poems*. The time he spent writing in self-imposed poverty and isolation came to an end in 1963 when he accepted a teaching position with the State University of New York at Buffalo in order to support his wife and son. He taught there until 1965 when he returned to Gloucester.

Two weeks into the fall semester during 1969, Olson began teaching at the University of Connecticut; however, the pain he had been experiencing in his left ear was debilitating and forced him to be hospitalized. After much testing, it was concluded that Olson had cancer of the liver which could not be treated. The cancer, it seems, had spread throughout his large frame—he was six foot eight. During the course of his hospitalization, the doctors discovered that the pain he had felt in his ear was due, ironically enough, to the maximus nerve.

Charles Olson was a tremendously influential figure in contemporary poetry. He had had many enthusiastic students who loved and revered him. One such student, Charles Boer, was saying goodbye to Olson, his friend and mentor, who already had slipped into the coma from which he would not emerge. According to Boer, among the incoherent words the poet mumbled came one word loud and clear—"Wonderful...wonderful."

The Kingfishers [*1949*]

1
What does not change / is the will to change

He woke, fully clothed, in his bed. He
remembered only one thing, the birds, how
when he came in, he had gone around the rooms
and got them back in their cage, the green one first,
she with the bad leg, and then the blue,
the one they had hoped was a male

Otherwise? Yes, Fernand, who had talked lispingly of Albers & Angkor
    Vat.
He had left the party without a word. How he got up, got into his coat,
I do not know. When I saw him, he was at the door, but it did not matter,
he was already sliding along the wall of the night, losing himself
in some crack of the ruins. That it should have been he who said, "The
    kingfishers!
who cares
for their feathers
now?"

His last words had been, "The pool is slime." Suddenly everyone,
ceasing their talk, sat in a row around him, watched
they did not so much hear, or pay attention, they
wondered, looked at each other, smirked, but listened,
he repeated and repeated, could not go beyond his thought
"The pool   the kingfishers' feathers were wealth   why
did the export stop?"

It was then he left

2
I thought of the E on the stone, and of what Mao said
la lumiere"
        but the kingfisher
de l'aurore"
        but the kingfisher flew west
est devant nous!

he got the color of his breast
from the heat of the setting sun!

The features are, the feebleness of the feet (syndactylism of the 3rd & 4th
    digit)
the bill, serrated, sometimes a pronounced beak, the wings
where the color is, short and round, the tail
inconspicuous.

But not these things are the factors. Not the birds.
The legends are
legends. Dead, hung up indoors, the kingfisher
will not indicate a favoring wind,
or avert the thunderbolt. Nor, by its nesting,
still the waters, with the new year, for seven days.
It is true, it does nest with the opening year, but not on the waters.
It nests at the end of a tunnel bored by itself in a bank. There,
six or eight white and translucent eggs are laid, on fishbones
not on bare clay, on bones thrown up in pellets by the birds.

                On these rejectamenta
(as they accumulate they form a cup-shaped structure) the young are born.
And, as they are fed and grow, this nest of excrement and decayed fish
    becomes
                    a dripping, fetid mass
Mao concluded:
                nous devons
                        nous lever
                                et agir!

        3
When the attentions change/the jungle
leaps in
            even the stones are split
                            they rive
Or,
enter
that other conqueror we more naturally recognize
he so resembles ourselves

But the E
cut so rudely on that oldest stone
sounded otherwise,
was differently heard

as, in another time, were treasures used:

(and, later, much later, a fine ear thought
a scarlet coat)

      "of green feathers   feet, beaks and eyes
      of gold

      "animals likewise,
      resembling snails

      "a large wheel, gold, with figures of unknown four-foots,
      and worked with tufts of leaves, weight
      3800 ounces

      "last, two birds, of thread and featherwork, the quills
      gold, the feet
      gold, the two birds perched on two reeds
      gold, the reeds arising from two embroidered mounds,
      one yellow, the other
      white.
          "And from each reed hung
          seven feathered tassels.

In this instance, the priests,
(in dark cotton robes, and dirty,
their dishevelled hair matted with blood, and flowing wildly
over their shoulders)
rush in among the people, calling on them
to protect their gods

And all now is war
where so lately there was peace,
and the sweet brotherhood, the use
of tilled fields.

4

Not one death but many
not accumulation but change, the feed-back proves, the feed-back is
the law
        Into the same river no man steps twice
        When fire dies air dies
        No one remains, nor is, one

Around an appearance, one common model, we grow up
many. Else how is it,
if we remain the same,
we take pleasure now
in what we did not take pleasure before? love
contrary objects? admire and/or find fault? use
other words, feel other passions, have
nor figure, appearance, disposition, tissue
the same?
        To be in different states without a change
        is not a possibility

We can be precise. The factors are
in the animal and/or the machine the factors are
communication and/or control, both involve
the message. And what is the message? The message is
a discrete or continuous sequence of measurable events distributed in time

is the birth of air, is
the birth of water, is
a state between
the origin and
the end, between
birth and the beginning of
another fetid nest

is change, presents
no more than itself

And the too strong grasping of it,
when it is pressed together and condensed,
loses it

This very thing you are

II

They buried their dead in a sitting posture
serpent   cane   razor   ray of the sun

And she sprinkled water on the head of the child, crying
"Cioa-coatl! Cioa-coatl!"
with her face to the west

Where the bones are found, in each personal heap
with what each enjoyed, there is always
the Mongolian louse

The light is in the east. Yes. And we must rise, act. Yet
in the west, despite the apparent darkness (the whiteness
which covers all), if you look, if you can bear, if you can, long enough

as long as it was necessary for him, my guide
to look into the yellow of that longest-lasting rose

so you must, and, in that whiteness, into that face, with what candor, look

and, considering the dryness of the place
the long absence of an adequate race

(of the two who first came, each a conquistador, one healed, the other
tore the eastern idols down, toppled
the temple walls, which, says the excuser
were black from human gore)

hear
hear, where the dry blood talks
where the old appetite walks

la piu saporita et migliore
che si possa truovar al mondo

where it hides, look
in the eye how it runs
in the flesh/chalk

> but under these petals
> in the emptiness
> regard the light, contemplate
> the flower

whence it arose

> with what violence benevolence is bought
> what cost in gesture justice brings
> what wrongs domestic rights involve
> what stalks
> this silence

> what pudor pejorocracy affronts
> how awe, night-rest and neighborhood can rot
> what breeds where dirtiness is law
> what crawls
> below

III

I am no Greek, hath not th'advantage.
And of course, no Roman:
he can take no risk that matters,
the risk of beauty least of all.

But I have my kin, if for no other reason than
(as he said, next of kin) I commit myself, and,
given my freedom, I'd be a cad
if I didn't. Which is most true.

It works out this way, despite the disadvantage.
I offer, in explanation, a quote:
si j'ai du goût, ce n'est guères
que pour la terre et les pierres

Despite the discrepancy (an ocean   courage   age)
this is also true: if I have any taste
it is only because I have interested myself
in what was slain in the sun

    I pose you your question:
shall you uncover honey/where maggots are?

    I hunt among stones

I, Maximus of Gloucester, To You

By ear, he sd.

But that which matters, that which insists, that which will last
where shall you find it, my people, how, where shall you listen
when all is become billboards, when all, even silence, is
when even the gulls,
my roofs,
when even you, when sound itself

        Where, Portygee Hill, she sang
        and over the water, at Tarr's
        (the water glowed, the light west,
        black, gold, the tide
        outward at evening

        The fixed bells rang, their voices
        came like boats over the oil-slicks,
        like milkweed hulls

        And a man slumped,
        attentionless,
        against pink shingles

            (sea city

2

one loves only form,
and form only comes
into existence when
the thing is born

     born of yourself, born
     of hay and cotton struts
     of street-pickings, wharves, weeds
     you carry in, my bird

        of a bone of a fish
        of a straw, or will
        of a color, of a bell
        of yourself, torn

        (o bird
        o kylix, o
        Antony of Padua
        sweep low, bless
        the roofs,
        the gentle steep ones
        on whose ridge-poles the gulls sit,
        from whey they depart

        And the flake-racks
        of my city

3

love is form, and cannot be without
important substance (the weight, say, 50 carats, each one of us, perforce,
our own goldsmith's scale (feather to feather added,
and what is mineral, what is curling hair, what string
you carry in your nervous beak, these
make bulk, these, in the end, are
sum
        (o my lady of good voyage
        in whose arm,

in whose left arm rests no boy
but a carefuly carved wood, a painted
schooner
   a delicate mast, a bow-sprit
                             for forwarding

4

the underpart is, though stemmed, uncertain
is, as sex is, as moneys are, facts
to be dealt with as the seas is, the demand
that they be played by, that they only can be, that they must
be played by, said he coldly,
the ear

But love is not easy,
and how shall you know,
New England, now
that pejorocracy is here, now
that street-cars, o Oregon, twitter
in the afternoon, offend
a gold-black loin?

how shall you strike,
swordfisherman, the blue-red back
when, last night, your aim
was mu-sick, mu-sick, mu-sick
and not the cribbage game?

    (o Gloucesterman,
    weave your birds and fingers
    new, your roof-tops
    clean shat on, racks
    sunned on

    American, braid
    with others like you, such
    extricable surface
    as faun and oral satyr lesbos vase
    o kill kill kill kill kill

          those
          who advertise you
          out

     5

in, the bow-sprit, bird, beak
in, the act is in, goes in, the form
what holds, what you make, what is
the object, strut, strut

what you are, what you must be, what you can
right now hereinafter erect

          Off-shore, by islands in the blood, I, Maximus, tell you
          (as I see it, over the waters, from this place
          where I am, where I hear, where I can still hear

          from where I carry you a feather
          as though, sharply, I picked up,
          in the first of morning delivered you,
          a jewel, it flashing
          more than a wing, than any old romantic thing
          than memory, than place, than any thing other than

          that which you also carry, than that which is
          (call it a nest) around the bend of, call it
          the next
          second

The Songs of Maximus

SONG 1

          colored pictures
of all things to eat: dirty
postcards

And words, words, words
all over everything
      No eyes or ears left
to do their own doings (all

invaded, appropriated, outraged, all senses

including the mind, that worker on what is

          And that other sense
made to give even the most wretched, or any of us, wretched,
that consolation (greased
                lulled
even the street-cars

song

SONG 2

    all
wrong
    And I am asked—ask myself (I, too, covered
with the gurry of it) where
shall we go from here, what can we do
when even the public conveyances
sing?
    how can we go anywhere,
even cross-town
        how get out of anywhere (the bodies
all buried
in shallow graves?

SONG 3

    This morning of the small snow
I count the blessings, the leak in the faucet
which makes of the sink time, the drop
of the water on water as sweet
as the Seth Thomas
in the old kitchen

my father stood in his drawers to wind (always
he forgot the 30th day, as I don't want to remember
the rent
      a house these days
so much somebody else's,
especially,
Congoleum's

        Or the plumbing,
that it doesn't work, this I like, have even used paper clips
as well as string to hold the ball up   And flush it
with my hand
        But that the car doesn't, that no moving things moves
without that song I'd void my ear of, the musickracket
of all ownership...

        Holes
in my shoes, that's all right, my fly
gaping, me out
at the elbows, the blessing
                that difficulties are once more

        "In the midst of plenty, walk
        as close to
        bare
            In the face of sweetness,
        piss
                In the time of goodness,
        go side, go
        smashing, beat them, go as
        (as near as you can

        tear

        In the land of plenty, have
        nothing to do with it
                    take the way of
        the lowest,
        including your legs, go
        contrary, go

sing

SONG 4

I know a house made of mud & wattles,
I know a dress just sewed
                    (saw the wind
blow its cotton
against her body
from the ankle
        so!
it was Nike
        And her feet: such bones
I could have had the tears
that lovely pedant had
who couldn't unwrap it himself, had to ask them to, on the schooner's deck

and he looked,
the first human eyes to look again
at the start of human motion (just last week
300,000,000 years ago
                    She
was going fast
across the square, the water
this time of year, that
scarce

And the fish

SONG 5

I have seen faces of want,
and have not wanted the FAO: Appleseed
's gone back to
what any of us
New England

SONG 6

you sing, you

who also

wants

Maximus, To Himself

I have had to learn the simplest things
last. Which made for difficulties.
Even at sea I was slow, to get the hand out, or to cross
a wet deck.
      The sea was not, finally, my trade.
But even my trade, at it, I stood estranged
from that which was most familiar. Was delayed,
and not content with the man's argument
that such postponement
is now the nature of
obedience,
      that we are all late
      in a slow time,
      that we grow up many
      And the single
      is not easily
      known

It could be, though the sharpness (the *achiote*)
I note in others,
makes more sense
than my own distances. The agilities

      they show daily
      who do the world's
      businesses
      And who do nature's
      as I have no sense
      I have done either

I have made dialogues,

have discussed ancient texts,
have thrown what light I could, offered
what pleasures
doceat allows
        But the known?
This, I have had to be given,
a life, love, and from one man
the world.
        Tokens.
        But sitting here
        I look out as a wind
        and water man, testing
        And missing
        some proof

I know the quarters
of the weather, where it comes from,
where it goes. But the stem of me,
this I took from their welcome,
or their rejection, of me

        And my arrogance
        was neither diminished
        nor increased,
        by the communication

    2

It is undone business
I speak of, this morning,
with the sea
stretching out
from my feet

            The Ring Of

it was the west wind caught her up, as
she rose

from the genital
wave, and bore her from the delicate
foam, home
to her isle

and those lovers
of the difficult, the hours
of the golden day welcomed her, clad her, were
as though they had made her, were wild
to bring this new thing born
of the ring of the sea pink
& naked, this girl, brought her
to the face of the gods, violets
in her hair

Beauty, and she
said no to zeus & them all, all were not or
was it she chose the ugliest
to bed with, or was it straight
and to expiate the nature of beauty, was it?

knowing hours, anyway,
she did not stay long, or the lame
was only one part, & the handsome
mars had her   And the child
had that name, the arrow of
as the flight of, the move of
his mother who adorneth

with myrtle the dolphin and words
they rise, they do who
are born of like
elements

A Newly Discovered 'Homeric' Hymn
(for Jane Harrison if she were alive)

Hail and beware the dead who will talk life until you are blue
in the face. And you will not understand what is wrong,
they will not be blue, they will have tears in their eyes,
they will seem to you so much more full of life
than the rest of us, and they will ask so much, not of you no
but of life, they will cry, isn't it this way, if it isn't
I don't care for it, and you will feel the blackmail, you will not
     know
what to answer, it will all have become one mass

Hail and beware them, for they come from where you have not
     been,
they come from where you cannot have come, they come into life
by a different gate. They come from a place which is not easily
     known,
it is known only to those who have died. They carry seeds
you must not touch, you must not touch the pot they taste of,
no one must touch the pot, no one must, in their season.

Hail and beware them, in their season. Take care. Prepare
to receive them, they carry what the living cannot do without,
but take the proper precautions, do the prescribed things, let
down the thread from the right shoulder. And from the forehead.
And listen to what they say, listen to the talk, hear
every word of it—they are drunk from the pot, they speak
like no living man may speak, they have the seeds in their mouth—
listen, and beware

Hail them solely that they have the seeds in their mouth, they
are drunk, you cannot do without a drunkenness, seeds can't,
they must be soaked in the contents of the pot, they must be all
     one mass.
But you who live cannot know what else the seeds must be. Hail
and beware the earth, where the dead come from. Life
is not of the earth. The dead are of the earth. Hail and beware
the earth, where the pot is buried.

Greet the dead in the dead man's time. He is drunk of the pot.
He speaks like spring does. He will deceive you. You are meant
to be deceived. You must observe the drunkenness. You are not to
drink. But you must hear, and see. You must beware.

Hail them, and fall off. Fall off! The drink is not yours,
it is not yours! You do not come
from the same place, you do not suffer as the dead do,
they do not suffer, they need, because they have drunk of the pot,
they need. Do not drink of the pot, do not touch it. Do not touch
them.

    Beware the dead. And hail them. They teach you
  drunkenness.
You have your own place to drink. Hail and beware them, when
  they come.

Cole's Island

I met Death—he was a sportsman—on Cole's
Island. He was a property-owner. Or maybe
Cole's Island, was his. I don't know. The
point was I was there, walking, and—as it
often is, in the woods—a stranger, suddenly
showing up, makes the very thing you were do-
ing no longer the same. That is suddenly
what you thought, when you were alone, and
doing what you were doing, changes because someone else
shows up. He didn't bother me, or say anything. Which is
not surprising, a person might not, in the circumstances;
or at most a nod or something. Or they would. But they wouldn't,
or you wouldn't think to either, if it was Death. And
He certainly was, the moment I saw him. There wasn't any question
about that even though he may have looked like a sort of country
gentleman, going about his own land. Not quite. Not it being He.
A fowler, maybe—as though he was used to
hunting birds, and was out, this morning, keeping

his hand in, so to speak, moving around, noticing
what game were about. And how they seemed. And how the woods
were. As a matter of fact just before he had shown up,
so naturally, and as another person might walk
up on a scene of your own, I had noticed
a cock and hen pheasant cross easily the
road I was on and had tried, in fact,
to catch my son's attention quick enough for him
to see before they did walk off into the bayberry
or arbor vitae along the road.

        My impression is we did—
that is, Death and myself, regard each other. And
there wasn't anything more than that, only that he had appeared,
and we did recognize each other—or I did, him and he seemed
to have no question
about my presence there, even though I was uncomfortable.
    That is,
Cole's Island
is a queer isolated and gated place, and I was only there by will
to know more of the topography of it lying as it does out
over the Essex River. And as it now is, with no tenants that one can speak
    of,
it's more private than almost any place one might imagine.
And down in that part of it where I did meet him (about half way between
    the
two houses over the river and the carriage house
at the entrance) it was as quiet and as much a piece
of the earth as any place can be. But my difficulty,
when he did show up, was immediately at least that I was
an intruder, by being there at all
and yet, even if he seemed altogether
used to Cole's Island, and, like I say, as though he owned it,
even if I was sure he didn't, I noticed him, and he me, and he
went on without anything extraordinary at all.

Maybe he had gaiters on, or almost
a walking stick, in other words much more
habited than I,
who was in chinos actually and

only doing what I had set myself to do here
& in other places on Cape Ann.
    It was his eye perhaps which makes me
render him as Death? It isn't true, there wasn't anything
that different about his eye,
    it was not one thing more than that he was Death instantly
that he came into sight. Or that I was aware there was a person
here as well as myself. And son.

    We did exchange some glance. That is the fullest possible
account I can give, of the encounter.

The Moon Is the Number 18

is a monstrance,
the blue dogs bay,
and the son sits,
grieving

is a grinning god, is
the mouth of, is
the dripping moon
while in the tower the cat
preens
and all motion
is a crab

and there is nothing he can do but what they do, watch
the face of waters, and fire

          The blue dogs paw,
          lick the droppings, dew
          or blood, whatever
          results are. And night,
          the crab, rays round

attentive as the cat to catch
human sound

The blue dogs rue,
as he does, as he would howl, confronting
the wind which rocks what was her, while prayers
striate the snow, words blow
as questions cross fast, fast
as flames, as flames form, melt
along any darkness

Birth is an instance as is a host, namely, death

The moon has no air

In the red tower
in that tower where she also sat
in that particular tower where watching & moving
        are,
there,
there where what triumph there is, is: there
is all substance, all creature
all there is against the dirty moon, against
number, image, sortilege—

alone with cat & crab,
and sound is, is, his
conjecture

LAWRENCE FERLINGHETTI [Born 1919]

Lawrence Ferlinghetti was born in Yonkers, New York. While still a child, Ferlinghetti's father died, his mother was placed in an insane asylum, and he was sent to an orphanage, where he stayed until a relative took him to France with her. He attended the University of North Carolina and served in the Naval Reserve from 1941-1945, after which he continued his studies at Columbia University and at the Sorbonne in Paris.

Ferlinghetti was one of the major influences in the Beat movement. He was co-founder of City Lights Bookstore, the first all paperback bookstore in the United States, and was editor of City Lights Books, which published many Beat poets including Gregory Corso and Allen Ginsberg. Ferlinghetti, like other Beat poets, celebrated the virtues of freedom and love, explored Eastern religion, experimented with drugs, and satirized society. However, his unique contribution derived out of his experimentation with jazz and poetry, creating a verse which emphasizes aural qualities over visual. During the sixties, he became very active in politics and incorporated the fervor of his activism into his poetry. Ferlinghetti is a poet who has always felt that poetry should be accessible to the masses, and his volume *A Coney Island of the Mind* is still one of the best selling books of verse ever.

He

(To the Allen Ginsberg of the 1950s. before "The Change")

He is one of the prophets come back
He is one of the wiggy prophets come back
He had a beard in the Old Testament
    but shaved it off in Paterson
He has a microphone around his neck
    at a poetry reading
    and he is more than one poet
    and he is an old man perpetually writing a poem
    about an old man
    whose every third thought is Death
    and who is writing a poem
    about an old man
    whose every third thought is Death
    and who is writing a poem
    Like the picture on a Quaker Oats box
    that shows a figure holding up a box
    upon which is a picture of a figure
    holding up a box
    and the figure smaller and smaller
    and further away each time
    a picture of shrinking reality itself
He is one of the prophets come back
    to see to hear to file a revised report
    on the present state
    of the shrinking world
He has buttonhooks in his eyes
    with which he fastens on
    to every foot of existence
    and onto every shoestring rumor
    of the nature of reality
    And his eye fixes itself
    on every stray person or thing
    and waits for it to move
    like a cat with a dead white mouse
    suspecting it of hiding
    some small clew to existence
    and he waits gently

for it to reveal itself
or herself or himself
and he is gentle as the lamb of God
made into mad cutlets
And he picks up every suspicious object
and he picks up every person or thing
examining it and shaking it
like a white mouse with a piece of string
who thinks the thing is alive
and shakes it to speak
and shakes it alive
and shakes it to speak
He is a cat who creeps at night
and sleeps his buddhahood in the violet hour
and listens for the sound of three hands about to clap
and reads the script of hs brainpan
his hieroglyph of existence
He is a talking asshole on a stick
he is a walkie-talkie on two legs
and he holds his phone to his ear
and he holds his phone to his mouth
and hears *Death death*
He has one head with one tongue hung
in the back of his mouth
and he speaks with an animal tongue
and man has devised a language
that no other animal understands
and his tongue sees and his tongue speaks
and his own ear hears what is said
and clings to his head
and hears *Death death*
and he has a tongue to say it
that no other animal understands
He is a forked root walking
with a knot-hole eye in the middle of his head
and his eye turns outward and inward
and sees and is mad
and is mad and sees
And he is the mad eye of the fourth person singular
of which nobody speaks

and he is the voice of the fourth person singular
in which nobody speaks
and which yet exists
with a long head and a foolscap face
and the long mad hair of death
of which nobody speaks
And he speaks of himself and he speaks of the dead
of his dead mother and his Aunt Rose
with their long hair and their long nails
that grow and grow
and they come back to his speech without a manicure
And he has come back with his black hair
and his black eye and his black shoes
and the big black book of his report
And he is a big black bird with one foot raised
to hear the sound of life reveal itself
on the shell of his sensorium
and he speaks to sing to get out of his skin
and he pecks with his tongue on the shell of it
and he knocks with his eye on the shell
and sees *light light* and hears *death death*
of which nobody speaks
For he is a head with a head's vision
and his is the lizard's look
and his unbuttoned vision is the door
in which he stands and waits and hears
the hand that knocks and claps and claps and knocks
his *Death Death*
For he is his own ecstatic illumination
and he is his own hallucination
and he is his own shrinker
and his eye turns in the shrinking head of the world
and hears his organ speak *Death Death*
a deaf music
For he has come at the end of the world
and he is the flippy flesh made word
and he speaks the word he hears in his flesh
and the word is *Death*

Death Death

      Death Death

Death Death

      Death Death

           Death

    Death Death

        Death Death

  Death Death

      Death Death

         Death Death

Death Death

    Death Death

      Death Death

         Death Death

Death

Constantly Risking Absurdity

Constantly risking absurdity
                and death
        whenever he performs
                above the heads
                        of his audience
    the poet like an acrobat
                climbs on rime
                    to a high wire of his own making
and balancing on eyebeams
                    above a sea of faces
            paces his way
                    to the other side of day
        performing entrechats
                    and sleight-of-foot tricks
    and other high theatrics
                    and all without mistaking
            any thing
                    for what it may not be

        For he's the super realist
                    who must perforce perceive
            taut truth
                    before the taking of each stance or step
    in his supposed advance
                    toward that still higher perch
where Beauty stands and waits
                    with gravity
                        to start her death-defying leap

    And he
        a little charleychaplin man
                    who may or may not catch
            his fair eternal form
                    spreadeagled in the empty air
            of existence

The Pennycandystore Beyond the El

The pennycandystore beyond the El
is where I first
                fell in love
                        with unreality
Jellybeans glowed in the semi-gloom
of that september afternoon
A cat upon the counter moved among
                                the licorice sticks
                and tootsie rolls
        and Oh Boy Gum

Outside the leaves were falling as they died
A wind had blown away the sun
A girl ran in
Her hair was rainy
Her breasts were breathless in the little room

Outside the leaves were falling
                and they cried
                        Too soon! too soon!

Monet's Lilies Shuddering

Monet never knew
                he was painting his 'Lilies' for
        a lady from the Chicago Art Institute
            who went to France and filmed
                today's lilies
                by the 'Bridge at Giverny'
                        a leaf afloat among them
        the film of which now flickers
        at the entrance to his framed visions
            with a Debussy piano soundtrack
flooding with a new fluorescence (fleur-essence?)
        the rooms and rooms

of waterlilies

Monet caught a Cloud in a Pond
                              in 1903
        and got a first glimpse
                        of its lilies
        and for twenty years returned
        again and again to paint them
                which now gives us the impression
                that he floated thru life on them
                                and their reflections
        which he also didn't know
                we would have occasion
                        to reflect upon

Anymore than he could know
        that John Cage would be playing a
        'Cello with Melody-driven Electronics'
                tonight at the University of Chicago
And making those Lilies shudder and shed
                                black light

The Third World

        This loud morning
                sensed a small cry in
                        the news
                                paper
                caught somewhere on
                        an inner page
                                I
                decide to travel for lunch &
                end up in an automat
                        White House Cafeteria
                looking thru a little window
                put a nickel in the slot
                and out comes

                    fried rice
          Taking a tour
of the rest of that building
                         I
               hear a small cry
     beyond the rice paddies
          between floors where
          the escalator sticks
and remember last night's dream of
     attending my own funeral
          at a drive-in mortuary
          not really believing
               I was that dead
          Someone throwing rice
               All the windows dry
Tipped the coffin open & laughed
                         into it
          and out falls
               old funnyface
               myself
          the bargain tragedian
     with a small cry
followed by sound of Che Guevara singing
          in the voice of Fidel

     Far over the Perfume River
                    the clouds pass
          carrying small cries

     The monsoon has set in
                    the windows weep
          I
          back up to
               the Pentagon
     on a flatbed truck
and unload the small brown bodies
               fresh from the blasted fields!

Stone Reality Meditation

Humankind can indeed bear
very much reality
That 'busy little monster
                    manunkind'
can bear it too
So may womankind
So can every kind
of clay and creature
Trees too can bear it
after the leaves have flown away
after the birds have blown away
'bare ruined choirs' bear it
as stones do
They too bear the 'heavy weight
of creation'
as we do
cast in clay and stoned in earth
Masters of ecstasy

An Elegy To Dispel Gloom

(After the assassinations of Mayor George Moscone and
Supervisor Harvey Milk in San Francisco, November, 1978)

Let us not sit upon the ground
and tell sad stories
of the death of sanity.
Two humans made of flesh
are meshed in death
and no more need be said.
It is pure vanity
to think that all humanity
be bathed in red
because one young mad man
one so bad man
lost his head.

The force that through the red fuze
drove the bullet
does not drive everyone
through the City of Saint Francis
where there's a breathless hush
in the air today
a hush at City Hall
and a hush at the Hall of Justice
a hush in Saint Francis Wood
where no bird
tries to sing
a hush on the Great Highway
and in the great harbor
upon the great ships
and on the Embarcadero
from the Mission Rock Resort
to the Eagle Cafe
a hush on the great red bridge
and on the great grey bridge
a hush in the Outer Mission
and at Hunter's Point
a hush at a hot potato stand on Pier 39
and a hush at the People's Temple
where no bird
tries its wings
a hush and a weeping
at the Convent of the Sacred Heart
on Upper Broadway
a hush upon the fleshpots
of Lower Broadway
a pall upon the punk rock
at Mabuhay Gardens
and upon the cafes and bookstores
of old North Beach
a hush upon the landscape
of the still wild West
where two sweet dudes are dead
and no more need be said.
Do not sit upon the ground and speak
of other senseless murderings

or worse disasters waiting
in the wings
Do not sit upon the ground and talk
of the death of things beyond
these sad sad happenings.
Such men as these do rise above
our worst imaginings.

Night Light

Night, night
Death's true self, Death's second self
Black is my true love's hair
Yet all, all is despair

Black night, black light
Death's true self
Black, black, black is my true love's hair
And all, all is despair

Night, night
Death's second self
where all is empty, all is despair
All gone, all down
All, all despair
And grey is my true love's hair

Yet sun bursts forth upon the land
And a butterfly lights in it
upon my hand
And lights these songs
and lights these songs
in air

I Am Waiting

I am waiting for my case to come up
and I am waiting
for a rebirth of wonder
and I am waiting for someone
to really discover America
and wail
and I am waiting
for the discovery
of a new symbolic western frontier
and I am waiting
for the American Eagle
to really spread its wings
and straighten up and fly right
and I am waiting
for the Age of Anxiety
to drop dead
and I am waiting
for the war to be fought
which will make the world safe
for anarchy
and I am waiting
for the final withering away
of all governments
and I am perpetually awaiting
a rebirth of wonder

I am waiting for the Second Coming
and I am waiting
for a religious revival
to sweep thru the state of Arizona
and I am waiting
for the Grapes of Wrath to be stored
and I am waiting
for them to prove
that God is really American
and I am waiting
to see God on television
piped onto church altars

if only they can find
the right channel
to tune in on
and I am waiting
for the Last Supper to be served again
with a strange new appetizer
and I am perpetually awaiting
a rebirth of wonder

I am waiting for my number to be called
and I am waiting
for the Salvation Army to take over
and I am waiting
for the meek to be blessed
and inherit the earth
without taxes
and I am waiting
for forests and animals
to reclaim the earth as theirs
and I am waiting
for a way to be devised
to destroy all nationalisms
without killing anybody
and I am waiting
for linnets and planets to fall like rain
and I am waiting for lovers and weepers
to lie down together again
in a new rebirth of wonder

I am waiting for the Great Divide to be crossed
and I am anxiously waiting
for the secret of eternal life to be discovered
by an obscure general practitioner
and I am waiting
for the storms of life
to be over
and I am waiting
to set sail for happiness
and I am waiting
for a reconstructed Mayflower

to reach America
with its picture story and tv rights
sold in advance to the natives
and I am waiting
for the lost music to sound again
in the Lost Continent
in a new rebirth of wonder

I am waiting for the day
that maketh all things clear
and I am awaiting retribution
for what America did
to Tom Sawyer
and I am waiting
for the American Boy
to take off Beauty's clothes
and get on top of her
and I am waiting
for Alice in Wonderland
to retransmit to me
her total dream of innocence
and I am waiting
for Childe Roland to come
to the final darkest tower
and I am waiting
for Aphrodite
to grow live arms
at a final disarmament conference
in a new rebirth of wonder

I am waiting
to get some intimations
of immortality
by recollecting my early childhood
and I am waiting
for the green mornings to come again
youth's dumb green fields come back again
and I am waiting
for some strains of unpremeditated art
to shake my typewriter

and I am waiting to write
the great indelible poem
and I am waiting
for the last long careless rapture
and I am perpetually waiting
for the fleeing lovers on the Grecian Urn
to catch each other up at last
and embrace
and I am awaiting
perpetually and forever
a renaissance of wonder

DENISE LEVERTOV [Born 1923]

Although Denise Levertov was born in Essex, England, she is nevertheless considered an American poet. She arrived in this country at the age of twenty-five after having served as a nurse in London during the Second World War. Married in 1947 to an American novelist, Mitchell Goodman, she was naturalized in 1955. Her poetry was greatly transformed by this emigration. In England, her writing was influenced by Herbert Read who wrote in a formally structured style that nostalgically harkened back to the poetry of the nineteenth century romantics. In this country she became strongly influenced by the modern poets: William Carlos Williams, Ezra Pound and Hilda Doolittle (H.D.), *et al.* When her husband introduced her to Robert Creeley, whom he had known from his days at Harvard, the two poets discovered a shared poetic ideology; this became the basis for Ms. Levertov's association with the Black Mountain Movement, even though she had never taught at the College from which the movement took its name. She has, however, taught at many colleges and universities including the University of California at Berkeley and the Massachusetts Institute of Technology. She has been awarded many grants and prizes for her poetry, among them are a Guggenheim Fellowship and a grant from the National Institute of Arts and Letters. In 1961 she was the poetry editor of *The Nation.* Denise Levertov's contribution to American poetry has been nothing less than prolific; to date she has had over thirty works published.

During the Eichmann Trial, Selections

III CRYSTAL NIGHT

From blacked-out streets
   (wide avenues swept by curfew,
   alleyways, veins
   of dark within dark)

from houses whose walls
   had for a long time known
the tense stretch of skin over bone
as their brick or stone listened—

   The scream!
The awaited scream rises,
the shattering
of glass and the cracking
of bone

a polar tumult as when
black ice booms, knives
of ice and glass
splitting and splintering the silence into
innumerable screaming needles of
yes, now it is upon us, the jackboots
are running in spurts of
sudden blood-light through the
broken temples

the veils
are rent in twain
terror has a white sound
every scream
of fear is a white needle freezing the eyes
the floodlights of their trucks throw
jets of white, their shouts
cleave the wholeness of darkness into
sectors of transparent white-clouded pantomime
where all that was awaited
is happening, it is Crystal Night

it is Crystal Night
these spikes which are not
pitched in the range of common hearing
whistle through time

smashing the windows of sleep and dream
smashing the windows of history
a whiteness scattering
in hailstones
each a mirror
for man's eyes.

Pleasures

1
I like to find
what's not found
at once, but lies

within something of another nature,
in repose, distinct.
Gull feathers of glass, hidden

in white pulp: the bones of squid
which I pull out and lay
blade by blade on the draining board—

tapered as if for swiftness, to pierce
the heart, but fragile, substance
belying design.   Or a fruit, *mamey,*

cased in rough brown peel, the flesh
rose-amber, and the seed:
the seed a stone of wood, carved and

polished, walnut-colored, formed
like a brazilnut, but large,
large enough to fill
the hungry palm of a hand.

I like the juicy stem of grass that grows
within the coarser leaf folded round,
and the butteryellow glow

in the narrow flute from which the morning-glory
opens blue and cool on a hot morning.

Cancion

When I am the sky
a glittering bird
slashes at me with the knives of song.

When I am the sea
fiery clouds plunge into my mirrors,
fracture my smooth breath with crimson sobbing.

When I am the earth
I feel my flesh of rock wearing down:
pebbles, grit, finest dust, nothing.

When I am a woman—O, when I am
a woman,
my wells of salt brim and brim,
poems force the lock of my throat.

The Goddess

She in whose lipservice
I passed my time,
whose name I knew, but not her face,
came upon me where I lay in Lie Castle!

Flung me across the room, and
room after room (hitting the walls, re-
bounding—to the last
sticky wall—wrenching away from it
pulled hair out!)
till I lay
outside the outer walls!

There in cold air
lying still where her hand had thrown me,
I tasted the mud that splattered my lips:
the seeds of a forest were in it,
asleep and growing! I tasted
her power!

The silence was answering my silence,
a forest was pushing itself
out of sleep between my submerged fingers.

I bit on a seed and it spoke on my tongue
of day that shone already among stars
in the water-mirror of low ground,
and a wind rising ruffled the lights:
she passed near me returning from the encounter,
she who plucked me from the close rooms,

without whom nothing
flowers, fruits, sleeps in season,
without whom nothing
speaks in its own tongue, but returns
lie for lie!

The Hands

Don't forget the crablike
hands, slithering
among the keys.

Eyes shut, the downstream
play of sound lifts away from
the present, drifts you
            off your feet : too easily let off.

So look: that almost painful
movement restores the pull, incites
            the head with the heart : a tension, as of
            actors at rehearsal, who move
this way, that way, on a bare stage, testing
            their diagonals, in common clothes.

Scenes from the Life of the Peppertrees

I
The peppertrees, the peppertrees!

Cats are stretching in the doorways,
sure of everything. It is morning.
            But the peppertrees
stand aside in diffidence, with berries
of modest red.
                        Branch above branch, an air
of lightness; of shadows
scattered lightly.
            A cat
closes upon its shadow.
Up and up goes the sun,
sure of everything.
            The peppertrees
                        shiver a little.
Robust
and soot-black, the cat
leaps to a low branch. Leaves
close about him.

II

The yellow moon dreamily
tipping buttons of light
down among the leaves. Marimba,
marimba—from beyond the
black street.
                    Somebody dancing,
somebody
          getting the hell
outta here. Shadows of cats
weave round the tree trunks,
the exposed knotty roots.

III

The man on the bed sleeping
defenseless. Look—
his bare long feet together
sideways, keeping each other
warm. And the foreshortened shoulders,
the head
barely visible. He is good.
Let him sleep.
                    But the third peppertree
          is restless, twitching
thin leaves in the light
of afternoon. After a while
it walks over and taps
on the upstairs window with a bunch
of red berries. Will he wake?

Wedding-Ring

My wedding-ring lies in a basket
as if at the bottom of a well.
Nothing will come to fish it back up
and onto my finger again.
                    It lies

among keys to abandoned houses,
nails waiting to be needed and hammered
into some wall,
telephone numbers with no names attached,
idle paperclips.
It can't be given away
for fear of bringing ill-luck.
It can't be sold
for the marriage was good in its own
time, though that time is gone.
Could some artificer
beat into it bright stones, transform it
into a dazzling circlet no one could take
for solemn betrothal or to make promises
living will not let them keep? Change it
into a simple gift I could give in friendship?

The Old Adam

A photo of someone else's childhood,
a garden in another country—world
he had no part in and has no power to imagine:

yet the old man who has failed his memory
keens over the picture—'Them happy days—
gone—gone for ever!'—glad for a moment to suppose

a focus for unspent grieving, his floating
sense of loss.
He wanders

asking the day of the week, the time,
over and over the wrong questions.
Missing his way in the streets

he acts out
the bent of his life,
the lost way

never looked for, life
unlived, of which he is dying
very slowly.

'A man,'
says his son, 'who never
made a right move in all his life.' A man

who thought **the dollar was sweet** and
couldn't make a buck, riding the subway
year after year to untasted sweetness,

loving his sons obscurely, incurious
who they were, these men, his sons—
a shadow of love, for love longs

to know the beloved, and a light goes with it
into the dark mineshafts of feeling...A man
who now, without knowing,

in endless concern for the smallest certainties,
looking again and again at a paid bill,
inquiring again and again, 'When was I here last?'

asks what it's too late to ask:
'Where is my life? Where is my life?
What have I done with my life?'

Rain Spirit Passing

Have you ever heard the rain at night
streaming its flaxen hair against
the walls of your house?

Have you ever heard the rain at night
drifting its black, shiny, seaweed hair
through multistoreyed arcades of leaves?

And have you risen then
from bed and felt your way
to the window, and raised the blind, and seen

       stillness, unmisted moonlight, the air
       dry? Street and garden
       empty and silent?

You had been lying awake; the rain
was no dream. Yet where is it?

When did that rain descend and descend,
filling your chalices
until their petals loosened

and wafted
down to rest
on grass and the wet ground,

and your roots in their burrows
stretched and sighed?

Come into Animal Presence

Come into animal presence.
No man is so guileless as
the serpent. The lonely white
rabbit on the roof is a star
twitching its ears at the rain.
The llama intricately
folding its hind legs to be seated
not disdains but mildly
disregards human approval.

What joy when the insouciant
armadillo glances at us and doesn't
quicken his trotting
across the track into the palm brush.

What is this joy? That no animal
falters, but knows what it must do?
That the snake has no blemish,
that the rabbit inspects his strange surroundings
in white star-silence? The llama
rests in dignity, the armadillo
has some intention to pursue in the palm-forest.
Those who were sacred have remained so,
holiness does not dissolve, it is a presence
of bronze, only the sight that saw it
faltered and turned from it.
An old joy returns in holy presence.

Writing in the Dark

It's not difficult.
Anyway, it's necessary.

Wait till morning, and you'll forget.
And who knows if morning will come.

Fumble for the light, and you'll be
stark awake, but the vision
will be fading, slipping
out of reach.

You must have paper at hand,
a felt-tip pen—ballpoints don't always flow,
pencil points tend to break. There's nothing
shameful in that much prudence: those are your tools.

Never mind about crossing your t's, dotting your i's—
but take care not to cover
one word with the next. Practice will reveal
how one hand instinctively comes to the aid of the other
to keep each line
clear of the next.

Keep writing in the dark:
a record of the night, or
words that pulled you from depths of unknowing,
words that flew through your mind, strange birds
crying their urgency with human voices,

or opened
as flowers of a tree that blooms
only once in a lifetime:

words that may have the power
to make the sun rise again.

LOUIS SIMPSON [Born 1923]

Louis Simpson was born in Jamaica, British West Indies, and grew up in Kingston, Jamaica. His father was a second generation Jamaican of Scottish descent, and his mother was from a family of Polish Jews. At seventeen he moved to New York and attended Columbia University. However, his schooling was interrupted in 1943 when he served in the U.S. Army as an infantryman, receiving two Purple Hearts and a Bronze Star. Simpson drew on his boyhood experiences in Jamaica, his European heritage, and his experiences in the war for much of his poetry. After the war he returned to Columbia University, earning a B.S. degree (1948), an M.A. (1950), and a Ph.D. (1959). He has worked as an editor and has taught at Columbia University and the University of California at Berkeley. Since 1967 he has been professor of English at the State University of New York at Stony Brook.

Simpson's early poetry was quite formal, but eventually his verse evolved to where the content was dictating the form. His language became more colloquial and his subject matter became rooted in the American experience; however, his poetry always maintained an educated and literate sensibility. In 1957, with Donald Hall and Robert Pack, Simpson edited the acclaimed anthology *New Poets of England and America*. He has also been the recipient of numerous honors and awards such as an American Academy of Arts and Letters Rome Fellowship, an Edna St. Vincent Millay Memorial Award, two Guggenheim Fellowships, and a Pulitzer Prize for *At the End of the Open Road*.

American Poetry

Whatever it is, it must have
A stomach that can digest
Rubber, coal, uranium, moons, poems.

Like the shark, it contains a shoe.
It must swim for miles through the desert
Uttering cries that are almost human.

A Story about Chicken Soup

In my grandmother's house there was always chicken soup
And talk of the old country—mud and boards,
Poverty,
The snow falling down the necks of lovers.

Now and then, out of her savings
She sent them a dowry. Imagine
The rice-powered faces!
And the smell of the bride, like chicken soup.

But the Germans killed them.
I know it's in bad taste to say it,
But it's true. The Germans killed them all.

* * *

In the ruins of Berchtesgaden
A child with yellow hair
Ran out of a doorway.

A German girl-child—
Cuckoo, all skin and bones—
Not even enough to make chicken soup.
She sat by the stream and smiled.

Then as we splashed in the sun
She laughed at us.
We had killed her mechanical brothers,
So we forgave her.

*   *   *

The sun is shining.
The shadows of the lovers have disappeared.
They are all eyes; they have some demand on me—
They want me to be more serious than I want to be.

They want me to stick in their mudhole
Where no one is elegant.

They want me to wear old clothes,
They want me to be poor, to sleep in a room with many others—

Not to walk in the painted sunshine
To a summer house,
But to live in the tragic world forever.

Walt Whitman at Bear Mountain

"...life which does not give the preference to any other life, of any previous period, which therefore prefers its own existence..."

Ortega y Gasset

Neither on horseback nor seated,
But like himself, squarely on two feet,
The poet of death and lilacs
Loafs by the footpath. Even the bronze looks alive
Where it is folded like cloth. And he seems friendly.

"Where is the Mississippi panorama
And the girl who played the piano?
Where are you, Walt?
The Open Road goes to the used-car lot.

"Where is the nation you promised?
These houses built of wood sustain
Colossal snows,
And the light above the street is sick to death.

"As for the people—see how they neglect you!
Only a poet pauses to read the inscription."

"I am here," he answered.
"It seems you have found me out.
Yet, did I not warn you that it was Myself
I advertised? Where my words not sufficiently plain?

"I gave no prescriptions,
And those who have taken my moods for prophecies
Mistake the matter."
Then, vastly amused—"Why do you reproach me?
I freely confess I am wholly disreputable.
Yet I am happy, because you have found me out."

A crocodile in wrinkled metal loafing...

Then all the realtors,
Pickpockets, salesmen, and the actors performing
Official scenarios,
Turned a deaf ear, for they had contracted
American dreams.

But the man who keeps a store on a lonely road,
And the housewife who knows she's dumb,
And the earth, are relieved.

All that grave weight of America
Cancelled! Like Greece and Rome.
The future in ruins!

The castles, the prisons, the cathedrals
Unbuilding, and roses
Blossoming from the stones that are not there...

The clouds are lifting from the high Sierras,
The Bay mists clearing.
And the angel in the gate, the flowering plum,
Dances like Italy, imagining red.

Hot Night on Water Street

A hot midsummer night on Water Street—
The boys in jeans were combing their blond hair,
Watching the girls go by on tired feet;
And an old woman with a witch's stare
Cried "Praise the Lord!" She vanished on a bus
With hissing air brakes, like an incubus.

Three hardware stores, a barbershop, a bar,
A movie playing Westerns—where I went
To see a dream of horses called *The Star*....
Some day, when this uncertain continent
Is marble, and men ask what was the good
We lived by, dust may whisper "Hollywood."

Then back along the river bank on foot
By moonlight...On the West Virginia side
An owlish train began to huff and hoot;
It seemed to know of something that had died.
I didn't linger—sometimes when I travel
I think I'm being followed by the Devil.

At the newsstand in the lobby, a cigar
Was talkative: "Since I've been in this town
I've seen one likely woman, and a car
As she was crossing Main Street knocked her down."
I was a stranger here myself, I said,
And bought the *New York Times*, and went to bed.

My Father in the Night Commanding No

My father in the night commanding No
Has work to do. Smoke issues from his lips;
    He reads in silence.
The frogs are croaking and the streetlamps glow.

And then my mother winds the gramophone;
The Bride of Lammermoor begins to shriek—
    Or reads a story
About a prince, a castle, and a dragon.

The moon is glittering above the hill.
I stand before the gateposts of the King—
    So runs the story—
Of Thule, at midnight when the mice are still.

And I have been in Thule! It has come true—
The journey and the danger of the world,
    All that there is
To bear and to enjoy, endure and do.

Landscapes, seascapes...where have I been led?
The names of cities—Paris, Venice, Rome—
    Held out their arms.
A feathered god, seductive, went ahead.

Here is my house. Under a red rose tree
A child is swinging; another gravely plays.
    They are not surprised
That I am here; they were expecting me.

And yet my father sits and reads in silence,
My mother sheds a tear, the moon is still,
    And the dark wind
Is murmuring that nothing ever happens.

Beyond his jurisdiction as I move
Do I not prove him wrong? And yet, it's true
    They will not change
There, on the stage of terror and of love.

The actors in that playhouse always sit
In fixed positions—father, mother, child
        With painted eyes.
How sad it is to be a little puppet!

Their heads are wooden. And you once pretended
To understand them! Shake them as you will,
        They cannot speak.
Do what you will, the comedy is ended.

Father, why did you work? Why did you weep
Mother? Was the story so important?
        "Listen!" the wind
Said to the children, and they fell asleep.

Chocolates

Once some people were visiting Chekhov.
While they made remarks about his genius
the Master fidgeted. Finally
he said, "Do you like chocolates?"

They were astonished, and silent.
He repeated the question,
whereupon one lady plucked up her courage
and murmured shyly, "Yes."

"Tell me," he said, leaning forward,
light glinting from his spectacles,
"what kind? The light, sweet chocolate
or the dark, bitter kind?"

The conversation became general.
They spoke of cherry centers,
of almonds and Brazil nuts.
Losing their inhibitions
they interrupted one another.

For people may not know what they think
about politics in the Balkans,
or the vexed question of men and women,

but everyone has a definite opinion
about the flavor of shredded coconut.
Finally someone spoke of chocolates filled with liqueur,
and everyone, even the author of *Uncle Vanya,*
was at a loss for words.

As they were leaving he stood by the door
and took their hands.
           In the coach returning to Peterburg
they agreed that it had been a most
unusual conversation.

Physical Universe

He woke at five and, unable
to go back to sleep,
went downstairs.

A book was lying on the table
where his son had done his homework.
He took it into the kitchen,
made coffee, poured himself a cup,
and settled down to read.

"There was a local eddy in the swirling gas
of the primordial galaxy,
and a cloud was formed, the protosun,
as wide as the present solar system.

This contracted. Some of the gas
formed a diffuse, spherical nebula,
a thin disk, that cooled and flattened.
Pulled one way by its own gravity,

the other way by the sun,
it broke, forming smaller clouds,
the protoplanets. Earth
was 2000 times as wide as it is now."

The earth was without form, and void,
and darkness was upon the face of the deep.

                                        *

"Then the sun began to shine,
dispelling the gases and vapors,
shrinking the planets, melting earth,
separating iron and silicate
to form the corn and mantle.
Continents appeared..."
history, civilization,
the discovery of America
and the settling of Green Harbor,
bringing us to Tuesday, the seventh of July.

Tuesday, the day they pick up the garbage!
He leaped into action,
took the garbage bag out of its container,
tied it with a twist of wire,
and carried it out to the tool-shed,
taking care not to let the screen-door slam,
and put it in the large garbage-can
that was three-quarters full.
He kept it in the tool-shed so the raccoons
couldn't get at it.

He carried the can out to the road,
then went back into the house
and walked around, picking up newspapers
and fliers for: "Thompson Seedless Grapes,
California's finest sweet eating";

"Scott Bathroom Tissue";

"Legislative report from Senator Ken LaValle."

He put all this paper in a box,
and emptied the waste baskets in the two
downstairs bathrooms,
and the basket in the study.

He carried the box out to the road,
taking care not to let the screen-door slam,
and placed the box next to the garbage.

Now let the garbage men come!

*

He went back upstairs.
Susan said, "Did you put out the garbage?"
But her eyes were closed.
She was sleeping, yet could speak in her sleep,
ask a question, even answer one.

"Yes," he said, and climbed into bed.
She turned around to face him,
with her eyes still closed.

He thought, perhaps she's an oracle,
speaking from the Collective Unconscious.
He said to her, "Do you agree with Darwin
that people and monkeys have a common ancestor?
Or should we stick to the Bible?"

She said, "Did you take out the garbage?"

"Yes," he said, for the second time.
Then thought about it. Her answer
had something in it of the sublime.
Like a *koan*...the kind of irrelevance
a Zen-master says to the disciple
who is asking riddles of the universe.

He put his arm around her,
and she continued to breathe evenly
from the depths of sleep.

KENNETH KOCH [Born 1925]

Kenneth Koch was born on February 27, in Cincinnati, Ohio, where he also grew up. From 1943 through 1946 he served in the United States Army as a rifleman, stationed in the Pacific. After his return, he received a B.A. from Harvard, where he met John Ashbery and Frank O'Hara. He obtained a doctorate from Columbia in 1959.

During his adolescence, Koch was interested in the stream of consciousness style of writing, but his ideas regarding poetry changed while he was at college. His association with John Ashbery and Frank O'Hara formed the nucleus of the New York School of poetry. This group was contemporary with the Beat Movement of the mid to late fifties; both were reacting to the general conservatism in poetry at that time. However, the New York poets differed from the Beat poets in that the former affected an elitist attitude regarding the artist and the *object d'art*, while the latter favored a Whitmanesque approach, in other words, writing for the "common man." Having begun as spontaneous phenomenons, both groups dissipated rapidly as each poet grew into his own particular style.

Koch spent three years living in Europe at which time he immersed himself in the humorous, surrealistic and psychologically eccentric poetry then popular in France. A few years after his return to America, his poetry had already lost some of its wild incomprehensibility but did not become realistic by any standard. A vision of the world that is slightly, and some times very much, askew is ever present in Koch's work. It is that very quality—"fresh air"—which he believes is sorely missing in much contemporary poetry, and a quality he has in abundance.

For the more than a dozen books of poetry he has had published, Koch has received numerous awards; among them are a Fulbright Fellowship in 1950 and again in 1978, a Guggenheim Fellowship in 1961, a National Endowment for the Arts grant in 1966, and a National Institute of Arts and Letters award in 1976. Lesser known are his accomplishments as a playwright; he has written many dramatic works, some of which can be found in *A Change of Hearts*, an anthology covering his work between the years 1951 and 1971. Expanding his role as an instructor, Koch, who has been a Professor of English at Columbia University until recently, has also authored books on teaching poetry writing to young children and to adults in nursing homes.

In Bed, Selections

Mornings in Bed

Are energetic mornings.

Snow in Bed

When we got out of bed
It was snowing.

Men in Bed

All over Paris
Men are in bed.

Beautiful Girl in Bed

Why I am happy to be here.

Long Relationship in Bed

The springs and the bedposts
Are ready the minute we come in.

Dolls in Bed

With little girls.

Hammer and Nails in Bed

To make it better
They are making it a better bed
And a bigger bed, firmer and larger

And finer bed. So the hammer and nails in the bed
And the carpenter's finger
And thumb and his eyes and his shoulder.
Bang! Bang! Snap! The hammer and nails in bed.

Sheep in Bed

The sheep got into the bed
By mistake.

Buying a New Bed

One of the first things you did
Was buy a new bed.

Window in Bed

I looked at you
And you looked back.

Married in Bed

We'll be married in bed.
The preachers, the witnesses, and all our families
Will also be in bed.

Poetry Bed

Whenas in bed
Then, then

Other Poetry Bed

Shall I compare you to a summer's bed?
You are more beautiful.

Orchids in Bed

She placed orchids in the bed
On that dark blue winter morning.

Lying in Bed

Bed with Spain in it
Bed with Gibraltar in it
Bed of art!

Lovers in Bed

Are lovers no more
Than lovers on the street.
(See Picasso's "Pair of Young Mountebanks," FC 533,
Greuze's "Noces," or hear Mozart's "Fleichtscausenmusik,"
    Köchel 427)

Some Bed

Once
Held
This
All

God in Bed

Christ
Was not
Born
(And did
Not die)
In a bed.

Léger in Bed

Above our apartment
In 1955
Lived Fernand Léger.

Shouting in Bed

We wake up
To the sound of shouts.

Friends in Bed

Sleep well.

Angelic Ceremony in Bed

Putting on the sheets.

Mystery of Bed

She takes it for granted
That he will stay up all night long.

Workmen in Bed

With workmen's wives
And workmen's girl friends
And other workmen
And dolls.

Acapulco in Bed

In Mexico, with blue shimmering water,
Acapulco is in bed.

My Intoxication in Bed

Was not long-lasting.
Was fantastic.
Did not lead me to be very well-mannered.
Wasn't completely romantic.

Basketball in Bed

The basketball is thrown on the bed.

Expensive Bed

At the Lutétia 500 francs a night
In the Hôpital St-Antoine 1000 francs a night

Theatrical Bed

Exceeded expectations
And received applause.

Sirens in Bed

My face is plastered to the window
When the sirens come.

Courtship in Bed

"Please. Tell me you like me."
"How did you get in this bed?"

Wet Dog in Bed

There is nothing like a wet dog in bed.

Dog Bed

In the dog bed
I cannot sleep.

Atomic Bed

Billions of—uncountable—electrons
Compose this bed.

Being in Bed

Belongs to everyone
Bed with Spain in it
Bed of art!

Snow in Bed (Later)

When it stopped snowing
We still hadn't gone to bed

Mending Sump

"Hiram, I think the sump is backing up.
The bathroom floor boards for above two weeks
Have seemed soaked through. A little bird, I think
Has wandered in the pipes, and all's gone wrong."
"Something there is that doesn't hump a sump,"
He said; and through his head she saw a cloud
That seemed to twinkle. "Hiram, well," she said,
"Smith is come home! I saw his face just now
While looking through your head. He's come to die
Or else to laugh, for hay is dried-up grass
When you're alone." He rose, and sniffed the air.
"We'd better leave him in the sump," he said.

Fresh Air

1

At the Poem Society a black-haired man stands up to say,
"You make me sick with all your talk about restraint and mature
    talent!
Haven't you ever looked out the window at a painting by Matisse,
Or did you always stay in hotels where there were too many

spiders crawling on your visages?
Did you ever glance inside a bottle of sparkling pop,
Or see a citizen split in two by the lightning?
I am afraid you have never smiled at the hibernation
Of bear cubs except that you saw in it some deep relation
To human suffering and wishes, oh what a bunch of crackpots!"
The black-haired man sits down, and the others shoot arrows at
    him.

A blond man stand up and says,
"He is right! Why should we be organized to defend the kingdom
Of dullness? There are so many slimy people connected with
    poetry,
Too, and people who know nothing about it!
I am not recommending that poets like each other and organize
    to fight them,
But simply that lightning should strike them."
Then the assembled mediocrities shot arrows at the blond-haired
    man.
The chairman stood up on the platform, oh he was physically
    ugly!
He was small-limbed and -boned and thought he was quite se-
    ductive,
But he was bald with certain hideous black hairs,
And his voice had the sound of water leaving a vaseline bathtub,
And he said, "The subject for this evening's discussion is poetry
On the subject of love between swans." And everyone threw
    candy hearts
At the disgusting man, and they stuck to his bib and tucker,
And he danced up and down on the platform in terrific glee
And recited the poetry of his little friends—but the blond man
    stuck his head
Out of a cloud and recited poems about the east and thunder,
And the black-haired man moved through the stratosphere chant-
    ing
Poems of the relationships between terrific prehistoric charcoal
    whales,
And the slimy man with candy hearts sticking all over him

Wilted away like a cigarette paper on which the bumblebees
   have urinated,
And all the professors left the room to go back to their duty,
And all that were left in the room were five or six poets
And together they sang the new poem of the twentieth century
Which, though influenced by Mallarmé, Shelley, Byron, and
   Whitman,
Plus a million other poets, is still entirely original

And is so exciting that it cannot be here repeated.
You must go to the Poem Society and wait for it to happen.
Once you have heard this poem you will not love any other,
Once you have dreamed this dream you will be inconsolable,
Once you have loved this dream you will be as one dead,
Once you have visited the passages of this time's great art!

   2
"Oh to be seventeen years old
Once again," sang the red-haired man, "and not know that poetry
Is ruled with sceptre of the dumb, the deaf, and the creepy!"
And the shouting persons battered his immortal body with stones
And threw his primitive comedy into the sea
From which it sang forth poems irrevocably blue.

Who are the great poets of our time, and what are their names?
Yeats of the baleful influence, Auden of the baleful influence,
   Eliot of the baleful influence
(Is Eliot a great poet? no one knows), Hardy, Stevens, Williams
   (is Hardy of our time?),
Hopkins (is Hopkins of our time?), Rilke (is Rilke of our time?),
   Lorca (is Lorca of our time?), who is still of our time?
Mallarmé, Valéry, Apollinaire, Eluard, Reverdy, French poets are
   still of our time,
Pasternak and Mayakovsky, is Jouve of our time?

Where are young poets in America, they are trembling in publish-
   ing houses and universities,
Above all they are trembling in universities, they are bathing the
   library steps with their spit,

They are gargling our innocuous (to whom?) poems about maple
    trees and their children,
Sometimes they brave a subject like the Villa d'Este or a light-
    house in Rhode Island,
Oh what worms they are! they wish to perfect their form.

Yet could not these young men, put in another profession,
Succeed admirably, say at sailing a ship? I do not doubt it, Sir,
    and I wish we could try them.

(A plane flies over the ship holding a bomb but perhaps it will
    not drop the bomb,
The young poets from the universities are staring anxiously at the
    skies,
Oh they are remembering their days on the campus when they
    looked up to watch birds excrete,
They are remembering the days they spent making their elegant
    poems.)

Is there no voice to cry out from the wind and say what it is like
    to be the wind,
To be roughed up by the trees and to bring music from the scat-
    tered houses
And the stones, and to be in such intimate relationship with the
    sea
That you cannot understand it? Is there no one who feels like a
    pair of pants?

3
Summer in the trees! "It is time to strangle several bad poets."
The yellow hobbyhorse rocks to and fro, and from the chimney
Drops the Strangler! The white and pink roses are slightly agitated
    by the struggle,
But afterwards beside the dead "poet" they cuddle up comfort-
    ingly against their vase. They are safer now, no one will com-
    pare them to the sea.

Here on the railroad train, one more time, is the Strangler.
He is going to get that one there, who is on his way to a poetry

reading.
Agh! Biff! A body falls to the moving floor.

In the football stadium I also see him,
He leaps through the frosty air at the maker of comparisons
Between football and life and silently, silently strangles him!

Here is the Strangler dressed in a cowboy suit
Leaping from his horse to annihilate the students of myth!

The Strangler's ear is alert for the names of Orpheus,
Cuchulain, Gawain, and Odysseus,

And for poems addressed to Jane Austen, F. Scott Fitzgerald,
To Ezra Pound, and to personages no longer living
Even in anyone's thoughts—O Strangler the Strangler!

He lies on his back in the waves of the Pacific Ocean.

   4
Supposing that one walks out into the air
On a fresh spring day and has the misfortune
To encounter an article on modern poetry
In *New World Writing,* or has the misfortune
To see some examples of some of the poetry
Written by the men with their eyes on the myth
And the Missus and the midterms, in the *Hudson Review,*
Or, if one is abroad, in *Botteghe Oscure,*
Or indeed in *Encounter,* what is one to do
With the rest of one's day that lies blasted to ruins
All bluely about one, what is one to do?
O surely one cannot complain to the President,
Nor even to the deans of Columbia College,
Nor to T.S. Eliot, nor to Ezra Pound,
And supposing one writes to the Princess Caetani,
"Your poets are awful!" what good would it do?
And supposing one goes to the *Hudson Review*
With a package of matches and sets fire to the building?
One ends up in prison with trial subscriptions
to the *Partisan, Sewanee,* and *Kenyon Review!*

5
Sun out! perhaps there is a reason for the lack of poetry
In these ill-contented souls, perhaps they need air!

Blue air, fresh air, come in, I welcome you, you are an art student,
Take off your cap and gown and sit down on the chair.
Together we shall paint the poets—but no, air! perhaps you
    should go to them, quickly,
Give them a little inspiration, they need it, perhaps they are out
    of breath,
Give the a little inhuman company before they freeze the Eng-
    lish language to death!

(And rust their typewriters a little, be sea air! be noxious! kill
    them, if you must, but stop their poetry!
I remember I saw you dancing on the surf on the Côte d'Azur,
And I stopped, taking my hat off, but you did not remember me,
Then afterwards, you came to my room bearing a handful of or-
    ange flowers
And we were together all through the summer night!)

That we might go away together, it is so beautiful on the sea,
    there are a few white clouds in the sky!

But no, air! you must go...Ah, stay!

But she has departed and...Ugh! what poisonous fumes and
    clouds! what a suffocating atmosphere!
Cough! whose are these hideous faces I see, what is this rigor
Infecting the mind? where are the green Azores,
Fond memories of childhood, had the pleasant orange trolleys,
A girl's face, red-white, and her breasts and calves, blue eyes,
    brown eyes, green eyes, fahrenheit
Temperatures, dandelions, and trains, O blue?!
Wind, wind, what is happening? Wind! I can't see any bird but
    the gull, and I feel it should symbolize...
Oh, pardon me, there's a swan, one two three swans, a great white
    swan, hahaha how pretty they are! Smack!
Oh! stop! help! yes, I see—disrespect to my superiors—forgive

me, dear Zeus, nice Zeus, parabolic bird, O feathered excel-
lence! white!
There is Achilles too, and there's Ulysses, I've always wanted to
see them, hahaha!
And here is Helen of Troy, I suppose she is Zeus too, she's so ter-
ribly pretty—hello, Zeus, my you are beautiful, Bang!
One more mistake and I get thrown out of the Modern Poetry
Association, help! Why aren't there any adjectives around?
Oh there are, there's practically nothing else—look, here's *grey,
utter, agonized, total, phenomenal, gracile, invidious, sundered,*
and *fused,*
Elegant, absolute, pyramidal, and ... Scream! But what can I
describe with these words? States!

States symbolized and divided by two, complex states, magic
states, states of consciousness governed by an aroused sincer-
ity, cockadoodle doo!
Another bird! is it morning? Help! where am I? Am I in the barn-
yard? Oink oink, scratch, moo! Splash!
My first lesson. "Look around you. What do you think and feel?"
Uhhh..."Quickly!" *This Connecticut landscape would have
pleased Vermeer.* Wham! A-Plus. "Congratulations!" I am pro-
moted.
OOOhhhhh I wish I were dead, what a headache! My second
lesson: "Rewrite your first lesson line six hundred times. Try
to make it into a magnetic field." I can do it too. But my poor
line! What a nightmare! Here comes a tremendous horse,
Trojan, I presume. No, it's my third lesson. "Look, look! Watch
him, see what he's doing? That's what we want you to do. Of
course it won't be the same as his at first, but..." I demur. Is
there no other way to fertilize minds?
Bang! I give in ... Already I see my name in two or three anthol-
ogies, a serving girl comes into the barn bringing me the an-
thologies,
She is very pretty and I smile at her a little sadly, perhaps it is
my last smile! Perhaps she will hit me! But no, she smiles in
return, and she takes my hand.
My hand, my hand! what is this strange thing I feel in my hand,
on my arm, on my chest, my face—can it be...? it is! AIR!
Air, air, you've come back! Did you have any success? "What do

you think?" I don't know, air. You are so strong, air.
And she breaks my chains of straw, and we walk down the road,
  behind us the hideous fumes!
Soon we reach the seaside, she is a young art student who places
  her head on my shoulder,
I kiss her warm red lips, and here is the Strangler, reading the
  Kenyon Review! Good luck to you, Strangler!

Goodbye, Helen! goodbye, fumes! goodbye, abstracted dried-up
  boys! goodbye, dead trees! goodbye, skunks!
Goodbye, manure! goodbye, critical manicure! goodbye, you big
  fat men standing on the east coast as well as the west giving
  poems the test! farewell, Valéry's stern dictum!
Until tomorrow, then, scum floating on the surface of poetry!
  goodbye for a moment, refuse that happens to land in poetry's
  boundaries! adieu, stale eggs teaching imbeciles poetry to bolster up
  your egos! adios, boring anomalies of these same stale
  eggs!
Ah, but the scum is deep! Come, let me help you! and soon we
  pass into the clear blue water. Oh GOODBYE, castrati of po-
  etry! farewell, stale pale skunky pentameters (the only honest
  English meter, gloop gloop!)! until tomorrow, horrors! oh,
  farewell!

Hello, sea! good morning, sea! hello, clarity and excitement, you
  great expanse of green—

O green, beneath which all of them shall drown!

You Were Wearing

You were wearing your Edgar Allan Poe printed cotton blouse.
In each divided up square of the blouse was a picture of Edgar Allan
  Poe.
Your hair was blonde and you were cute. You asked me, "Do most
  boys think that most girls are bad?"

I smelled the mould of your seaside resort hotel bedroom on your hair
  held in place by a John Greenleaf Whittier clip.
"No," I said, "it's girls who think that boys are bad." Then we read
  Snowbound together
And ran around in an attic, so that a little of the blue enamel was
  scraped off my George Washington, Father of His Country, shoes.

Mother was walking in the living room, her Strauss Waltzes comb in
  her hair.
We waited for a time and then joined her, only to be served tea in
  cups painted with picutres of Herman Melville
As well as with illustrations from his book *Moby Dick* and from his
  novella, *Benito Cereno.*
Father came in wearing his Dick Tracy necktie: "How about a drink,
  everyone?"
I said, "Let's go outside a while," Then we went onto the porch and
  sat on the Abraham Lincoln swing.
You sat on the eyes, mouth, and beard part, and I sat on the knees.
In the yard across the street we saw a snowman holding a garbage can
  lid smashed into a likeness of the mad English king, George the
  Third.

ROBERT CREELEY [Born 1926]

Robert Creeley was born in Arlington, Massachusetts, on May 21. He studied at Harvard but left in the middle of his education to serve with the American Field Service in India and Burma during the final year of World War II. He returned to Harvard in 1946 but dropped out school with only one term incomplete. Creeley then remained in New England for a few years before traveling to Mallorca, Spain, where he founded the Divers Press. In 1954 he was invited to teach at Black Mountain College by Charles Olson. There he established and edited the *Black Mountain Review*, a small, but innovative, magazine that facilitated the growth of American poetry in a new direction: post-modernism. At Black Mountain College, Creeley was influenced by the bold and controversial poetics of Charles Olson, as put forth in the essay, "Projective Verse." This essay shatters the notion of poems as recollections, and redefines the poem as an action wherein discoveries unfold in the reading and the reader experiences the poem with all its spontaneity in tact:

> Each way the turn
> twists, to be apprehended.
> (from "The Turn")

Olson was also influenced by Creeley and would frequently quote his friend's summation of the new poetics: "Form is never more than the extension of content." Creeley stayed at Black Mountain until its closing in 1956. He then took up residence in New Mexico where he taught; and in 1960 he received his M.A. degree from the University of New Mexico. Six years later he accepted the teaching position he has today at the State University of New York at Buffalo, where Charles Olson had also taught for a time during the early sixties.

For You

Like watching rings extend in water
this time of life.

For My Mother:
Genevieve Jules Creeley
April 8, 1887-October 7, 1972

Tender, semi-
articulate flickers
of your

presence, all
those years
past

now, eighty-
five, impossible to
count them

one by one, like
addition, sub-
traction, missing

not one. The last
curled up, in
on yourself,

position you take
in the bed, hair
wisped up

on your head, a
top knot, body
skeletal, eyes

closed against,
in must be,
further disturbance—

breathing a skim
of time, lightly
kicks the intervals—

days, days and
years of it,
work, changes,

sweet flesh caught
at the edges,
dignity's faded

dilemma. It
is *your* life, oh
no one's

forgotten anything
ever. They want
to make you

happy when
they remember. Walk
a little, get

up, now, die
safely,
easily, into

singleness, too
tired with it
to keep

on and on.
Waves break at
the darkness

under the road, sounds
in the faint
night's softness. Look

at them, catching
the light, white
edge as they turn—

always again
and again. Dead
one, two,

three hours—
all these minutes
pass. Is it,

was it, ever
you alone
again, how

long you kept
at it, your
pride, your

lovely, confusing
discretion. Mother, I
love you—for

whatever that
means,
meant—more

than I know, body
gave me my
own, generous,

inexorable place
of you. I feel
the mouth's sluggish-

ness, slips on
turns of things
said, to you,

too soon, too late,
want to
go back to beginning,

smells of the hospital
room, the doctor
she responds

to now, the
order—get me
there. "Death's

let you out—"
comes true,
this, that,

endlessly circular
life, and we
came back

to see you one
last
time, this

time? Your head
shuddered,
it seemed, your

eyes wanted,
I thought,
to see

who it was.
I am here,
and will follow.

The Name

Be natural
wise
as you can be,
my daughter,

let my name
be in you flesh
I gave you
in the act of

loving your mother,
all your days
her ways,
the woman in you

brought from
sensuality's measure
no other,
there was no thought

of it but such
pleasure all women
must be in her,
as you, But not wiser,

not more of nature
than her hair,
the eyes
she gives you.

There will not be another
woman such as you
are. Remember
your mother,

the way you came,
the days of waiting.

Be natural,
daughter, wise

as you can be,
all my daughters,
be women
for men

when that time comes.
Let the rhetoric
stay with me
your father. Let

me talk about it,
saving you such
vicious self-
exposure, let you

pass it on
in you. I cannot
be more than the man
who watches.

Kore

As I was walking
   I came upon
chance walking
   the same road upon.

As I sat down
   by chance to move
later
   if and as I might,

light the wood was,
   light and green,
and what I saw
   before I had not seen.

It was a lady
    accompanied
by goat men
    leading her.

Her hair held earth.
    Her eyes were dark.
A double flute
    made her move.

"O love,
    where are you
leading
    me now?"

The Language

Locate *I*
love you some-
where in

teeth and
eyes, bite
it but

take care not
to hurt, you
want so

much so
little. Words
say everything.

I
love you
again,

then what
is emptiness
for. To

fill, fill.
I heard words
and words full

of holes
aching. Speech
is a mouth.

The Rescue

The man sits in a timelessness
with the horse under him in time
to a movement of legs and hooves
upon a timeless sand.

Distance comes in from the foreground
present in the picture as time
he reads outward from
and comes from that beginning.

A wind blows in
and out and all about the man
as the horse ran
and runs to come in time.

A house is burning in the sand.
A man and horse are burning.
The wind is burning.
They are running to arrive.

A Gift of Great Value

Oh that horse I see so high
when the world shrinks into its
relationships, my mother
sees as well as I.

She was born, but I bore with her.
This horse was a mighty occasion!
The intensity of its feet! The height
of its immense body!

Now then in wonder at evening, at
the last small entrance of the night,
my mother calls it, and I
call it *my father.*

With angry face, with no
rights, with impetuosity and
sterile vision—and a great
wind we ride.

The World

I wanted so ably
to reassure you, I wanted
the man you took to be me,

to comfort you, and got
up, and went to the window,
pushed back, as you asked me to,

the curtain, to see
the outline of the trees
in the night outside.

The light, love,
the light we felt then,
greyly, was it, that

came in, on us, not
merely my hands or yours,
or a wetness so comfortable,

but in the dark then
as you slept, the grey
figure came so close

and leaned over,
between us, as you
slept, restless, and

my own face had to
see it, and be seen by it,
the man it was, your

grey lost tired bewildered
brother, unused, untaken—
hated by love, and dead,

but not dead, for an
instant, saw me, myself
the intruder, as he was not.

I tried to say, it is
all right, she is
happy, you are no longer

needed. I said,
he is dead, and he
went as you shifted

and woke, at first afraid,
then knew by my own knowing
what had happened—

and the light then
of the sun coming
for another morning
in the world.

Fire

Clear smoke,
a fire in the far off
haze of summer,
burning somewhere.

What is
a lonely heart for
if not
for itself alone.

Do the questions
answer themselves,
all wonder
brought to a reckoning?

When you are done,
I am done,
then it seems that
one by one

we can leave it all,
to go on.

Time

Moment to
moment the
body seems

to me to
be there: a
catch of

air, pattern
of space—Let's
walk today

all the way
to the beach,
let's think

of where we'll be
in two years'
time, of where

we *were*. Let
the days go.
Each moment is

of such paradoxical
definition—a
waterfall that would

flow backward
if it could. It
can? My time,

one thinks,
is drawing to
some close. This

feeling comes
and goes. No
measure ever serves

enough, enough—
so "finish it"
gets done, alone.

Just Friends

Out of the table endlessly rocking,
sea shells and firm,
I saw a face appear
which called me dear.

To be loved is half the battle
I thought.
To be
is to be better than is not.

Now when you are old what will you say?
You don't say,
she said.
That was on a Thursday.

Friday night I left
and haven't been back since.
Everything is water
if you look long enough.

For Fear

For fear I want
to make myself again
under the thumb
of old love, old time

subservience
and pain, bent
into a nail that will
not come out.

Why, love, does it
make such a difference
not to be heard
in spite of self

or what we may feel,
one for the other,
but as a hammer
to drive again

bent nail
into old hurt?

Song

Those rivers run from that land
to sea. The wind
finds trees to move,
then goes again.

And me, why me
on any day might be
favored with kind prosperity
or sunk in wretched misery.

I cannot stop the weather
by putting together
myself and another
to stop those rivers.

Or hold the wind
with my hand from the tree,
the mind from the thing,
love from her or me.

Be natural, while alive.
Dead, we die to that
also, and go another
course, I hope.

And me, why me
on any day might be
favored with kind prosperity
or sunk in wretched misery.

You I want back of me
in the life we have here,
waiting to see
what becomes of it.

Call, call loud,
I will hear you, or if
not me, the wind will
for the sake of the tree.

ALLEN GINSBERG [Born 1926]

Allen Ginsberg is the most important poet of the Beat generation. He was born in Newark, New Jersey, the son of poet Louis Ginsberg and Naomi Ginsberg, a Russian immigrant. He attended Columbia University and met author William Burroughs in New York. Burroughs introduced Ginsberg to many modern writers including Kafka and Rimbaud. He lived, on and off, with Burroughs and with Jack Kerouac and would take trips on merchant ships, work as a night porter or dishwasher, and work on completing his studies at Columbia, where he graduated in 1948.

Many incidents in Ginsberg's life have passed into legend, and he is known as much for his celebrity as for his poetry. Some of these incidents concerned his years at Columbia, such as being expelled in his sophmore year for writing obscenities in the dust of his dormitory window or having to spend eight months in a mental institution upon graduation because an addict friend used his apartment to store stolen goods. Ginsberg pleaded insanity to avoid being prosecuted as an accomplice. However, the most important incident involves having a hallucination of William Blake reciting his poems. First he heard "Ah! Sunflower" and then he heard "The Sick Rose." Ginsberg experienced this almost as a religious conversion.

Ginsberg worked at odd jobs and was even a market researcher, but he soon left for the Bohemian lifestyle of San Francisco. There he met many poets who became part of the San Francisco Renaissance such as Robert Duncan, Kenneth Rexroth, Gary Snyder, and Lawrence Ferlinghetti, whose City Lights Bookstore published "Howl." Ginsberg's reading of this poem was one of the signature events for the Beat generation, and "Howl" became one of the most circulated poems ever, though it was temporarily banned by the San Francisco police for being obscene. Both Jack Kerouac and William Carlos Williams influenced the writing of this poem, and Ginsberg acknowledged the volume, *Howl and Other Poems*, as an experiment paying tribute to William Blake and Walt Whitman.

Ginsberg spent the sixties travelling, giving poetry readings, studying with Buddhist teachers in India, and participating in anti-war protests and rallies to repeal harsh drug laws and anti-homosexual legislation. Ginsberg's other notable works include *Kaddish and Other Poems*, the title poem chronicling the life of his mother and her struggle with mental illness; *Empty Mirror: Early Poems, Reality Sandwiches,* and *The Fall of America*, which was written during his travels throughout America. He has received grants from the Guggenheim Foundation, the National Institute of Arts and Letters and the National Endowment for the Arts. He, along with Adrienne Rich, was a cowinner of the National Book Award for Poetry in 1974.

Ode to Failure

Many prophets have failed, their voices silent
ghost-shouts in basements nobody heard dusty laughter in family attics
nor glanced them on park benches weeping with relief under empty sky
Walt Whitman viva'd local losers—courage to Fat Ladies in the Freak
Show!
    nervous prisoners whose mustached lips dripped sweat on chow lines—
Mayakovsky cried, Then die! my verse, did like the workers' rank & file
    fusilladed in Petersburg!
Prospero burned his Power books & plummeted his magic wand to the
    bottom of dragon seas
Alexander the Great failed to find more worlds to conquer!
O Failure I chant your terrifying name, accept me your 54 year
old Prophet
epicking Eternal Flop! I join your Pantheon of mortal bards,
& hasten this
    ode with high blood pressure
rushing to the top of my skull as if I wouldn't last another minute,
like the Dying Gaul! to
You, Lord of blind Monet, deaf Beethoven, armless Venus
de Milo, headless
    Winged Victory!
I failed to sleep with every bearded rosy-cheeked boy I jacked off over
My tirades destroyed no Intellectual Unions of KGB & CIA
in turtlenecks
    & underpants, their woolen suits and tweeds
I never dissolved Plutonium or dismantled the nuclear Bomb
before my skull
    lost hair
I have not yet stopped the Armies of entire Mankind in
their march toward
    World War III
I never got to Heaven, Nirvana, X, Whatchamacallit, I never left Earth,
I never learned to die.

Wales Visitation

White fog lifting & falling on mountain-brow
    Trees moving in rivers of wind
                             The clouds arise
    as on a wave, gigantic eddy lifing mist
    above teeming ferns exquisitely swayed
                          along a green crag
    glimpsed thru mullioned glass in valley raine—

Bardic, O Self, Visitacione, tell naught
    but what seen by one man in a vale in Albion,
    of the folk, whose physical sciences end in Ecology,
                  the wisdom of earthly relations,
    of mouths & eyes interknit ten centuries visible
    orchards of mind language manifest human,
of the satanic thistle that raises its horned symmetry
    flowering above sister grass-daisies' pink tiny
                bloomlets angelic as lightbulbs—

Remember 160 miles from London's symmetrical thorned tower
    & network of TV pictures flashing bearded your Self
    the lambs on the tree-nooked hillside this day bleating
    heard in Blake's old ear, & the silent thought of Wordsworth in
                        eld Stillness
    clouds passing through skeleton arches of Tintern Abbey—
    Bard Nameless as the Vast, babble to Vastness!
All the Valley quivered, one extended motion, wind
            undulating on mossy hills
    a giant wash that sank white fog delicately down red runnels
            on the mountainside
    whose leaf-branch tendrils moved asway
            in granitic undertow down—
and lifted the floating Nebulous upward, and lifted the arms of the
                              trees
    and lifted the grasses an instant in balance
    and lifted the lambs to hold still
    and lifted the green of the hill, in one solemn wave

A solid mass of Heaven, mist-infused, ebbs thru the vale,
   a wavelet of Immensity, lapping gigantic through Llanthony
                                         Valley,
   the length of all England, valley upon valley under Heaven's ocean
                                  tonned with cloud-hang,
      Heaven balanced on a grassblade—
Roar of the mountain wind slow, sigh of the body,
    One Being on the mountainside stirring gently
      Exquisite scales trembling everywhere in balance,
one motion thru the cloudy sky-floor shifting on the million
                                 feet of daisies,
one Majesty the motion that stirred wet grass quivering
    to the farthest tendril of white fog poured down
      through shivering flowers on the mountain's
                      head—
No imperfection in the budded mountain,
    Valleys breathe, heaven and earth move together,
   daisies push inches of yellow air, vegetables tremble
      green atoms shimmer in grassy mandalas,
sheep speckle the mountainside, revolving their jaws with empty
                                 eyes,

     horses dance in the warm rain,
   tree-lined canals network through live farmland,
    blueberries fringe stone walls
    on hill breasts nippled with hawthorn,
   pheasants croak up meadow-bellies haired with fern—
Out, out on the hillside, into the ocean sound, into delicate
      gusts of wet air,
Fall on the ground, O great Wetness, O Mother, No harm on
                      thy body!
Stare close, no imperfection in the grass,
     each flower Buddha-eye, repeating the story,
     the myriad-formed soul
Kneel before the foxglove raising green buds, mauve bells drooped
    doubled down the stem trembling antennae,
  & look in the eyes of the branded lambs that stare
    breathing stockstill under dripping hawthorn—
I lay down mixing my beard with the wet hair of the mountainside,

smelling the brown vagina-moist ground, harmless,
        tasting the violet thistle-hair, sweetness—
One being so balanced, so vast, that its softest breath
        moves every floweret in the stillness on the valley floor,
    trembles lamb-hair hung gossamer rain-beaded in the grass,
lifts trees on their roots, birds in the great draught
        hiding their strength in the rain, bearing same weight,

Groan thru breast and neck, a great Oh! to earth heart
                Calling our Presence together
        The great secret is no secret
            Senses fit the winds,
                Visible is visible,
        rain-mist curtains wave through the bearded vale,
            grey atoms wet the wind's Kaballah
Crosslegged on a rock in dusk rain,
        rubber booted in soft grass, mind moveless,
    breath trembled in white daisies by the roadside,
            Heaven breath and my own symmetric
        Airs wavering thru antlered green fern
drawn in my navel, same breath as breathes thru Capel-Y-Ffn,
            Sounds of Aleph and Aum
                through forests of gristle,
        my skull and Lord Hereford's Knob equal,
            All Albion one.
What did I notice? Particulars! The
        vision of the great One is myriad—
    smoke curls upward from ash tray,
            house fire burned low,
The night, still wet & moody black heaven
                starless
    upward in motion with wet wind.

My Sad Self
To Frank O'Hara

Sometimes when my eyes are red
I go up on top of the RCA Building
        and gaze at my world, Manhattan—
            my buildings, streets I've done feats in,
                lofts, beds, coldwater flats
—on Fifth Ave below which I also bear in mind,
        its ant cars, little yellow taxis, men
            walking the size of specks of wool—
Panorama of the bridges, sunrise over Brooklyn machine,
        sun go down over New Jersey where I was born
            & Paterson where I played with ants—
my later loves on 15th Street,
        my greater loves of Lower East Side,
            my once fabulous amours in the Bronx
                faraway—
paths crossing in these hidden streets,
        my history summed up, my absences
            and ecstasies in Harlem—
—sun shining down on all I own
        in one eyeblink to the horizon
            in my last eternity—

                                    matter is water.

Sad,
    I take the elevator and go
            down, pondering,
and walk on the pavements staring into all man's

                                    plateglass, faces,
            questioning after who loves,
    and stop, bemused
            in front of an automobile shopwindow
standing lost in calm thought,
            traffic moving up & down 5th Avenue blocks
                behind me
            waiting for a moment when...
Time to go home & cook supper & listen to
            the romantic war news on the radio

                                        ...all movement stops
& I walk in the timeless sadness of existence,
    tenderness flowing thru the buildings,
        my fingertips touching reality's face,
    my own face streaked with tears in the mirror
    of some window—at dusk—
                                        where I have no desire—
    for bonbons—or to own the dresses or Japanese
        lampshades of intellection—

Confused by the spectacle around me,
    Man struggling up the street
        with packages, newspapers,
            ties, beautiful suits
        toward his desire
    Man, woman, streaming over the pavements
        red lights clocking hurried watches &
        movements at the curb—

And all these streets leading
    so crosswise, honking, lengthily,
            by avenues
    stalked by high buildings or crusted into slums
            thru such halting traffic
                                        screaming cars and engines
so painfully to this
    countryside, this graveyard
        this stillness
                                        on deathbed or mountain
    once seen
            never regained or desired
                                        in the mind to come
where all Manhattan that I've seen must disappear.

JAMES MERRILL [Born 1926]

James Merrill was born in New York City to an affluent family; his father was one of the founders of what became the Merrill Lynch investment firm. Merrill attended Amherst College, but his education was interrupted temporarily when he served in the army toward the end of World War II. In 1947 he received a B.A. and travelled extensively after graduation. For the past twenty-five years he has divided his time between Athens, Greece, and Stonington, Connecticut.

Merrill's literary style is distinguished by his exquisite verse technique and his ability to weave autobiographical details into his poetry. Frequent themes that Merrill focuses on are loss and recovery, sexual, erotic experience, and the nature of the universe described from every perspective, such as historically, scientifically and paranormally. One of the strongest influences on Merrill's writing is Proust, as evidenced by the way he incorporates narrative or epic qualities into his verse. Merrill's poetry has always been lauded for its elegance, but, over the years as his subject matter became more personal, his critical acclaim and popularity have grown significantly. *Braving the Elements* (1972) received the Bollingen Award, *Nights and Days* (1966) and *Mirabell* (1978) won prizes from *Poetry* magazine and National Book Awards, and *Divine Comedies* (1976) was awarded the Pulitzer Prize for Poetry.

The Broken Home

Crossing the street,
I saw the parents and the child
At their window, gleaming like fruit
With evening's mild gold leaf.

In a room on the floor below,
Sunless, cooler—a brimming
Saucer of wax, marbly and dim—
I have lit what's left of my life.

I have thrown out yesterday's milk
And opened a book of maxiums.
The flame quickens. The word stirs.

Tell me, tongue of fire,
That you and I are as real
At least as the people upstairs.

My father, who had flown in World War I,
Might have continued to invest his life
In cloud banks well above Wall Street and wife.
But the race was run below, and the point was to win.

Too late now, I make out in his blue gaze
(Through the smoked glass of being thirty-six)
The soul eclipsed by twin black pupils, sex
And business; time was money in those days.

Each thirteenth year he married. When he died
There were already several chilled wives
In sable orbit—rings, cars, permanent waves.
We'd felt him warming up for a green bride.

He could afford it. He was "in his prime"
At three score ten. But money was not time.

When my parents were younger this was a popular act:
A veiled woman would leap from an electric, wine-dark car
To the steps of no matter what—the Senate or the Ritz Bar—
And bodily, at newsreel speed, attack

No matter whom—Al Smith or José Maria Sert
or Clemenceau—veins standing out on her throat
As she yelled *War mongerer! Pig! Give us the vote!*,
And would have to be hauled away in her hobble skirt.

What had the man done? Oh, made history.
Her business (he had implied) was giving birth,
Tending the house, mending the socks.

Always that same old story—
Father Time and Mother Earth,
A marriage on the rocks.

One afternoon, red, satyr-thighed
Michael, the Irish setter, head
Passionately lowered, led
The child I was to a shut door. Inside,

Blinds beat sun from the bed.
The green-gold room throbbed like a bruise.
Under a sheet, clad in taboos
Lay whom we sought, her hair undone, outspread,

And of a blackness found, if ever now, in old
Engravings where the acid bit.
I must have needed to touch it
Or the whiteness—was she dead?
Her eyes flew open, startled strange and cold.
The dog slumped to the floor. She reached for me. I fled.

Tonight they have stepped out onto the gravel.
The party is over. It's the fall
Of 1931. They love each other still.

She: Charlie, I can't stand the pace.
He: Come on, honey—why, you'll bury us all!

A lead soldier guards my windowsill:
Kahaki rifle, uniform, and face.
Something in me grows heavy, silvery, pliable.

How intensely people used to feel!
Like metal poured at the close of a proletarian novel,
Refined and glowing from the crucible,
I see those two hearts, I'm afraid,
Still. Cool here in the graveyard of good and evil,
They are even so to be honored and obeyed.

...Obeyed, at least, inversely. Thus
I rarely buy a newspaper, or vote.
To do so, I have learned, is to invite
The tread of a stone guest with my house.

Shooting this rusted bolt, though, against him,
I trust I am no less time's child than some
Who on the heath impersonate Poor Tom
Or on the barricades risk life and limb.

Nor do I try to keep a garden, only
An avocado in a glass of water—
Roots pallid, gemmed with air. And later,

When the small gilt leaves have grown
Fleshy and green, I let them die, yes, yes,
And start another. I am earth's no less.

A child, a red dog roamed the corridors,
Still, of the broken home. No sound. The brilliant
Rag runners halt before wide-open doors.
My old room! Its wallpaper—cream, medallioned
With pink and brown—brings back the first nightmares,
Long summer colds, and Emma, sepia-faced,
Perspiring over broth carried upstairs
Aswim with golden fats I could not taste.

The real house became a boarding-school.
Under the ballroom ceiling's allegory
Someone at last may actually be allowed
To learn something; or, from my window, cool
With the unstiflement of the entire story,
Watch a red setter stretch and sink in cloud.

The Mad Scene

Again last night I dreamed the dream called Laundry.
In it, the sheets and towels of a life we were going to share,
The milk-stiff bibs, the shroud, each rag to be ever
Trampled or soiled, bled on or groped for blindly,
Came swooning out of an enormous willow hamper
Onto moon-marbly boards. We had just met. I watched
From outer darkness. I had dressed myself in clothes
Of a new fiber that never stains or wrinkles, never
Wears thin. The opera house sparkled with tiers
And tiers of eyes, like mine enlarged by belladonna,
Trained inward. There I saw the cloud-clot, gust by gust,

Form, and the lightning bite, and the roan mane unloosen.
Fingers were running in panic over the flute's nine gates.
Why did I flinch? I loved you. And in the downpour laughed
To have us wrung white, gnarled together, one
Topmost mordent of wisteria,
As the lean tree burst into grief.

The Parnassians

Theirs was a language within ours, a loge
Hidden by bee-stitched hanging from the herd.
The mere exchanged glance between word and word
Took easily the place, the privilege,
Of words themselves. Here therefore all was tact.
Pairs at first blush ill-matched, like *turd* or *monstrance*,
Tracing their cousinage by consonants,
Communed, ecstatic, through the long entr'acte.

Without our common meanings, though, that world
Would have slid headlong to apocalypse.
We'd built the Opera, changed the scenery, trod
Grapes for the bubbling flutes mild fingers twirled;
As footmen, by no eyelid's twitch betrayed
Our scorn and sound investment of their tips.

Last Words

My life, your light green eyes
Have lit on me with joy.
There's nothing I don't know
Or shall not know again,
Over and over again.
It's noon, it's dawn, it's night,
I am the dog that dies
In the deep street of Troy
Tomorrow, long ago—
Part of me dims with pain,
Becomes the stinging flies,
The bent head of the boy.
Part looks into your light
And lives to tell you so.

An Urban Convalescence

Out for a walk, after a week in bed,
I find them tearing up part of my block
And, chilled through, dazed and lonely, join the dozen
In meek attitudes, watching a huge crane
Fumble luxuriously in the filth of years.
Her jaws dribble rubble. An old man
Laughs and curses in her brain,
Bringing to mind the close of *The White Goddess*.

As usual in New York, everything is torn down
Before you have had time to care for it.
Head bowed, at the shrine of noise, let me try to recall
What building stood here. Was there a building at all?
I have lived on this same street for a decade.

Wait. Yes. Vaguely a presence rises
Some five floors high, of shabby stone
—Or am I confusing it with another one
In another part of town, or of the world?—
And over its lintel into focus vaguely
Misted with blood (my eyes are shut)
A single garland sways, stone fruit, stone leaves,
Which years of grit had etched until it thrust
Roots down, even into the poor soil of my seeing.
When did the garland become part of me?
I ask myself, amused almost,
Then shiver once from head to toe,

Transfixed by a particular cheap engraving of garlands
Bought for a few francs long ago,
All calligraphic tendril and cross-hatched rondure,
Ten years ago, and crumpled up to stanch
Boughs dripping, whose white gestures filled a cab,
And thought of neither then nor since.
Also, to clasp them, the small, red-nailed hand

Of no one I can place. Wait. No. Her name, her features
Lie toppled underneath that year's fashions.
The words she must have spoken, setting her face
To fluttering like a veil, I cannot hear now,
Let alone understand.

So that I am already on the stair,
As it were, of where I lived,
When the whole structure shudders at my tread
And soundlessly collapses, filling
The air with motes of stone.
Onto the still erect building next door
Are pressed levels and hues—
Pocked rose, streaked greens, brown whites.
Who drained the pousse-café?
Wire and pipes, snapped off at the roots, quiver.

Well, that is what life does. I stare
A moment longer, so. And presently
The massive volume of the world
Closes again.

Upon that book I swear
To abide by what it teaches:
Gospels of ugliness and waste,
Of towering voids, of soiled gusts,
Of a shrieking to be faced.
Full into, eyes astream with cold—

With cold?
All right then. With self-knowledge.

Indoors at last, the pages of *Time* are apt
To open, and the illustrated mayor of New York,
Given a glimpse of how and where I work,
To note yet one more house that can be scrapped.

Unwillingly I picture
My walls weathering in the general view.

It is not even as though the new
Buildings did very much for architecture.

Suppose they did. The sickness of our time requires
That these as well be blasted in their prime.
You would think the simple fact of having lasted
Threatened our cities like mysterious fires.

There are certain phrases which to use in a poem
Is like rubbing silver with quicksilver. Bright
But facile, the glamour deadens overnight.
For instance, how "the sickness of our time"

Enhances, then debases, what I feel.
At my desk I swallow in a glass of water
No longer cordial, scarcely wet, a pill
They had told me not to take until much later.

With the result that back into my imagination
The city glides, like cities seen from the air,
Mere smoke and sparkle to the passenger
Having in mind another destination

Which now is not that honey-slow descent
Of the Champs-Elysées, her hand in his,
But the dull need to make some kind of house
Out of the life lived, out of the love spent.

The Octopus

There are many monsters that a glassen surface
Restrains. And none more sinister
Than vision asleep in the eye's tight translucence.
Rarely it seeks now to unloose
Its diamonds. Having divined how drab a prison
The purest mortal tissue is,
Rarely it wakes. Unless, coaxed out by lusters
Extraordinary, like the octopus

From the gloom of its tank half-swimming half-drifting
Toward anything fair, a handkerchief
Or child's face dreaming near the glass, the writher
Advances in a godlike wreath
Of its own wrath. Chilled by such fragile reeling
A hundred blows of a boot-heel
Shall not quell, the dreamer wakes and hungers.
Percussive pulses, drum or gong,
Build in his skull their loud entrancement,
Volutions of a Hindu dance.
His hands move clumsily in the first conventional
Gestures of assent.
He is willing to undergo the volition and fervor
Of many fleshlike arms, observe
These in their holiness of indirection
Destroy, adore, evolve, reject—
Till on glass rigid with his own seizure
At length the sucking jewels freeze.

The Peacock

I speak to the unbeautiful of this bird
        Celestially bored,
That on gnarled gray feet under willows trails
Too much of himself, like Proust, a long brocade
Along, not seen but felt; that's never spared,
        Most mortal of his trials,
    Lifting this burden up in pride.

The outspread tail is drab seen from the back
        But it's worthwhile to look
At what strenuous midribs make the plumage stretch.
Then, while it teeters in the light wind, ah
He turns, black, buff, green, gold, that zodiac
        Of-no, not eyes so much
    As idiot mouths repeating: I.

Consider other birds: the murderous swan
      And dodo now undone,
The appalling dove, hens' petulant sisterhood;
And now this profile that no cry alarms,
Tense with idlesse, as though already on
      A terrace in boxwood
    Or graven in a coat of arms;

And in all these, the comic flaw of nature
      No natural hand can suture,
A lessening—whether by want of shape they fail,
Of song, or will to live, or something else.
How comforting to think blest any creature
      So vain, so beautiful!
    But some have known such comfort false.

A beatitude of trees which shall inherit
      Whoever's poor in spirit
Receives the peacock into cumbersome shade.
Some who have perfect beauty do not grieve,
As I, when beauty passes. They've known merit
      In word, emotion, deed:
    Lone angels round each human grave.

Foliage of Vision

As landscapes richen after rain, the eye
Atones, turns fresh after a fit of tears.
When all the foliage of vision stirs
I glimpse the plump fruit hanging, falling, fallen
Where wasps are sputtering. In the full sky
Time, a lean wasp sucks at the afternoon.

The tiny black and yellow agent of rot
Assaults the plum, stinging and singing. What
A marvel is the machinery of decay!

How rare the day's wrack! What fine violence
Went to inject its gall in the glad eye!
The plum lies all brocaded with corruption.

There is no wit in weeping, yet I wept
To hear the insect wrath and rhythm of time
Surround the plum that fell like a leper's thumb.
The hours, my friend, are felicitous imagery,
Yet I became their image to watch the sun
Dragging with it a scarlet palace down.

The eye attunes, pastoral warbler, always.
Joy in the cradle of calamity
Wakes though dim voices work at lullaby.
Triumph of vision: the act by which we see
Is both the landscape-gardening of our dream
And the root's long revel under the clipped lawn.

I think of saints with hands pierced and wrenched eyes
Sensational beyond the art of sense,
As though whatever they saw was about to be
While feeling alters in its imminence
To palpable joy; of Dante's ascent in hell
To greet with a cleansed gaze the petaled spheres;

Of Darwin's articulate ecstasy as he stood
Before a tangled bank and watched the creatures
Of air and earth noble among much leafage
Dancing an order rooted not only in him
But in themselves, bird, fruit, wasp, limber vine,
Time and disaster and the limping blood.

FRANK O'HARA [1926-1966]

Frank O'Hara was born in Baltimore, Maryland, but grew up in a suburb of Massachusetts. As a youngster, he wanted to be a concert pianist and studied music seriously until he entered Harvard. Once there he changed his major to English, deciding to become a writer instead. At Harvard he met John Ashbery and first published his writing in the *Harvard Advocate*. During trips to New York he met Kenneth Koch, James Schuyler, Jackson Pollock, Larry Rivers, and other painters with whom he would later associate. In fact, O'Hara, Ashbery, Koch, Schuyler, and Barbara Guest were all part of a group referred to as the New York school of poets, which took its name from their association with the 1950 New York abstract-expressionist painters. Following his years at Harvard, O'Hara went to the University of Michigan upon the urging of his professor, John Ciardi, but soon missed New York and returned in 1951. He was the first New York poet to write art criticism and soon became editorial associate for *Art News*. He also began a long relationship with the Museum of Modern Art, starting as a clerk and ending up as the associate curator.

O'Hara had a casual attitude toward his career as a poet. He did not court publishers, editors or academic alliances, though he was quite a knowledgeable poet who was aware of current trends in his field. His interests in poetry ranged from William Carlos Williams to W.H. Auden to the French symbolist Apollinaire to the surrealist Vladimir Mayakovski. He was also familiar with Charles Olson's essay "Projective Verse" before it gained renown. His professional break came when he was included in Donald Allen's *New American Poetry* (1960), which brought many new, young poets to the public's attention. It was his own volume, *Lunch Poems*, however, which solidified his reputation and earned him a small but faithful following, which grew tremendously after his *Collected Poems* was published posthumously in 1971.

Steps

How funny you are today New York
like Ginger Rogers in *Swingtime*
and St. Bridget's steeple leaning a little to the left

here I have just jumped out of a bed full of V-days
(I got tired of D-days) and blue you there still
accepts me foolish and free
all I want is a room up there
and you in it

and even the traffic halt so thick is a way
for people to rub up against each other
and when their surgical appliances lock
they stay together
for the rest of the day (what a day)
I go by to check a slide and I say
that painting's not so blue

where's Lana Turner
she's out eating
and Garbo's backstage at the met
everyone's taking their coat off
so they can show a rib-cage to the rib-watchers
and the park's full of dancers with their tights and shoes
in little bags
who are often mistaken for worker-outers at the West Side Y
why not
the Pittsburgh Pirates shout because they won
and in a sense we're all winning
we're alive

the apartment was vacated by a gay couple
who moved to the country for fun
they moved a day too soon
even the stabbings are helping the population explosion
though in the wrong country

and all those liars have left the U N
the Seagram Building's no longer rivalled in interest
not that we need liquor (we just like it)

and the little box is out on the sidewalk
next to the delicatessen
so the old man can sit on it and drink beer
and get knocked off it by his wife later in the day
while the sun is still shining

oh god it's wonderful
to get out of bed
and drink too much coffee
and smoke too many cigarettes
and love you so much

Poem

Lana Turner has collapsed!
I was trotting along and suddenly
it started raining and snowing
and you said it was hailing
but hailing hits you on the head
hard so it was really snowing and
raining and I was in such a hurry
to meet you but the traffic
was acting exactly like the sky
and suddenly I see a headline
LANA TURNER HAS COLLAPSED!
there is no snow in Hollywood
there is no rain in California
I have been to lots of parties
and acted perfectly disgraceful
but I never actually collapsed
oh Lane Turner we love you get up

Ode: Salute to the French Negro Poets

From near the sea, like Whitman my great predecessor, I call
to the spirits of other lands to make fecund my existence

do not spare your wrath upon our shores, that trees may grow
upon the sea, mirror of our total mankind in the weather

one who no longer remembers dancing in the heat of the moon may call
across the shifting sands, trying to live in the terrible western world

here where to love at all's to be a politician, as to love a poem
is pretentious, this may sound tendentious but it's lyrical

which shows what lyricism has been brought to by our fabled times
where cowards are shibboleths and one specific love's traduced

by shame for what you love more generally and never would avoid
where reticence is paid for by a poet in his blood or casing to be

blood! blood that we have mountains in our veins to stand of jackals
in the pillaging of our desires and allegiances, Aimé Césaire

for if there is fortuity it's in the love we bear each other's differences
in race which is the poetic ground on which we rear our smiles

standing in the sun of marshes as we wade slowly toward the
culmination
of a gift which is categorically the most difficult relationship

and should be sought as such because it is our nature, nothing
inspires us but the love we want upon the frozen face of earth

and utter disparagement turns into praise as generations read the
message
of our hearts in adolescent closets who once shot at us in doorways

or kept us from living freely because they were too young then to know
what they would ultimately need from a barren and heart-sore life

the beauty of America, neither cool jazz nor devoured Egyptian heroes,
lies in
lives in the darkness I inhabit in the midst of sterile millions

the only truth is face to face, the poem whose words become your
mouth
and dying in black and white we fight for what we love, not are

Why I Am Not a Painter

I am not a painter, I am a poet.
Why? I think I would rather be
a painter, but I am not. Well,

for instance, Mike Goldberg
is starting a painting. I drop in.
"Sit down and have a drink" he
says. I drink; we drink. I look
up. "You have SARDINES in it."
"Yes, it needed something there."
"Oh." I go and the days go by
and I drop in again. The painting
is going on, and I go, and the days
go by. I drop in. The painting is
finished. "Where's SARDINES?"
All that's left is just
letters, "It was too much," Mike says.

But me? One day I am thinking of
a color: orange. I write a line
about orange. Pretty soon it is a
whole page of words, not lines.
Then another page. There should be
so much more, not of orange, of
words, of how terrible orange is
and life. Days go by. It is even in

prose, I am a real poet. My poem
is finished and I haven't mentioned
orange yet. It's twelve poems, I call
it ORANGES. And one day in a gallery
I see Mike's painting, called SARDINES.

A True Account of Talking
to the Sun at Fire Island

The Sun woke me this morning loud
and clear, saying "Hey! I've been
trying to wake you up for fifteen
minutes. Don't be so rude, you are
only the second poet I've ever chosen
to speak to personally
                    so why
aren't you more attentive? If I could
burn you through the window I would
to wake you up. I can't hang around
here all day."
            "Sorry, Sun, I stayed
up late last night talking to Hal."

"When I woke up Mayakovsky he was
a lot more prompt" the Sun said
petulantly. "Most people are up
already waiting to see if I'm going
to put in an appearance."
                    I tried
to apologize "I missed you yesterday."
"That's better" he said "I didn't
know you'd come out. You may be
wondering why I've come so close?"
"Yes" I said beginning to feel hot
wondering if maybe he wasn't burning me
anyway.

"Frankly I wanted to tell you
I like your poetry. I see a lot
on my rounds and you're okay. You may
not be the greatest thing on earth, but
you're different. Now, I've heard some
say you're crazy, they being excessively
calm themselves to my mind, and other
crazy poets think that you're a boring
reactionary. Not me.
                    Just keep on
like I do and pay no attention. You'll
find that people always will complain
about the atmosphere, either too hot
or too cold too bright or too dark, days
too short or too long.
                    If you don't appear
at all one day they think you're lazy
or dead. Just keep right on, I like it.

And don't worry about your lineage
poetic or natural. The Sun shines on
the jungle, you know, on the tundra
the sea, the ghetto. Wherever you were
I knew it and saw you moving. I was waiting
for you to get to work.
                    And now that you
are making your own days, so to speak,
even if no one reads you but me
you won't be depressed. Not
everyone can look up, even at me. It
hurts their eyes."
                    "Oh Sun, I'm so grateful to you!"

"Thanks and remember I'm watching. It's
easier for me to speak to you out
here. I don't have to slide down
between buildings to get your ear.
I know you love Manhattan, but
you ought to look up more often.
                                        And

always embrace things, people earth
sky stars, as I do, freely and with
the appropriate sense of space. That
is your inclination, known in the heavens
and you should follow it to hell, if
necessary, which I doubt.

                                    Maybe we'll

speak again in Africa, of which I too
am specially fond. Go back to sleep now
Frank, and I may leave a tiny poem
in that brain of yours as my farewell."

"Sun, don't go!" I was awake
at last. "No, go I must, they're calling
me."
            "Who are they?"
                    Rising he said "Some
day you'll know. They're calling to you
too." Darkly he rose, and then I slept.

Hôtel Transylvanie

Shall we win at love or shall we lose

                                    can it be

that hurting and being hurt is a trick forcing the love
we want to appear, that the hurt is a card
and is it black? is it red? is it a paper, dry of tears
chevalier, change your expression! the wind is sweeping over
the gaming tables ruffling the cards/they are black and red
like a Futurist torture and how do you know it isn't always there
waiting while doubt is the father that has you kidnapped by friends

        yet you will always live in a jealous society of accident
you will never know how beautiful you are or how beautiful
the other is, you will continue to refuse to die for yourself

you will continue to sing on trying to cheer everyone up
and they will know as they listen with excessive pleasure that you're
dead
          and they will not mind that they have let you entertain
at the expense of the only thing you want in the world/you are amusing
as a game is amusing when someone is forced to lose as in a game must

          oh *hôtel*, you should be merely a bed
surrounded by walls where two souls meet and do nothing but breathe
breathe in breathe out fuse illuminate confuse *stick* dissemble
but not as cheaters at cards have something to win/you have only to be
as you are being, as you must be, as you always are, as you shall be
forever
no matter what fate deals you or the imagination discards like a tyrant
as the drums descend and summon the hatchet over the tinselled
realities

you know that I am not here to fool around, that I must win or die
I expect you to do everything because it is of no consequence/no duel
you must rig the deck you must make me win at whatever cost to the
reputation
of the establishment/sublime moment of dishonest hope/I must win
for if the floods of tears arrive they will wash it all away
                                                    and then
you will know what it is to want something, but you may not be allowed
to die as I have died, you may only be allowed to drift downstream
to another body of inimical attractions for which you will
substitute/distrust
and I will have had my revenge on the black bitch of my nature which you
                              love as I have never loved myself

but I hold on/I am lyrical to a fault/I do not despair being too foolish
where will you find me, projective verse, since I will be gone?
for six seconds of your beautiful face I will sell the hotel and commit
an uninteresting suicide in Louisiana where it will take them a long time
to know who I am/why I came there/what and why I am and made to
happen

Les Etiquettes Jaunes

I picked up a leaf
today from the sidewalk
This seems childish.

Leaf! you are so big!
How can you change your
color, then just fall!

As if there were no
such thing as integrity!

You are too relaxed
to answer me. I am too
frightened to insist.

Leaf! don't be neurotic
like the small chameleon.

For James Dean

Welcome me, if you will,
as the ambassador of a hatred
who knows it cause
and does not envy you your whim
of ending him.

For a young actor I am begging
peace, gods. Alone
in the empty streets of New York
I am its dirty feet and head
and he is dead.

He has banged into your wall
of air, your hubris, racing
towards your heights and you
have cut him from your table
which is built, how unfairly
for us! not on trees, but on clouds.

I speak as one whose filth
is like his own, of pride
and speed and your terrible
example nearer than the sirens' speech,
a spirit eager for the punishment
which is your only recognition.

Peace! to be true to a city
of rats and to love the envy
of the dreary, smudged mouthers
of an arcane dejection
smoldering quietly in the perception
of hopelessness and scandal
at unnatural vigor. Their dreams
are their own, as are the toilets
of a great railway terminal
and the sequins of a very small,
very fat eyelid.
                    I take this
for myself, and you take up
the triad of my life between your teeth,
tin thread and tarnished with abuse,
you still shall hear
as long as the beast in me maintains
its taciturn power to close my lids
in tears, and my loins move yet
in the ennobling pursuit of all the worlds
you have left me alone in, and would be
the dolorous distraction from,
while you summon your army of anguishes
which is a million hooting blood vessels

on the eyes and in the ears
at that instant before death.

                                                    And

the menials who surrounded him critically,
languorously waiting for a
final impertinence to rebel
and enslave him, starlets and other
glittering things in the hog-wallow,
lunging mireward in their inane
mothlike adoration of niggardly
care and stagnant respects

paid themselves, you spared,
as a hospital preserves its orderlies
Are these your latter-day saints,
these unctuous starers, muscular
somnambulists, these stages for which
no word's been written hollow
enough, these exhibitionists in
well-veiled booths, these navel-suckers?

Is it true that you high ones, celebrated
among amorous flies, hated the
prodigy and invention of his nerves?
To withhold your light
from painstaking paths!
your love
should be difficult, as his was hard.

Nostrils of pain down avenues
of luminous spit-globes breathe in
the fragrance of his innocent flesh
like smoke, the temporary lift,
the post-cancer excitement
of vile manners and veal-thin lips,
obscure in the carelessness of your scissors.

Men cry from the grave while they still live
and now I am this dead man's voice,
stammering, a little in the earth.

I take up
the nourishment of his pale green eyes,
out of which I shall prevent
flowers from growing, your flowers.

Poem
"A la recherche de Gertrude Stein"

When I am feeling depressed and anxious sullen
all you have to do is take your clothes off
and all is wiped away revealing life's tenderness
that we are flesh and breathe and are near us
as you are really as you are I become as I
really am alive and knowing vaguely what is
and what is important to me above the intrusions
of incident and accidental relationships
which have nothing to do with my life

when I am in your presence I feel life is strong
and will defeat all its enemies and all of mine
and all of yours and yours in you and mine in me
sick logic and feeble reasoning are cured
by the perfect symmetry of your arms and legs
spread out making an eternal circle together
creating a golden pillar beside the Atlantic
the faint line of hair dividing your torso
gives my mind rest and emotions their release
into the infinite air where since once we are
together we always will be in this life come what may

To John Ashbery

I can't believe there's not
another world where we will sit
and read new poems to each other
high on a mountain in the wind.
You can be Tu Fu, I'll be Po Chü-i
and the Monkey Lady'll be in the moon,
smiling at our ill-fitting heads
as we watch snow settle on a twig.
Or shall we be really gone? this
is not the grass I saw in my youth!
and if the moon, when it rises
tonight, is empty—a bad sign,
meaning "You go, like the blossoms."

Autobiographia Literaria

When I was a child
I played by myself in a
corner of the schoolyard
all alone.

I hated dolls and I
hated games, animals were
not friendly and birds
flew away.

If anyone was looking
for me I hid behind a
tree and cried out "I am
an orphan."

And here I am, the
center of all beauty!
writing these poems!
Imagine!

W.D. SNODGRASS [Born 1926]

W.D. Snodgrass was born on January 5 in Wilkinsberg, Pennsylvania. He grew up in Beaver Falls and was educated at Geneva College. Serving during the last years of World War II in the United States Navy, Snodgrass returned to school in 1947 at the State University of Iowa where he studied with Robert Lowell who was directing the Writer's Workshop there. In 1959 Snodgrass had his first book, *Heart's Needle*, published and was awarded the Pulitzer Prize for it the following year. The list of prizes and awards won by Snodgrass is quite lengthy as is the list of colleges and universities at which he has taught. He has directed several writing workshops and has translated *Traditional Hungarian Songs* among other works. Five books of his poetry have been published since that first widely acclaimed book, but it was that first work which made his reputation as a Confessional poet in the style of Lowell, Sexton, and Plath. Clearly autobiographical, *Heart's Needle* draws its energy from the pain of the gradual estrangement from his daughter after his divorce. In 1977 Snodgrass published *The Fuhrer Bunker: A Cycle of Poems in Progress*. This work is written in a dramatic style where the pronoun "I" would never be confused with the identity of the poet—as it could be in *Heart's Needle*. Thus, labeling Snodgrass as a Confessional poet misrepresents a poet grown beyond convenient tags. His most recent book, published in 1984, is *Belladonna*.

Mhtis Outis

For R. M. Powell

He fed them generously who were his flocks,
Picked, shatterbrained, for food. Passed as a goat
Among his sheep, I cast off. Though hurled rocks
And prayers deranged by torment tossed our boat,
I could not silence, somehow, this defiant
Mind. From my fist into the frothed wake ran
The white eye's gluten of the living giant
I had escaped, by trickery, as no man.

Unseen where all seem stone blind, pure disguise
Has brought me home alone to No Man's land
To look at nothing I dare recognize.
My dead blind guide, you lead me here to claim
Still waters that will never wash my hand,
To kneel by my old face and know my name.

At the Park Dance

As the melting park
darkens, the firefly winks
to signal loving strangers
from their pavilion
lined with Easter colored
lights, fading out together

until they merge with
weathered huge trees and join
the small frogs, those warm singers;
and they have achieved
love's vanishing point
where all perspectives mingle,

where even the most
close things are indistinct
or lost, where bright worlds shrink,
they will grope to find
blind eyes make all one world;
their unseen arms, horizons.

Beyond, jagged stars
are glinting like jacks hurled
farther than eyes can gather;
on the dancefloor, girls
turn, vague as milkweed floats
bobbing from childish fingers.

April Inventory

The green catalpa tree has turned
All white; the cherry blooms once more.
In one whole year I haven't learned
A blessed thing they pay you for.
The blossoms snow down in my hair;
The trees and I will soon be bare.

The trees have more than I to spare.
The sleek, expensive girls I teach,
Younger and pinker every year,
Bloom gradually out of reach.
The pear tree lets its petals drop
Like dandruff on a tabletop.

The girls have grown so young by now
I have to nudge myself to stare.
This year they smile and mind me how
My teeth are falling with my hair.
In thirty years I may not get
Younger, shrewder, or out of debt.

The tenth time, just a year ago,
I made myself a little list
Of all the things I'd ought to know,
Then told my parents, analyst,
And everyone who's trusted me
I'd be substantial, presently.

I haven't read one book about
A book or memorized one plot.
Or found a mind I did not doubt.

I learned one date. And then forgot.
And one by one the solid scholars
Get the degrees, the jobs, the dollars.

And smile above their starchy collars.
I taught my classes Whitehead's notions;
One lovely girl, a song of Mahler's.
Lacking a source-book or promotions,
I showed one child the colors of
A luna moth and how to love.

I taught myself to name my name,
To bark back, loosen love and crying;
To ease my woman so she came,
To ease an old man who was dying.
I have not learned how often I
Can win, can love, but choose to die.

I have not learned there is a lie
Love shall be blonder, slimmer, younger;
That my equivocating eye
Loves only by my body's hunger;
That I have forces, true to feel,
Or that the lovely world is real.

While scholars speak authority
And wear their ulcers on their sleeves,
My eyes in spectacles shall see

These trees procure and spend their leaves.
There is a value underneath
The gold and silver in my teeth.

Though trees turn bare and girls turn wives,
We shall afford our costly seasons;
There is a gentleness survives
That will outspeak and has its reasons.
There is a loveliness exists,
Preserves us, not for specialists.

The Campus on the Hill

Up the reputable walks of old established trees
They stalk, children of the *nouveaux riches*; chimes
Of the tall Clock Tower drench their heads in blessing:
"I don't wanna play at your house;
I don't like you anymore."
My house stands opposite, on the other hill,
Among meadows, with the orchard fences down and
        falling;
Deer come almost to the door.
You cannot see it, even in this clearest morning.
White birds hang in the air between
Over the garbage landfill and those homes thereto
        adjacent,
Hovering slowly, turning, settling down
Like the flakes sifting imperceptibly onto the little town
In a waterball of glass.
And yet, this morning, beyond this quiet scene,
The floating birds, the backyards of the poor,
Beyond the shopping plaza, the dead canal, the hillside
        lying tilted in the air,
Tomorrow has broken out today:
Riot in Algeria, in Cyprus, in Alabama;
Aged in wrong, the empires are declining,

And China gathers, soundlessly, like evidence.
What shall I say to the young on such a morning?—
Mind is the one salvation?—also grammar?—
No; my little ones lean not toward revolt. They
Are the Whites, the vaguely furiously driven, who resist
Their souls with such passivity
As would make Quakers swear. All day, dear Lord, all day
They wear their godhead lightly.
They look out from their hill and say,
To themselves, "We have nowhere to go but down;
The great destination is to stay."
Surely the nations will be reasonable;
They look at the world—don't they?—the world's way?
The clock just now has nothing more to say.

Old Apple Trees

Like battered old millhands, they stand in the orchard—
Like drunk legionnaires, heaving themselves up,
Lurching to attention. Not one of them wobbles
The same way as another. Uniforms won't fit them—
All those cramps, humps, bulges. Here, a limb's gone;
There, rain and corruption have eaten the whole core.
They've all grown too tall, too thick, or too something.
Like men bent too long over desks, engines, benches,
Or bent under mailsacks, under loss.
They've seen too much history and bad weather, grown
Around rocks, into high winds, diseases, grown
Too long to be wilful, too long to be changed.

Oh, I could replant, bulldoze the lot,
Get nursery stock, all the latest ornamentals,
Make the whole place look like a suburb,
Each limb sleek as a teeny bopper's—pink
To the very crotch—each trunk smoothed, ideal
As the fantasy life of an adman.
We might just own the Arboreal Muscle Beach:

each tree disguised as its neighbor. Or each disguised
As if not its neighbor—each doing its own thing
Like executives' children.

                    At least I could prune,
At least I should trim the dead wood; fill holes
Where rain collects and decay starts. Well, I should;
I should. There's a red squirrel nest here someplace.
I live in the hope of hearing one saw-whet owl.
Then, too, they're right about Spring. Bees hum
Through these branches like lascivious intentions. The white
Petals drift down, sift across the ground; this air's so rich

Monet: "Les Nymphéas"

The eyelids glowing, some chill morning.
O world half-known through opening, twilit lids
    Before the vague face clenches into light;
O universal waters like a cloud,
    like those first clouds of half-created matter;
O all things rising, rising like the fumes
    From waters falling, O forever falling;
Infinite, the skeletal shells that fall, relinquished,
    The snowsoft sift of the diatoms, like selves
Downdrifting age upon age through milky oceans;
    O slow downdrifting of the atoms;
O island nebulae and O the nebulous islands
    Wandering these mists like false fires, which are
        true,
Bobbing like milkweed, like warm lanterns bobbing
    Through the snowfilled windless air, blinking and
        passing
As we pass into the memory of women
    Who are passing. Within those depths
What ravening? What devouring rage?
    How shall our living know its ends of yielding?

These things have taken me as the mouth an orange—
    That acrid sweet juice entering every cell;
And I am shared out. I become these things:
    These lilies, if these things are water lilies
Which are dancers growing dim across no floor;
    These mayflies; whirled dust orbiting in the sun;
This blossoming diffused as rushlights; galactic
        vapors;
    Fluorescence into which we pass and penetrate;
O soft as the thighs of women;
    O radiance, into which I go on dying...

Inquest

Under the lamp your hands do not seem red.
What if the vicious histories didn't lie
And, in good time, might cover you with shame?—
You seldom hope to see yourself as dead.

How can you guess what vices on your head
Might shine like dead wood for some distant eye?
Of course you have your faults; you make no claim
To sainthood, but your hands do not look red.

It's no crime to be envied or well-fed;
You aimed at no man's life. Who would deny
Yours is the human and the normal aim?
You scarely want to see yourself as dead.

Only last week the commentators said
Not even foreign generals need die
For circumstantial crimes. You would proclaim
Your own guilt if you saw your own hands red.

If you were hungry, who'd give up his bread
Without a fight? A person has to try
To feed himself; earn his own wealth and fame;
Nobody wants to see himself as dead.

Still, men go back to wars. They're not misled
By the old lies. They know the reasons why.
When you can't praise the world your world became
And see no place where your own hands are red,

It must be someone, then—how have they fled
The justice you had hoped you could apply?
You've hanged your enemies, shown up their game,
So now you don't dare see yourself as dead

And things lose focus. You can lie in bed
Repeating Men do starve. Their children cry.
They really cry. They do not cry your name.
Go back to sleep, your hands do not feel red.

Or sit in some dark newsreel to be led
Through barbed wire and the white dead piled boot high
Your palms sweat; you feel just about the same.
Your last hope is to see yourself as dead

And yet you did not bleed when those were bled.
The humans carry knives. "It is not I!"
The screen goes white you see no one to blame.
Till you endure to see yourself as dead
Your blood in your own hands would not seem red.

No man should come here except on a working pass;
No man should leave here without going to confession.
All Fall, apples nearly crack the boughs;
They hang here red as candles in the
White oncoming snow.

Tonight we'll drive down to the bad part of town
To the New Hungarian Bar or the Klub Polski,
To the Old Hellas where we'll eat the new spring lamb;
Drink good *mavrodaphne*, say, at the Laikon Bar,
Send drinks to the dancers, those meatcutters and laborers
Who move in their native dances, the archaic forms.
Maybe we'll still find our old crone selling chestnuts,

Whose toothless gums can spit out fifteen languages,
Who turns, there, late at night, in the center of the floor,
Her ancient dry hips wheeling their slow, slow *tsamikos;*
We'll stomp under the tables, whistle, we'll all hiss
Till even the belly dancer leaves, disgraced.

We'll drive back, lushed and vacant, in the first dawn;
Out of the light gray mists may rise our flowering
Orchard, the rough trunks holding their formations
Like elders of Colonus, the old men of Thebes
Tossing their white hair, almost whispering.

Soon, each one of us will be taken
By dark powers under this ground
That drove us here, that warped us.
Not one of us got it his own way.
Nothing like anyone of us
Will be seen again, forever.
Each of us held some noble shape in mind.
It seemed better that we kept alive.

After Experience Taught Me...

After experience taught me that all the ordinary
Surroundings of social life are futile and vain;

I'm going to show you something very
Ugly: someday, it might save your life.

Seeing that none of the things I feared contain
In themselves anything either good or bad

What if you get caught without a knife;
Nothing—even a loop of piano wire;

Excepting only in the effect they had
Upon my mind, I resolved to inquire

Take the first two fingers of this hand;
Fork them out—kind of a "V for Victory"—

Whether there might be something whose discovery
Would grant me supreme, unending happiness.

And jam them into the eyes of your enemy.
You have to do this hard. Very hard. Then press

No virtue can be thought to have priority
Over this endeavor to preserve one's being.

Both fingers down around the cheekbone
And setting your foot high into the chest

No man can desire to act rightly, to be blessed,
To live rightly, without simultaneously

You must call up every strength you own
And you can rip off the whole facial mask.

Wishing to be, to act, to live. He must ask
First, in other words, to actually exist.

And you, whiner, who wastes your time
Dawdling over the remorseless earth,
What evil, what unspeakable crime
Have you made your life worth?

The Führer Bunker, Selections

Magda Goebbels

— 19 April, 1945

(Planning to destroy first her six
children by Goebbels, then herself,
Magda prepares to move to the
bunker.)

i

How can you do the things you know you'll do?—
One last act to bring back integrity.
I've got just one desire left: to be true.

You can't pick how you'll live. Our times will screw
Your poor last virtues from you, ruthlessly.
How can you do the things you know you'll do?

My mother drove me on: get married to
Quandt. Rich. Kind enough. If elderly.
I've got just one desire left: to be true.

He turned me against Friedlander, the Jew—
My stepfather who'd raised me lovingly.
How can you do the things you know you'll do?

Quandt trapped me with young Ernst. He planned to sue
Till I found his old tax books. And the key.
I've got just one desire left: to be true.

Those thin books brought me in the revenue
For leisure, for the best society.
How can you do the things you know you'll do?

And then I heard Him speak: our Leader, who
Might have been talking to no one but me.
I've got just one desire left: to be true
Till death to Him. And what I know I'll do.

ii

How can you live through what life brings you to?
Who's showed us, ever, the least loyalty?
All of us find it hard just to be true.

The Chief was wild for me; yet we all knew
He couldn't marry—He needs to be free.
How can you live through what life brings you to?

They said why not take Joseph, then; *in lieu,*
The Chief would visit our place secretly.
All of us find it hard just to be true.

Joseph said *he'd* play false. But he came through;
He kept that single promise faithfully.
How can you live through what life brings you to?

I, too, found lovers, given time. Some few
Were his good friends—his staff, his ministry.
All of us find it hard just to be true.

He wanted Lida; I took Karl. Then who
But the Chief sealed us shut—a family!
How can you live through what life brings you to?

So now I won't leave Joseph; I'll die, too.
The children? They'll just have to come with me.
All of us find it hard just to be true
Till death to all this false world brings you to.

iii

The children? They'll just have to come with me.
At their age, how could they find their own way?
We must preserve them from disloyalty.

They're too good for the world we all foresee.
If they were old enough, we know they'd say

It's right and just they'll have to come with me.

My father left—divorced—when I was three
So how could I leave them alone today?
We must preserve them from disloyalty.

They've been the fist behind my policy
Since Joseph and that Slav girl ran astray;
It's right and just they'll have to come with me.

I slammed his door on him. "Of course you're free.
It's time they learned who cares and who'll betray."
We must preserve them from disloyalty.

My father came; he said Joseph would be
Ruin to us all. I turned him away.
It's right and just they'll have to come with me.

He begged to visit them. He will not see
Them till he dies. That's just the price he'll pay.
We must preserve them from disloyalty
And this false world. They'll have to come with me.

                              iv

You try to spare them the worst misery;
Who knows what cold force they'd be subject to?
How could we let them fall to treachery,

Disgrace, to brute foes? At the best, they'd see
Scorn in the face of every Red or Jew.
You try to spare them the worst misery.

In evil days, models of constancy
Are the one thing that will still see men through.
How could we let them fall to treachery

When they've once known our Leader? Yet if He,
If we go, just how many could stay true?
You try to spare them the worst misery

Of wanting this, that. From our own past, we
Know things they might have to say or do.
How could we let them fall to treachery.

To making base terms with an enemy,
Denying us and our best ideals, too?
You try to spare them the worst misery

But they'd still want to live. What if they'd be
Happy—they could prove all we thought untrue.
How could we let them fall to treachery
And their own faults? You end their misery.

JOHN ASHBERY [Born 1927]

John Ashbery was born in Rochester, New York. He attended Harvard University, where he majored in literature, and Columbia University, receiving his M.A. in 1951. In 1955 he was awarded a Fulbright Scholarship to study in France and remained there for a decade. While in France, Ashbery wrote art criticism for the European edition of the *New York Herald Tribune* and served as foreign correspondent for *Art News*. Upon his return to the United States in 1965, he became the executive editor of *Art News*.

Critics have traced some of Ashbery's influences to Wallace Stevens, the French symbolists, and painters such as Willem de Kooning and Jackson Pollack. However, because of his constant experimentation— a commonplace among New York poets such as Ashbery, Frank O'Hara and Kenneth Koch—and the frequent inaccessibility of his verse, it is difficult to see his work as an outgrowth of any of these influences. Instead, the difficulty of his poetry becomes its most unique characteristic. The difficulty does not stem from complex imagery, symbolism or allusions; rather, it lies in the onslaughts of small details, memories, and lines that seem to have no referent. However, it is not Ashbery's intention to have his poetry simplify the world but rather to have it portray the fragmentation, the complexity and, at times, the unintelligibility of the world. In 1956 Ashbery's volume, *Some Trees*, was selected for the Yale Younger Poets Series. Since then his poetry has continued to receive numerous awards, culminating in the National Book Award, the National Book Critics Circle Award, and the Pulitzer Prize for *Self-Portrait in a Convex Mirror* (1975).

Endless Variation

At some point in the pageant there is a moment
Of complete quiet. That is when you grab the urchin
By the hair and hold his head firmly
In the rush of water from the hydrant
As he metamorphoses by turns into a frog,
An ostrich, a rhinoceros, an electric eel,
And further things too solemn to identify, as though
They had waited for the others to give up before
Asserting a definitive muteness. And as there is no longer
Anything to interpret, you must now return

To the debate, the quarrel of the ancients and moderns,
That flutes more shrilly as each succeeding century
Resumes it. What must happen on the stage?
And in whose interest is it all, finally?
It is wise to pay attention so that the final plea
Of the defense will mean something, before the case is rested,
Though we know it will end in a tie again.
Yet the result is always the product of an elsewhere
Beyond these sounds, these signs that build an argument
That falls short, every time. It would be the same
If no one had left home, except for the tingle
Of frost in the air, overruled, expectant, that means us well.

The Instruction Manual

As I sit looking out of a window of the building
I wish I did not have to write the instruction manual on the uses of a
new metal.
I look down into the street and see people, each walking with an inner
peace,
And envy them—they are so far away from me!
Not one of them has to worry about getting out this annual on
schedule.
And, as my way is, I begin to dream, resting my elbows on the desk
and leaning out of the window a little,
Of dim Guadalajara! City of rose-colored flowers!
City I wanted most to see, and most did not see, in Mexico!
But I fancy I see, under the press of having to write the instruction
manual,
Your public square, city, with its elaborate little bandstand!
The band is playing *Scheherazade* by Rimsky-Korsakov.
Around stand the flower girls, handing out rose- and lemon-colored
flowers,
Each attractive in her rose-and-blue striped dress (Oh! such shades of
rose and blue),
And nearby is the little white booth where women in green serve you
green and yellow fruit.
The couples are parading; everyone is in a holiday mood.
First, leading the parade, is a dapper fellow
Clothed in deep blue. On his head sits a white hat
And he wears a mustache, which has been trimmed for the occasion.
His dear one, his wife, is young and pretty; her shawl is rose, pink, and
white.
Her slippers are patent leather, in the American fashion,
And she carries a fan, for she is modest, and does not want the crowd
to see her face too often.
But everybody is so busy with his wife or loved one
I doubt they would notice the mustachioed man's wife.
Here come the boys! They are skipping and throwing little things on
the sidewalk
Which is made of gray tile. One of them, a little older, has a toothpick
in this teeth.

He is silenter than the rest, and affects not to notice the pretty young
   girls in white.
But his friends notice them, and shout their jeers at the laughing girls.
Yet soon all this will cease, with the deepening of their years,
And love bring each to the parade grounds for another reason.
But I have lost sight of the young fellow with the toothpick.
Wait—there he is—on the other side of the bandstand,
Secluded from his friends, in earnest talk with a young girl
Of fourteen or fifteen. I try to hear what they are saying
But it seems they are just mumbling something—shy words of love,
   probably.
She is slightly taller than he, and looks quietly down into his sincere
   eyes.
She is wearing white. The breeze ruffles her long fine black hair against
   her olive cheek.
Obviously she is in love. The boy, the young boy with the toothpick, he
   is in love too;
His eyes show it. Turning from this couple,
I see there is an intermission in the concert.
The paraders are resting and sipping drinks through straws
(The drinks are dispensed from a large glass crock by a lady in dark
   blue),
And the musicians mingle among them, in their creamy white uniforms,
   and talk
about the weather, perhaps, or how their kids are doing at school.
Let us take this opportunity to tiptoe into one of the side streets.
Here you may see one of those white houses with green trim
That are so popular here. Look—I told you!
It is cool and dim inside, but the patio is sunny.
An old woman in gray sits there, fanning herself with a palm leaf fan.
She welcomes us to her patio, and offers us a cooling drink.
"My son is in Mexico City," she says. "He would welcome you too
If he were here. But his job is with a bank there.
Look, here is a photograph of him."
And a dark-skinned lad with pearly teeth grins out at us from the worn
   leather frame.
We thank her for her hospitality, for it is getting late
And we must catch a view of the city, before we leave, from a good
   high place.
That church tower will do—the faded pink one, there against the fierce

blue of the sky. Slowly we enter.
The caretaker, an old man dressed in brown and gray, asks us how long
  we have been in the city, and how we like it here.
His daughter is scrubbing the steps—she nods to us as we pass into the
  tower.
Soon we have reached the top, and the whole network of the city
  extends before us.
There is the rich quarter, with its houses of pink and white, and its
  crumbling, leafy terraces.
There is the poorer quarter, its homes a deep blue.
There is the market, where men are selling hats and swatting flies
And there is the public library, painted several shades of pale green and
  beige.
Look! There is the square we just came from, with the promenaders.
There are fewer of them, now that the heat of the day has increased,
But the young boy and girl still lurk in the shadows of the bandstand.
And there is the home of the little old lady—
She is still sitting in the patio, fanning herself.
How limited, but how complete withal, has been our experience of
  Guadalajara!
We have seen young love, married love, and the love of an aged mother
  for her son.
We have heard the music, tasted the drinks, and looked at colored
  houses.
What more is there to do, except stay? And that we cannot do.
And as a last breeze freshens the top of the weathered old tower, I turn
  my gaze
Back to the instruction manual which has made me dream of Guada-
  lajara.

Some Trees

These are amazing: each
Joining a neighbor, as though speech
Were a still performance.
Arranging by chance

To meet as far this morning
From the world as agreeing
With it, you and I
Are suddenly what the trees try

To tell us we are:
That their merely being there
Means something; that soon
We may touch, love, explain.

And glad not to have invented
Such comeliness, we are surrounded:
A silence already filled with noises,
A canvas on which emerges

A chorus of smiles, a winter morning.
Placed in a puzzling light, and moving,
Our days put on such reticence
These accents seem their own defense.

Fear of Death

What is it now with me
And is it as I have become?
Is there no state free from the boundary lines
Of before and after? The window is open today

And the air pours in with piano notes
In its skirts, as though to say, "Look, John,
I've brought these and these"—that is,
A few Beethovens, some Brahmses,

A few choice Poulenc notes...Yes,
It is being free again, the air, it has to keep coming back
Because that's all it's good for.
I want to stay with it out of fear

That keeps me from walking up certain steps,
Knocking at certain doors, fear of growing old
Alone, and of finding no one at the evening end
Of the path except another mayself

Nodding a curt greeting: "Well, you've been awhile
But now we're back together, which is what counts."
Air in my path, you could shorten this,
But the breeze has dropped, and silence is the last word.

The Tennis Court Oath

What had you been thinking about
the face studiously bloodied

heaven blotted region
I go on loving you like water but
there is a terrible breath in the way all of this
You were not elected president, yet won the race
All the way through fog and drizzle
When you read it was sincere the coasts
stammered with unintentional villages the
horse strains fatigued I guess...the calls...
I worry

the water beetle head
why of course reflecting all
then you redid you were breathing
I thought going down to mail this
of the kettle you jabbered as easily in the yard
you come through but
are incomparable the lovely tent
mystery you don't want surrounded the real
you dance
in the spring there was clouds

The mulatress approached in the hall—the
lettering easily visible along the edge of the *Times*
in a moment the bell would ring but there was time
for the carnation laughed here are a couple of "other"

to one in yon house

The doctor and Philip had come over the road
turning in toward the corner of the wall his hat on
reading it carelessly as if to tell you your fears were justified
the blood shifted you know those walls
wind off the earth had made him shrink
undeniably an oboe now the young

were there there was candy
to decide the sharp edge of the garment
like a particular cry not intervening called the dog "he's coming! he's
    coming" with an emotion felt it sink into peace

there was no turning back but the end was in sight
he chose this moment to ask her in detail about her family and the
    others
The person. pleaded—"have more of these
not stripes on the tunic—or the porch chairs
will teach you about men—what it means"
to be one in a million pink stripe
and now could go away the three approached the doghouse
the reef. Your daughter's
dream of my son understand prejudice
darkness in the hole
the patient finished
They could all go home now the hole was dark
lilacs blowing across his face glad he brought you

A Boy

I'll do what the raids suggest,
Dad, and that other livid window,
But the tide pushes an awful lot of monsters
And I think it's my true fate.

It had been raining but
It had not been raining.

No one could begin to mop up this particular mess.
Thunder lay down in the heart.
"My child, I love any vast electrical disturbance."
Disturbance! Could the old man, face in the rainweed,

Ask more smuttily? By night it charged over plains,
Driven from Dallas and Oregon, always *whither,*

Why not now? The boy seemed to have fallen
From shelf to shelf of someone's rage.

That night it rained on the boxcars, explaining
The thought of the pensive cabbage roses near the boxcars.
My boy. isn't there something I asked you once?
What happened? It's also farther to the corner
Aboard the maple furniture. *He*
Couldn't lie. He's tell 'em by their syntax.

But listen now in the flood.
They're throwing up behind the lines.
Dry fields of lightning rise to receive
The observer, the mincing flag. *An unendurable age.*

GALWAY KINNELL [Born 1927]

Galway Kinnell was born in Providence, Rhode Island, and was educated at Princeton. It was during college that he first began writing poetry, and poems from these early years are included in two volumes, *First Poems 1946-1954* and *The Avenue Bearing the Initial of Christ into the New World: Poems 1946-1964*. In 1955 he studied in Paris on a Fulbright Scholarship and has since travelled and lived in Europe, Iran, and throughout the United States. While living in the southern U.S., he became active in the Civil Rights movement, and in 1963 he was a field worker for the Congress of Racial Equality.

Kinnell's early poetry was quite traditional in terms of meter and rhyme, and it focused predominantly on Christian themes. However, he soon felt that rhyme was too restricting and moved to free verse. Kinnell points to Walt Whitman as a major influence on his poetry because of his loose style and colloquial phrasings. As his body of work grew, Kinnell returned to many of the same themes consistently: the power of the wilderness, the spiritual dimension of life so often suppressed by civilization, mortality, and death. Kinnell has been the recipient of numerous grants and awards which include a Rockefeller Grant (1967), a Guggenheim Fellowship (1974), and the Pulitzer Prize for poetry in 1982.

The Bear

1

In late winter
I sometimes glimpse bits of steam
coming up from
some fault in the old snow
and bend close and see it is lung-colored
and put down my nose
and know
the chilly, enduring odor of bear.

2

I take a wolf's rib and whittle
it sharp at both ends
and coil it up
and freeze it in blubber and place it out
on the fairway of the bears.

And when it has vanished
I move out on the bear tracks,
roaming in circles
until I come to the first, tentative, dark
splash on the earth.

And I set out
running, following the splashes
of blood wandering over the world.
At the cut, gashed resting places
I stop and rest,
at the crawl-marks

where he lay out on his belly
to overpass some stretch of bauchy ice
I lie out
dragging myself forward with bear-knives in my fists.

3

On the third day I begin to starve,
at nightfall I bend down as I knew I would
at a turd sopped in blood,
and hesitate, and pick it up,
and thrust it in my mouth, and gnash it down,
and rise
and go on running.

4

On the seventh day,
living by now on bear blood alone,
I can see his upturned carcass far out ahead, a scraggled,
steamy hulk,
the heavy fur riffling in the wind.

I come up to him
and stare at the narrow-spaced, petty eyes,
the dismayed
face laid back on the shoulder, the nostrils
flared, catching
perhaps the first taint of me as he
died.

I hack
a ravine in his thigh, and eat and drink,
and tear him down his whole length
and open him and climb in
and close him up after me, against the wind,
and sleep.

5

And dream
of lumbering flatfooted
over the tundra,
stabbed twice from within,

splattering a trail behind me,
splattering it out no matter which way I lurch,
no matter which parabola of bear-transcendence,
which dance of solitude I attempt,
which gravity-clutched leap,
which trudge, which groan.

6

Until one day I totter and fall—
fall on this
stomach that has tried so hard to keep up,
to digest the blood as it leaked in,
to break up
and digest the bone itself: and now the breeze
blows over me, blows off
the hideous belches of ill-digested bear blood
and rotted stomach
and the ordinary, wretched odor of bear,

blows across
my sore, lolled tongue a song
or screech, until I think I must rise up
and dance. And I lie still.

7

I awaken I think. Marshlights
reappear, geese
come trailing again up the flyway.
In her ravine under old snow the dam-bear
lies, licking
lumps of smeared fur
and drizzly eyes into shapes
with her tongue. And one
hairy-soled trudge stuck out before me,
the next groaned out,

the next,
the next,
the rest of my days I spend
wandering: wondering
what, anyway,
was that sticky infusion, that rank flavor of blood, that
   poetry, by which I lived?

In Fields of Summer

The sun rises,
The goldenrod blooms,
I drift in fields of summer,
My life is adrift in my body,
It shines in my heart and hands, in my teeth,
It shines up at the old crane
Who holds out his drainpipe of a neck
And creaks along in the blue,

And the goldenrod shines with its life, too,
And the grass, look,
The great field wavers and flakes,
The rumble of bumblebees keeps deepening,
A phoebe flutters up,
A lark bursts up all dew.

Cells Breathe in the Emptiness

1

When the flowers turn to husks
And the great trees suddenly die
And rocks and old weasel bones lose
The little life they suddenly had
And the air quells and goes so still
It gives the ears something like the bends,
It is an eerie thing to keep vigil,
The senses racing in the emptiness.

2

From the compost heap
Now arises the sound of the teeth
Of one of those sloppy green cabbageworms
Eating his route through a cabbage,
Now snarling like a petite chainsaw, now droning on...

A butterfly blooms on a buttercup,
From the junkpile flames up a junco.

3

How many plants are really very quiet animals?
How many inert molecules are ready to break into life?

Vapor Trail Reflected in the Frog Pond

1

The old watch: their
thick eyes
puff and foreclose by the moon. The young, heads
trailed by the beginnings of necks,
shiver,
in the guarantee they shall be bodies.
In the frog pond
the vapor trail of a SAC bomber creeps,

I hear its drone, drifting, high up
in immaculate ozone.

2

And I hear,
coming over the hills, America singing,
her varied carols I hear:
crack of deputies' rifles practicing their aim on stray dogs
    at night,
sput of cattleprod,
TV groaning at the smells of the human body,
curses of the soldier as he poisons, burns, grinds, and stabs
the rice of the world,
with open mouth, crying strong, hysterical curses.

3

And by rice paddies in Asia
bones
wearing a few shadows
walk down a dirt road, smashed
bloodsuckers on their heel, knowing
the flesh a man throws down in the sunshine
dogs shall eat
and the flesh that is upthrown in the air
shall be seized by birds,
shoulder blades smooth, unmarked by old feather-holes,
hands rivered
by blue, erratic wanderings of the blood,
eyes crinkled up
as they gaze up at the drifting sun that gives us our lives,
seed dazzled over the footbattered blaze of the earth.

For Robert Frost

1

Why do you talk so much
Robert Frost ? One day
I drove up to Ripton to ask,

I stayed the whole day
And never got the chance
To put the question.

I drove off at dusk
Worn out and aching
In both ears. Robert Frost,

Were you shy as a boy?
Do you go on making up
For some long stint of solitude?

Is it simply that talk
Doesn't have to be metered and rhymed?
Or is gab distracting from something worse?

2

I saw you once on the TV,
Unsteady at the lectern,
The flimsy white leaf
Of hair standing straight up
In the wind, among top hats,
Old farmer and son
Of worse winters than this,
Stopped in the first dazzle

Of the District of Columbia,
Suddenly having to pay
For the cheap onionskin,

The worn-out ribbon, the eyes
Wrecked from writing poems
For us—stopped,
Lonely before millions,
The paper jumping in your grip,

And as the Presidents
Also on the platform
Began flashing nervously
Their Presidential smiles
For the harmless old guy,
And poets watching on the TV
Started thinking. Well that's
The end of *that* tradition,

And the managers of the event
Said, Boys this is it,
This sonofabitch poet
Is gonna croak,
Putting the paper aside
You drew forth
From your great faithful heart
The poem.

3

Once, walking in winter in Vermont,
In the snow, I followed a set of footprints
That aimed for the woods. At the verge
I could make out, "far in the pillared dark,"
An old creature in a huge, clumsy overcoat,
Lifting his great boots through the drifts,
Going as if to die among "those dark trees"
Of his own country. I watched him go,

Past a house, quiet, warm and light,
A farm, a countryside, a woodpile in its slow
Smokeless burning, alder swamps ghastly white,
Tumultuous snows, blanker whitenesses,
Into the pathless woods, one eye weeping,

The dark trees, for which no saying is dark enough,
Which mask the gloom and lead on into it,
The bare, the withered, the deserted.

There were no more cottages.
Soft bombs of dust falling from the boughs,
The sun shining no warmer than the moon,
He had outwalked the farthest city light,
And there, clinging to the perfect trees,
A last leaf. What was it?
What was that whiteness?—white, uncertain—
The night too dark to know.

4

He turned. *Love,*
Love of things, duty, he said,
And made his way back to the shelter
No longer sheltering him, the house
Where everything real was turning to words,

Where he would think on the white wave,
Folded back, that rides in place on the obscure
Pouring of this life to the sea—
And invent on the broken lips of darkness
The seal of form and the *mot juste.*

5

Poet of the country of white houses,
Of clearings going out to the dark wall of woods
Frayed along the skyline, you who nearly foreknew
The next lines of poems you suddenly dropped,
Who dwelt in access to that which other men
Have burnt all their lives to get near, who heard
The high wind, in gusts, seething
From far off, headed through the trees exactly
To this place where it must happen, who spent

Your life on the point of giving away your heart
To the dark trees, the dissolving woods,
Into which you go at last, heart in hand, deep in:
When we think of a man who was cursed
Neither with the mystical all-lovingness of Walt Whitman
Nor with Melville's anguish to know and to suffer,
And yet cursed...a man, what shall I say,
Vain, not fully convinced he was dying, whose calling
Was to set up in the wilderness of his country,
At whatever cost, a man, who would be his own man,
We think of you. And from the same doorway
At which you lived, between the house and the woods,
We see your old footprints going away across
The great Republic, Frost, up memorized slopes,
Down hills floating by heart on the bulldozed land.

The Homecoming of Emma Lazarus

1

Having no father anymore, having got up
In England without hope, having sailed the strewn
Atlantic and been driven under Bedloe
In the night, where the Green Lady lifts
Over that slow, bleating, most tragic of harbors,

Her burning hand, Emma came floating home,
To the thick, empty whistling of the tugs.
Thoreau's pocket compass had been her keepsake,
She made her way in without it, through the fog,
It was hard for her, in fact, coming in to die,

A little unfair, her father having died already.
In the attic on Union Square? Thrown out? Ah,
Somewhere in the mess of things! From Governor's Island
A bugler's lonelienst notes roll slowly in,
And birds rock in the fog on the slapping waves.

2

As a child she had chased a butterfly
Through Battery Park, the only one decorating
Manhattan that afternoon, its clumsy, wind-thin
Wings making cathedral windows in the sun,

While the despised grandmother
With the gleety lashes, cruddy with age,
Of the eyebeams, held on. Alas, the crone's
Doughy ears must also have been golden in the sun!

It was towards you, gilded in the day's going down,
Green Lady, that we crawled—but from what ground of nausea
Had we turned, what relinquished plot of earth
Had we spit at, which was, anyway, the earth?

3

Dark haired, ephebic Emma, you knew
The night you floated into New York Harbor
Atlantis had sunk while you were abroad,
You could see the rainbows of it shining queerly
The many thousand leagues of your life away—

Weekends on Union Square, from his shaving mug
You blew bubbles crawling with colors that buoyed
Into the sunshine, you made up little rhymes,
You skipped rope, at your father's knee he put
Lilacs in your hair. Everybody loved you!

And on the last ride across 14th,
Did the English success suddenly become nothing,
Did the American childhood, including the odd affliction,
Your neurotic longing to be English, turn out
To be the one paradise you died longing for?

4

Facing the Old World the Green Lady whispers, "Eden!"
Seeing her looking so trim in American verdigris

They thought she was saying how it was here,
Seeing her looking to sea we heard the pure nostalgia,
Vacuumed in the wind from the Dry Cleaning Store
She may, herself, have wondered what she meant.

She crouches on the floor. She read once,
In the paper, a poem she had composed herself.
Was it just poetry, all that? It was pretty,
There is nothing she can do about it, it really was.
Her arm lies along the bench, her hand
Hangs over the edge as if she has just let something drop.

She has wept a long time now, and now poetry
Can do no more to her. Her shoulder shrugs as though
To drive away birds which, anyway, weren't intending
To alight. In the Harbor the conscript bugler
Blows the old vow of acceptance into the night—
It fades, and the wounds of all we had accepted open.

The Comfort of Darkness

Darkness swept the earth in my dream,
Cold crowded the streets with its wings
Cold talons pursued each river and stream
Into the mountains, found out their springs
And drilled the dark world with ice.
An enormous wreck of a bird
Closed on my heart in the darkness
And sank into sleep as it shivered.

Not even the heat of your blood, nor the pure
Light falling endlessly from you, like rain,
Could stay in my memory there
Or comfort me then.
Only the comfort of darkness,
The ice-cold, unfreezable brine,
Could melt the cries into silence,
Your bright hands into mine.

Westport

From the hilltop we could overlook
The changes on the world. Behind us
Spread the forest, that half a continent away
Met our fathers on the Atlantic shore.
Before us lay a narrow belt of brush.
Everywhere beyond, shifting like an ocean,
Swell upon swell of emerald green,
The prairies of the west were blowing.

We mounted and set out, small craft
Into the green. The grasses brushed
The bellies of the horses, and under
The hooves the knotted centuries of sod
Slowed the way. Here and there the grey
Back of a wolf breached and fell, as in the grass
Their awkward voyages appeared and vanished.

Then rain lashed down in a savage squall.
All afternoon it drove us west. "It will be
A long, hard journey," the boy said, "and look,
We are blown like the weed." And indeed we were...
O wild indigo, O love-lies-bleeding,
You, prince's feather, pigweed, and bugseed,
Hold your ground as you can. We toss ahead
Of you in the wild rain, and we barely touch
The sad ambages compassed for yourselves.

When the storm abated, a red streak in the west
Lit up the raindrops on the land before us.
"Yes," I said, "it will be a hard journey..."

And the shining grasses were bowed towards the west
As if one craving had killed them. "But at last,"
I added, "the hardness is the thing you thank."
So out of forest we sailed onto plains.
And from the dark afternoon came a bright evening.

Now out of evening we discovered night
And heard the cries of the prairie and the moan
Of wind through the roots of its clinging flowers.

W.S. MERWIN [Born 1927]

William Stanley Merwin was born in New York City but grew up in New Jersey and Pennsylvania. As a child he wrote hymns for his father, who was a Presbyterian minister. Merwin graduated from Princeton University in 1947 and continued graduate studies there in foreign languages. While at Princeton he met the poet John Berryman, who taught creative writing, and fellow student Galway Kinnell. After completing his studies Merwin lived in Europe, and in 1950 he tutored Robert Graves' son in Mallorca. Unlike many of his contemporaries, Merwin never supported himself by teaching; rather, he spent his time translating from French, Latin, Greek, and Chinese, writing and giving poetry readings. He has also been playwright-in-residence at the Poet's Theatre in Cambridge, Massachusetts, and poetry editor of *The Nation* during the early sixties.

Though Merwin began his career in the fifties, it was not until the following decades that he achieved popularity and acclaim. Over the years, his poetry has gone through various phases. His early poems were balanced and typically dealt with myth. By 1960, with *The Drunk in the Furnace*, his poety was more relaxed and colloquial. Since then he has experimented with surrealism and has moved toward more personal explorations. Merwin has been the recipient of numerous distinctions and awards including being chosen for the Yale Younger Poets Series, the Bollingen prize, and the Pulitzer Prize for Poetry.

The Drunk in the Furnace

For a good decade
The furnace stood in the naked gully, fireless
And vacant as any hat. Then when it was
No more to them than a hulking black fossil
To erode unnoticed with the rest of the junk-hill
By the poisonous creek, and rapidly to be added
        To their ignorance,

They were afterwards astonished
To confirm, one morning, a twist of smoke like a pale
Resurrection, staggering out of its chewed hole,
And to remark then other tokens that someone,
Cosily bolted behind the eye-holed iron
Door of the drafty burner, had there established
        His bad castle.

Where he gets his spirits
It's a mystery. But the stuff keeps him musical:
Hammer-and-anvilling with poker and bottle
To his jugged bellowings, till the last groaning clang
As he collapses onto the rioting
Springs of a litter of car-seats ranged on the grates,
        To sleep like an iron pig.

In their tar-paper church
On a text about stoke-holes that are sated never
Their Reverend lingers. They nod and hate trespassers.
When the furnace wakes, though, all afternoon
Their witless offspring flock like piped rats to its siren
Crescendo, and agape on the crumbling ridge
        Stand in a row and learn.

The Asians Dying

When the forests have been destroyed their darkness remains
The ash the great walker follows the possessors
Forever
Nothing they will come to is real
Nor for long
Over the watercourses
Like ducks in the time of the ducks
The ghosts of the villages trail in the sky
Making a new twilight

Rain falls into the open eyes of the dead
Again again with its pointless sound
When the moon finds them they are the color of everything

The nights disappear like bruises but nothing is healed
The dead go away like bruises
The blood vanishes into the poisoned farmlands
Pain the horizon
Remains
Overhead the seasons rock
They are paper bells
Calling to nothing living

The possessors move everywhere under Death their star
Like columns of smoke they advance into the shadows
Like thin flames with no light
They with no past
And fire their only future

Fog-Horn

Surely that moan is not the thing
That men thought they were making, when they
Put it there, for their own necessities.
That throat does not call to anything human
But to something men had forgotten,
That stirs under fog. Who wounded that beast
Incurably, or from whose pasture
Was it lost, full grown, and time closed round it
With no way back? Who tethered its tongue
So that its voice could never come
To speak out in the light of clear day,
But only when the shifting blindness
Descends and is acknowledged among us,
As though from under a floor it is heard,
Or as though from behind a wall, always
Nearer than we had remembered? If it
Was we that gave tongue to this cry
What does it bespeak in us, repeating
And repeating, insisting on something
That we never meant? We only put it there
To give warning of something we dare not
Ignore, lest we should come upon it
Too suddenly, recognize it too late,
As our cries were swallowed up and all hands lost.

The Removal
To the Endless Tribe

1
The Procession

When we see
the houses again
we will know that we are asleep at last

when we see
tears on the road
and they are ourselves

we are awake
the tree has been cut
on which we were leaves
the day does not know us
the river where we cross does not taste salt

the soles of our feet are black stars
but ours is the theme
of the light

2
The Homeless

A clock keeps striking
and the echoes move in files
their faces
have been lost
flowers of salt
tongues from lost languages
doorways closed with pieces of night

3
A Survivor

The dust never settles
but through it tongue tongue comes walking
shuffling like breath
but the old speech
is still in its country
dead

4
The Crossing of the Removed

At the bottom of the river
black ribbons cross under
and the water tries to soothe them
the mud tries to soothe them
the stones turn over and over trying
to comfort them
but they will not be healed

where the rims cut
and the shadows
sawed carrying
mourners
and some that had used horses
and had the harness
dropped it in half way over
on the far side the ribbons come out
invisible

5
A Widow is Taken

I call leave me here
the smoke on the black path
was my children
I will not walk
from the house I warmed
but they carry me through the light
my blackening face
my red eyes
everywhere I leave
one white footprint

the trackers will follow us into the cold
the water is high
the boats have been stolen away
there are no shoes
and they pretend that I am a bride
on the way to a new house

6
The Reflection

Passing a broken window
they see
into each of them the wedge of blackness
pounded
it is nothing
it splits them

loose hair
bare heels
at last they are gone
filing on in vacant rooms

The River of Bees

In a dream I returned to the river of bees
Five orange trees by the bridge and
Beside two mills my house
Into whose courtyard a blind man followed
The goats and stood singing
Of what was older

Soon it will be fifteen years

He was old he will have fallen into his eyes

I took my eyes
A long way to the calendars
Room after room asking how shall I live

One of the ends is made of streets
One man processions carry through it
Empty bottles their
Image of hope
It was offered to me by name

Once once and once
In the same city I was born
Asking what shall I say

He will have fallen into his mouth
Men think they are better than grass

I return to his voice rising like a forkful of hay

He was old he is not real nothing is real
Nor the noise of death drawing water

We are the echo of the future

On the door it says what to do to survive
But we were not born to survive
Only to live

Footprints on the Glacier

Where the wind
year round out of the gap
polishes everything
here this day are footprints like my own
the first ever
frozen
pointing up into the cold

and last night someone
marched and marched on the candle flame
hurrying
a painful road
and I heard the echo a long time afterwards
gone and some connection of mine

I scan the high slopes for a dark speck
that was lately here
I pass my hands
over the melted wax
like a blind man
they are all
moving into their season at last
my bones face each other trying
to remember a question

nothing moves while I watch
but here the black trees
are the cemetery of a great battle
and behind me as I turn
I hear names leaving the bark
in growing numbers and flying north

Leviathan

This is the black sea-brute bulling through wave-
    wrack,
Ancient as ocean's shifting hills, who in sea-toils
Travelling, who furrowing the salt acres
Heavily, his wake hoary behind him,
Shoulders spouting, the fist of his forehead
Over wastes gray-green crashing, among horses
    unbroken
From bellowing fields, past bone-wreck of vessels,
Tide-ruin, wash of lost bodies bobbing
No longer sought for, and islands of ice gleaming,
Who ravening the rank flood, wave-marshalling,
Overmastering the dark sea-marches, finds home
And harvest. Frightening to foolhardiest
Mariners, his size were difficult to describe:
The hulk of him is like hills heaving,
Dark, yet as crags of drift-ice, crowns cracking in
    thunder,
Like land's self by night black-looming, surf churning
    and trailing
Along his shores' rushing, shoal-water boding
About the dark of his jaws; and who should moor at
    his edge
And fare on afoot would find gates of no gardens,
But the hill of dark underfoot diving,
Closing overhead, the cold deep, and drowning.
He is called Leviathan, and named for rolling,

First created he was of all creatures,
He has held Jonah three days and nights,
He is that curling serpent that in ocean is,
Sea-fright he is, and the shadow under the earth.
Days there are, nonetheless, when he lies
Like an angel, although a lost angel
On the waste's unease, no eye of man moving,
Bird hovering, fish flashing, creature whatever
Who after him came to herit earth's emptiness.
Froth at flanks seething sooths to stillness,
Waits with one eye he watches
Dark of night sinking last, with one eye dayrise
As at first over foaming pastures. He makes no cry
Though that light is a breath. The sea curling,
Star-climbed, wind-combed, cumbered with itself still
As at first it was, is the hand not yet contented
Of the Creator. And he waits for the world to begin.

Lemuel's Blessing

Let Lemuel bless with the wolf, which is a
dog without a master, but the Lord hears
his cries and feeds him in the desert.
CHRISTOPHER SMART: Jubilate Agno

You that know the way,
Spirit,
I bless your ears which are like cypruses on a mountain
With their roots in wisdom. Let me approach.
I bless your paws and their twenty nails which tell
    their own prayer
And are like dice in command of their own com-
    binations.
Let me not be lost.
I bless your eyes for which I know no comparison.
Run with me like the horizon, for without you
I am nothing but a dog lost and hungry,
Ill-natured, untrustworthy, useless.

My bones together bless you like an orchestra of flutes.
Divert the weapons of the settlements and lead their
    dogs a dance.
Where a dog is shameless and wears servility
In his tail like a banner,
Let me wear the opprobrium of possessed and
    possessors
As a thick tail properly used
To warm my worst and my best parts. My tail and my
    laugh bless you.

Lead me past the error at the fork of hesitation.
Deliver me

From the ruth of the lair, which clings to me in the
    morning,
Painful when I move, like a trap;
Even debris has its favorite positions but they are not
    yours;
From the ruth of kindness, with its licked hands;
I have sniffed baited fingers and followed
Toward necessities which were not my own: it would
    make me
An habitué of back steps, faithful custodian of fat
    sheep;

From the ruth of prepared comforts, with its
Habitual dishes sporting my name and its collars and
    leashes of vanity;

From the ruth of approval, with its nets, kennels, and
    taxidermists;
It would use my guts for its own rackets and instru-
    ments, to play its own games and music;
Teach me to recognize its platforms, which are con-
    structed like scaffolds;

From the ruth of known paths, which would use my
    feet, tail, and ears as curios,
My head as a nest for tame ants,

My fate as a warning.

I have hidden at wrong times for wrong reasons.
I have been brought to bay. More than once.
Another time, if I need it,
Create a little wind like a cold finger between my
    shoulders, then
Let my nails pour out a torrent of aces like grain from
    a threshing machine;
Let fatigue, weather, habitation, the old bones, finally,
Be nothing to me,
Let all lights but yours be nothing to me.
Let the memory of tongues not unnerve me so that I
    stumble or quake.
But lead me at times beside the still waters;
There when I crouch to drink let me catch a glimpse
    of your image
Before it is obscured with my own.

Preserve my eyes, which are irreplaceable.
Preserve my heart, veins, bones,
Against the slow death building in them like hornets
    until the place is entirely theirs.
Preserve my tongue and I will bless you again and
    again.

Let my ignorance and my failings
Remain far behind me like tracks made in a wet
    season,
At the end of which I have vanished,
So that those who track me for their own twisted ends
May be rewarded only with ignorance and failings.
But let me leave my cry stretched out behind me like
    a road
On which I have followed you.
And sustain me for my time in the desert
On what is essential to me.

Blind William's Song

Stand from my shadow where it goes
threaded upon a white dream,
from my clear eyes that take no light
and give no mercy.

I stood in clean Monday and heard
seventy tongues of fire
burn down from their talk.
I am the ash that walk.

Tuesday was dusty feet;
I shall not be the first
who walked and did not know
the earth, the middle earth.

Wednesday, if it came,
I was a blown curse
and who are you not withered?
Tempt not my memory.

But though I was, on Thursday,
in that late morning,
multiple as rain
and fell as rain falls

and have been on Friday
say a white horse racing
—since I see no motion
all speed is easy—

I have not been the sea
(my dry bone forbids me)
whose blind repeated loss
any loud tide will serve.

Lull the stones over me,
I that on Saturday
closed about myself
and raged and was the grave.

Sunday I lie down
within without my body;
all colored creation
is tamed white by time.

ADRIENNE RICH [Born 1929]

Adrienne Rich was born into a middle-class family in Baltimore, Maryland. As a youngster, she enjoyed reading from her father's library (which included such poets as Tennyson, Keats, Blake, and Swinburne). It was under his guidance that she began to write poetry. In 1951, she graduated from Radcliffe College and had her first book of poetry, *A Change of World*, picked by W. H. Auden for the Yale Younger Poets Series during the same year. The following years brought her many distinctions such as travelling throughout Europe and England on a Guggenheim Fellowship, winning the Ridgely Torrence Memorial Award for her second collection, *The Diamond Cutters and Other Poems*, receiving a Bollingen Foundation Grant for translating Dutch Poetry, and winning the Shelley Memorial Award for *The Will to Change*. By the mid sixties, Rich became more politically active. She participated in various rallies, such as protesting the war in Indochina. By the early seventies, she became more involved with the Women's Movement and radical feminism. In fact, much of her later poetry deals with the politics of sexuality, as well as the experience of being a woman. Her latest volumes of poetry include *Of Women Born: Motherhood as Experience and Institution* (1985) and *Your Native Land, Your Life: Poems* (1986).

Diving into the Wreck

First having read the book of myths,
and loaded the camera,
and checked the edge of the knife-blade,

I put on
the body-armor of black rubber
the absurd flippers
the grave and awkward mask.
I am having to do this
not like Cousteau with his
assiduous team
aboard the sun-flooded schooner
but here alone.

There is a ladder.
The ladder is always there
hanging innocently
close to the side of the schooner.
We know what it is for,
we who have used it.
Otherwise
it's a piece of maritime floss
some sundry equipment.

I go down.
Rung after rung and still
the oxygen immerses me
the blue light
the clear atoms
of our human air.
I go down.
My flippers cripple me,
I crawl like an insect down the ladder
and there is no one
to tell me when the ocean
will begin.

First the air is blue and then
it is bluer and then green and then
black I am blacking out and yet
my mask is powerful
it pumps my blood with power
the sea is another story
the sea is not a question of power
I have to learn alone
to turn my body without force
in the deep element.

And now: it is easy to forget
what I came for
among so many who have always
lived here
swaying their crenellated fans
between the reefs
and besides
you breathe differently down here.

I came to explore the wreck.
The words are purposes.
The words are maps.
I came to see the damage that was done
and the treasures that prevail.
I stroke the beam of my lamp
slowly along the flank
of something more permanent
than fish or weed

the thing I came for
the wreck and not the story of the wreck
the thing itself and not the myth

the drowned face always staring
toward the sun
the evidence of damage
worn by salt and sway into this threadbare beauty
the ribs of the disaster
curving their assertion
among the tentative haunters.

This is the place.
And I am here, the mermaid whose dark hair
streams black, the merman in his armored body
We circle silently
about the wreck
we dive into the hold.
I am she: I am he

whose drowned face sleeps with open eyes
whose breasts still bear the stress
whose silver, copper, vermeil cargo lies
obscurely inside barrels

half-wedged and left to rot
we are the half-destroyed instruments
that once held to a course
the water-eaten log
the fouled compass

We are, I am, you are
by cowardice or courage
the one who find our way
back to this scene
carrying a knife, a camera
a book of myths
in which
our names do not appear.

Planetarium

Thinking of Caroline Herschel (1750-1848)
astronomer, sister of William; and others.

A woman in the shape of a monster
a monster in the shape of a woman
the skies are full of them

a woman   'in the snow
among the Clocks and instruments
or measuring the ground with poles'
in her 98 years to discover
8 comets

she whom the moon ruled
like us
levitating into the night sky
riding the polished lenses

Galaxies of women, there
doing penance for impetuousness
ribs chilled
in those spaces   of the mind

An eye,

        'virile, precise and absolutely certain'
        from the mad webs of Uranusborg

                                    encountering the NOVA

every impulse of light exploding
from the core
as life flies out of us

        Tycho whispering at last
        'Let me not seem to have lived in vain'

What we see, we see
and seeing is changing

the light that shrivels a mountain
and leaves a man alive

Heartbeat of the pulsar
heart sweating through my body

The radio impulse
pouring in from Taurus

I am bombarded yet   I stand

I have been standing all my life in the
direct path of a battery of signals
the most accurately transmitted most
untranslatable language in the universe
I am a galactic cloud so deep   so invo-
luted that a light wave could take 15
years to travel through me   And has
taken   I am an instrument in the shape
of a woman trying to translate pulsations
into images   for the relief of the body
and the reconstruction of the mind.

Snapshots of a Daughter-in-Law

1.
You, once a belle in Shreveport,
with henna-colored hair, skin like a peachbud
still have your dresses copied from that time,
and play a Chopin prelude
called by Cortot: "*Delicious recollections
float like perfume through the memory.*"

Your mind now, moldering like wedding-cake,
heavy with useless experience, rich
with suspicion, rumor, fantasy,
crumbling to pieces under the knife-edge
of mere fact. In the prime of your life.

Nervy, glowering, your daughter
wipes the teaspoons, grows another way.

2.

Banging the coffee-pot into the sink
she hears the angels chiding, and looks out
past the raked gardens to the sloppy sky.
Only a week since They said: *Have no patience.*

The next time it was: *Be insatiable.*
Then: *Save yourself; others you cannot save.*
Sometimes she's let the tapstream scald her arm,
a match burn to her thumbnail,

or held her hand above the kettle's snout
right in the woolly steam. They are probably angels,
since nothing hurts her anymore, except
each morning's grit blowing into her eyes.

3.

A thinking woman sleeps with monsters.
The beak that grips her, she becomes. And Nature,
that sprung-lidded, still commodious

steamer-trunk of *tempora* and *mores*
gets stuffed with it all: the mildewed orange-flowers,
the female polls, the terrible breast
of Boadicea beneath flat foxes' heads and orchids.

Two handsome women, gripped in argument,
each proud, acute, subtle, I hear scream
across the cut glass and majolica
like Furies cornered from their prey:
The argument *ad feminam,* all the old knives
that have rusted in my back, I drive in yours,
ma semblable, ma soeur!

4.

Knowing themselves too well in one another:
their gifts no pure fruition, but a thorn,
the prick filed sharp against a hint of scorn...
Reading while waiting

for the iron to heat,
writing. *My Life had stood—a Loaded Gun—*
in that Amherst pantry while the jellies boil and scum,
or, more often,
iron-eyed and beaked and purposed as a bird,
dusting everything on the whatnot every day of life.

5.
Dulce ridens, dulce loquens,
she shaves her legs until they gleam
like petrified mammoth-tusk.

6.
When to her lute Corinna sings
neither words nor music are her own;
only the long hair dipping
over the cheek, only the song
of silk against her knees
and these
adjusted in reflections of an eye.

Poised, trembling and unsatisfied, before
an unlocked door, that cage of cages,
tell us, you bird, you tragical machine—
is this *fertilisante douleur?* Pinned down
by love, for you the only natural action,
are you edged more keen
to prise the secrets of the vault? has Nature shown
her household books to you, daughter-in-law,
that her sons never saw?

7.
To have in this uncertain world some stay
which cannot be undermined, is
of the utmost consequence."
                                              Thus wrote
a woman, partly brave and partly good,
who fought with what she partly understood.
Few men about her would or could do more,
hence she was labeled harpy, shrew and whore.

8.
"You all die at fifteen," said Diderot,
and turn part legend, part convention.
Still, eyes inaccurately dream
behind closed windows blankening with steam.
Deliciously, all that we might have been,
all that we were—fire, tears,
wit, taste, martyred ambition—
stirs like the memory of refused adultery
the drained and flagging bosom of our middle years.

9.
Not that it is done well, but
that it is done at all? Yes, think
of the odds! or shrug them off forever.
This luxury of the precocious child,
Time's precious chronic invalid,—
would we, darlings, resign it if we could?
Our blight has been our sinecure:
mere talent was enough for us—
glitter in fragments and rough drafts.

Sigh no more, ladies.

                                                Time is male

and in his cups drinks to the fair.
Bemused by gallantry, we hear
our mediocrities over-praised,
indolence read as abnegation,
slattern thought styled intuition,
every lapse forgiven, our crime
only to cast too bold a shadow
or smash the mold straight off.

For that, solitary confinement,
tear gas, attrition shelling.
Few applicants for that honor.

10.
                                                                    Well,
she's long about her coming, who must be
more merciless to herself than history.
Her mind full to the wind, I see her plunge
breasted and glancing through the currents,
taking the light upon her
at least as beautiful as any boy

or helicopter,
                                                      poised, still coming,
her fine blades making the air wince

but her cargo
no promise then:
delivered
palpable
ours.

The Stranger

Looking as I've looked before, straight down the heart
of the street to the river
walking the rivers of the avenues
feeling the shudder of the caves beneath the asphalt
watching the lights turn on in the towers
walking as I've walked before
like a man, like a woman, in the city
my visionary anger cleansing my sight
and the detailed perceptions of mercy
flowering from that anger

if I come into a room out of the sharp misty light
and hear them talking a dead language
if they ask me my identity
what can I say but
I am the androgyne
I am the living mind you fail to describe
in your dead language
the lost noun, the verb surviving

only in the infinitive
the letters of my name are written under the lids
of the newborn child

Orion

Far back when I went zig-zagging
through tamarack pastures
you were my genius, you
my cast-iron viking, my helmed
lion-heart king in prison.
Years later now you're young

my fierce half-brother, staring
down from that simplified west
your breast open, your belt dragged down
by an oldfashioned thing, a sword
the last bravado you won't give over
though it weighs you down as you stride

and the stars in it are dim
and maybe have stopped burning.
But you burn, and I know it;
as I throw back my head to take you in
an old transfusion happens again:
divine astronomy is nothing to it.

Indoors I bruise and blunder,
break faith, leave ill enough
alone, a dead child born in the dark.
Night cracks up over the chimney,
pieces of time, frozen geodes
come showering down in the grate.

A man reaches behind my eyes
and finds them empty
a woman's head turns away
from my head in the mirror
children are dying my death
and eating crumbs of my life.

Pity is not your forte.
Calmly you ache up there
pinned aloft in your crow's nest,
my speechless pirate!
You take it all for granted
and when I look you back

it's with a starlike eye
shooting its cold and egotistical spear
where it can do least damage.
Breathe deep! No hurt, no pardon
out here in the cold with you
you with your back to the wall.

Prospective Immigrants
Please Note

Either you will
go through this door
or you will not go through.

If you go through
there is always the risk
of remembering your name.

Things look at you doubly
and you must look back
and let them happen.

If you do not go through
it is possible
to live worthily

to maintain your attitudes
to hold your position
to die bravely

but much will blind you,
much will evade you,
at what cost who knows?

The door itself
makes no promises.
It is only a door.

GREGORY CORSO [Born 1930]

Gregory Corso was born on March 26, in New York City, to young Italian parents. His mother was sixteen when he was born, his father, seventeen. After one year, his mother left, returning to Italy. His father did not assume custody of Gregory until eleven years later after remarrying. By that time Gregory had been sent to live in an orphanage and from there to various foster homes. At age eleven he moved in with his father and stepmother. Unhappy there, he ran away repeatedly. At seventeen Corso was sentenced to three years at Clinton Prison for theft. The young boy who often told his father, "I want very much to write," always received the same admonishment, "a poet-writer aint got no place in this world." His father's words were in a sense prophetic for it was outside of society, in prison, that Corso found a place to read, think, feel, and write. When he entered prison he had only a sixth grade education; but, by the time he was released, he was "well read and in love with Chatterton, Marlowe and Shelley." Out of prison and working in the garment district, he was having a drink in a local bar when by chance he met Beat poet Allen Ginsberg, who taught Corso about contemporary poetry and helped him adjust to life outside institutions. The next pivotal point in Corso's career came four years later when a friend brought him to Harvard. He thrived in the academic climate and wrote prolifically. *The Vestal Lady on Brattle*, his first book, was published with the money contributed by over fifty students from Radcliffe and Harvard. Since that time he had approximately ten books published and has been a member of the English Department at the State University of New York at Buffalo from 1965-1970. Although his books have been fairly few and far between these last few years, in 1976 he began raising a ten month old baby boy who like himself had been abandoned. Thus, it seems he has managed to transform the woes of his childhood into love and compassion and, of course, art.

Marriage
for Mr. and Mrs. Mike Goldberg

Should I get married? Should I be good?
Astound the girl next door
with my velvet suit and faustus hood?
Don't take her to movies but to cemeteries
tell all about werewolf bathtubs and forked clarinets
then desire her and kiss her and all the preliminaries
and she going just so far and I understanding why
not getting angry saying You must feel! It's beautiful to feel!
Instead take her in my arms
lean against an old crooked tombstone
and woo her the entire night the constellations in the sky—

When she introduces me to her parents
back straightened, hair finally combed, strangled by a tie,
should I sit knees together on their 3rd-degree sofa
and not ask Where's the bathroom?
How else to feel other than I am,
a young man who often thinks Flash Gordon soap—
O how terrible it must be for a young man
seated before a family and the family thinking
We never saw him before! He wants our Mary Lou!

After tea and homemade cookies they ask What do you do?
Should I tell them? Would they like me then?
Say All right get married, we're losing a daughter
but we're gaining a son—
And should I then ask Where's the bathroom?

O God, and the wedding! all her family and her friends
and only a handful of mine all scroungy and bearded
just waiting to get at the drinks and food—
And the priest! he looking at me as if I masturbated
asking me Do you take this woman
for your lawful wedded wife?
And I, trembling what to say, say Pie Glue!

I kiss the bride all those corny men slapping me on the back:
She's all yours, boy! Ha-ha-ha!
And in their eyes you could see
some obscene honeymoon going on—
Then all that absurd rice and clanky cans and shoes
Niagara Falls! Hordes of us! Husbands! Wives! Flowers!
All streaming into cozy hotels
All going to do the same thing tonight
The indifferent clerk he knowing what was going to happen
The lobby zombies they knowing what
The whistling elevator man he knowing
The winking bellboy knowing
Everybody knows! I'd be almost inclined not to do anything!
Stay up all night! Stare that hotel clerk in the eye!
Screaming: I deny honeymoon! I deny honeymoon!
running rampant into those almost climactic suites
yelling Radio belly! Cat shovel!
O I'd live in Niagara forever! in a dark cave beneath the Falls
I'd sit there the Mad Honeymooner
devising ways to break marriages, a scourge of bigamy
a saint of divorce—

But I should get married I should be good
How nice it'd be to come home to her
and sit by the fireplace and she in the kitchen
aproned young and lovely wanting my baby

and so happy about me she burns the roast beef
and comes crying to me and I get up from my big papa chair
saying Christmas teeth! Radiant brains! Apple deaf!
God what a husband I'd make! Yes, I should get married!
So much to do! like sneaking into Mr. Jones' house late at night
and cover his golf clubs with 1920 Norwegian books
Like hanging a picture of Rimbaud on the lawnmower
Like pasting Tannu Tuva postage stamps
all over the picket fence
Like when Mrs. Kindhead comes to collect
for the Community Chest
grab her and tell her There are unfavorable omens in the sky!
And when the mayor comes to get my vote tell him

When are you going to stop people killing whales!
And when the milkman comes leave him a note in the bottle
Penguin dust, bring me penguin dust, I want penguin dust—

Yet if I should get married and it's Connecticut and snow
and she gives birth to a child and I am sleepless, worn,
up for nights, head bowed against a quiet window,
the past behind me,
finding myself in the most common of situations
a trembling man
knowledged with responsibility not twig-smear
nor Roman coin soup—
O what would that be like!
Surely I'd give it for a nipple a rubber Tacitus
For a rattle a bag of broken Bach records
Tack Della Francesca all over its crib
Sew the Greek alphabet on its bib
And build for its playpen a roofless Parthenon—

No, I doubt I'd be that kind of father
not rural not snow no quiet window
but hot smelly tight New York City
seven flights up, roaches and rats in the walls
a fat Reichian wife screeching over potatoes Get a job!
And five nose-running brats in love with Batman

And the neighbors all toothless and dry haired
like those hag masses of the 18th century
all wanting to come in and watch TV
The landlord wants his rent
Grocery store Blue Cross Gas & Electric Knights of Columbus
Impossible to lie back and dream Telephone snow,
ghost parking—
No! I should not get married I should never get married!

But—imagine if I were married to a beautiful
sophisticated woman
tall and pale wearing an elegant black dress
and long black gloves
holding a cigarette holder in one hand

and a highball in the other
and we lived high up in a penthouse with a huge window
from which we could see all of New York
and even farther on clearer days
No, can't imagine myself married to that pleasant prison dream—

O but what about love? I forget love
not that I am incapable of love
it's just that I see love as odd as wearing shoes—
I never wanted to marry a girl who was like my mother
And Ingrid Bergman was always impossible
And there's maybe a girl now but she's already married
And I don't like men and—
but there's got to be somebody!
Because what if I'm 60 years old and not married,
all alone in a furnished room with pee stains on my underwear
and everybody else is married! All the universe married but me!

Ah, yet well I know that were a woman possible
as I am possible
then marriage would be possible—
Like SHE in her lonely alien gaud waiting her Egyptian lover
so I wait—bereft of 2,000 years and the bath of life.

Zizi's Lament

I am in love with the laughing sickness
it would do me a lot of good if I had it—
I have worn the splendid gowns of Sudan,
carried the magnificent halivas of Boudodin Bros.,
kissed the singing Fatimas of the pimp of Aden,
wrote glorious psalms in Hakhaliba's cafe,
but I've never had the laughing sickness
so what good am I?

The fat merchant offers me opium, kief, hashish, even camel
juice,

all is unsatisfactory—
O bitter damned night! you again! must I yet
pluck out my unreal teeth
undress my unlaughable self
put to sleep this melancholy head?
I am nothing without the laughing sickness.

My father's got it, my grandfather had it;
surely my Uncle Fez will get it, but me, me
who it would do the most good,
will I ever get it?

Uccello

            They will never die on that battlefield
nor the shade of wolves recruit their hoard like brides of
wheat on all horizons   waiting there to consume battle's end
            There will be no dead to tighten their loose bellies
no heap of starched horses to redsmash their bright eyes
            or advance their eat of dead
            They would rather hungersulk with mad tongues
than believe that on that field no man dies

            They will never die who fight so embraced
breath to breath   eye knowing eye   impossible to die
or move   no light seeping through   no maced arm
nothing but horse outpanting horse   shield brilliant upon
shield   all made starry by the dot ray of a helmeted eye
ah   how difficult to fall between those knitted lances
And those banners! angry as to flush insignia across its
            erasure of sky
            You'd think he'd paint his armies by the coldest rivers
have rows of iron skulls flashing in the dark
            You'd think it impossible for any man to die
each combatant's mouth is a castle of song
each iron fist a dreamy gong   flail resounding flail
                        like cries of gold

how I dream to join such battle!
a silver man on a black horse with red standard and striped
    lance   never to die but to be endless
            a golden prince of pictorial war

The Mad Yak

I am watching them churn the last milk
        they'll ever get from me.
They are waiting for me to die;
They want to make buttons out of my bones.
Where are my sisters and brothers?
That tall monk there, loading my uncle,
        he has a new cap.
And that idiot student of his—
        I never saw that muffler before.
Poor uncle, he lets them load him.
How sad he is, how tired!
I wonder what they'll do with his bones?
And that beautiful tail!
How many shoelaces will they make of that!

The Vestal Lady on Brattle

Within a delicate grey ruin
the vestal lady on Brattle
is up at dawn, as is her custom,
with the raise of a shade.

Swan-boned slippers revamp her aging feet;
she glides within an outer room...
pours old milk for an old cat.

Full-bodied and randomly young she clings,
peers down; hovers over a wine-filled vat,
and with outstretched arms like wings,
revels in the forming image of child below.

Despaired, she ripples a sunless finger
across the liquid eyes; in darkness
the child spirals down; drowns.
Pain leans her forward—face absorbing all—
mouth upon broken mouth, she drinks...

Within a delicate grey ruin
the vestal lady on Brattle
is up and about, as is her custom,
drunk with child.

But I Do Not Need Kindness

I have known the strange nurses of Kindness,
I have seen them kiss the sick, attend the old,
give candy to the mad!
I have watched them, at night, dark and sad,
rolling wheelchairs by the sea!
I have known the fat pontiffs of Kindness,
the little old grey-haired lady,
the neightborhood priest,
the famous poet
the mother,
I have known them all!
I have watched them, at night, dark and sad,
pasting posters of mercy
          on the stark posts of despair.

2
I have known Almighty Kindness Herself!
I have sat beside Her pure white feet,
gaining Her confidence!

We spoke of nothing unkind,
but one night I was tormented by those strange nurses,
those fat pontiffs
The little old lady rode a spiked car over my head!
The priest cut open my stomach, put his hands in me,
and cried:—Where's your soul? Where's your soul!—
The famous poet picked me up
and threw me out of the window!
The mother abandoned me!
I ran to Kindness, broke into Her chamber,
and profaned!
with an unnamable knife I gave Her a thousand wounds,
and inflicted them with filth!
I carried Her away, on my back, like a ghoul!
down the cobble-stoned night!
Dogs howled! Cats fled! All windows closed!
I carried Her ten flights of stairs!
Dropped Her on the floor of my small room,
and kneeling beside her, I wept. I wept.

3
But what is Kindness? I have killed Kindness,
but what is it?
You are kind because you live a kind life.
St. Francis was kind.
The landlord is kind.
A cane is kind.
Can I say people, sitting in parks, are kinder?

Hello

It is disastrous to be a wounded deer.
I'm the most wounded, wolves stalk,
and I have my failure, too.
My flesh is caught on the Inevitable Hook!
As a child I saw many things I did not want to be.
Am I the person I did not want to be?
That talks-to-himself person?
That neighbors-make-fun-of-person?
Am I he who, on the museum steps, sleeps on his side?
Do I wear the cloth of a man who has failed?
Am I the looney man?
In the great serenade of things,
          am I the most cancelled passage?

Waterchew!

He climbs the stair
The steps are old and carpeted   he climbs
He climbs the stair each step is another step
I sit on my bed   he climbs
I get up   bolt the door   put out the lights
I go to the window   I can't scream
I sit back on my bed with a smile   it's all a dream
A knock!
Hail Waterchew! big gubbling goopy mouth
Ho hairy clodbound oaf of beauty   hail!

I renounce the present like a king blessing an epic
I must beat the noon with a gold bassoon
In Waterchew I sleep Norse-proud
On ship deck furs I   O how deep into fear must I wedge
The strangeness I follow fools!

Vision of Rotterdam

September 1957 summoned by my vision-agent
via ventriloquial telegram
delivered by the dumb mouths stoned upon Notre Dame given golden
       fare & 17th Century diagram
I left the gargoyle city
And
Two suitcases filled with despair
              arrived in Rotterdam

Rotterdam is dying again
                 steamers & tankers
              unload an awful sight
May 1940 stevedors lead forth a platoon of lukemia
Pleasure ships send metalvoiced rats teeheeing a propaganda of ruin
A cargo of scream deafens the tinhorn of feeble War
Bombers overhead
              Young blond children in white blouses
              crawl in the streets gnawing their houses
The old the sick the mad leave their wheelchairs & cells and kneel in
       adoration before the gentle torpedo of miracles
Bombers unanswrable to the heart
              vitalize a Sunday afternoon dream
Bombs like jewels surprise

Explosion explosion explosion
Avalanche on medieval stilts brought down 1940
Mercy leans against her favorite bombardment
       and forgives the bomb

Alone
Eyes on the antique diagram
       I wander down the ruin and see
              amid a madness of coughing bicycles
the scheme of a new Rotterdam humming in the vacancy

GARY SNYDER [Born 1930]

Gary Snyder was born in San Francisco during the Depression but grew up in Washington and Oregon. It was in the surrounding mountains, forests, and sea that Snyder developed his love for nature. He recorded his childhood adventures in his first book of poetry, *Riprap* (1959). Snyder attended Reed College where he studied literature and anthropology, and in 1953 he entered the University of California at Berkeley to study Oriental languages. In 1955 he met Allen Ginsberg, Jack Kerouac, Kenneth Rexroth and others who were to comprise the Beat movement and wage a rebellion against American mass culture. He lived with Kerouac in a cabin for a few months, and that experience led Kerouac to use Snyder as the inspiration for Japhy Ryder in *The Dharma Bums*. It was during this period that Snyder wrote the poems resulting in his volume *Myths & Texts* (1960), which was the outgrowth of his interest in Indian myths and folktales. Eastern religion also fascinated Snyder and that fascination led Snyder to Japan two times. The second time, during the sixties, Snyder stayed for several years to study Zen Buddhism. His experiences during this extended stay are recounted in his prose work *Earth House Hold* (1969). Upon his return to the States, Snyder became more actively involved in environmental causes. His 1974 collection, *Turtle Island*, which centers on his desire to restore a feeling of respect for our planet, won the Pulitzer Prize for poetry in 1975.

Riprap

Lay down these words
Before your mind like rocks.
                placed solid, by hands
In choice of place, set
Before the body of the mind
                in space and time:
Solidity of bark, leaf, or wall
                riprap of things:
Cobble of milk way,
                straying planets,
These poems, people,
                lost ponies with
Dragging saddles—
                And rocky sure-foot trails.
The worlds like an endless
                four-dimensional
Game of Go.
                ants and pebbles
In the thin loam, each rock a word
                a creek-washed stone
Granite: ingrained
                with torment of fire and weight
Crystal and sediment linked hot
                all change, in thoughts,
As well as things.

Milton by Firelight

"O hell, what do mine eyes
              with grief behold?"
Working with an old
Singlejack miner, who can sense

The vein and cleavage
In the very guts of rock, can
Blast granite, build
Switchbacks that last for years
Under the beat of snow, thaw, mule-hooves.
What use, Milton, a silly story
Of our lost general parents,
              eaters of fruit?

The Indian, the chainsaw boy,
And a string of six mules
Came riding down to camp
Hungry for tomatoes and green apples.
Sleeping in saddle-blankets
Under a bright night-sky
Han River slantwise by morning.
Jays squall
Coffee boils

In ten thousand years the Sierras
Will be dry and dead, home of the scorpion.
Ice-scratched slabs and bent trees.

No paradise, no fall,
Only the weathering land
The wheeling sky,
Man, with his Satan
Scouring the chaos of the mind.
Oh Hell!

Fire down
Too dark to read, miles from a road
The bell-mare clangs in the meadow
That packed dirt for a fill-in
Scrambling through loose rocks
On an old trail
All of a summer's day.

Water

Pressure of sun on the rockslide
Whirled me in dizzy hop-and-step descent,
Pool of pebbles buzzed in a Juniper shadow,
Tiny tongue of a this-year rattlesnake flicked,
I leaped, laughing for little boulder-color coil—
Pounded by heat raced down the slabs to the creek
Deep tumbling under arching walls and stuck
Whole head and shoulders in the water:
Stretched full on cobble—ears roaring
Eyes open aching from the cold and faced a trout.

Things to Do Around a Lookout

Wrap up in a blanket in cold weather and just read.
Practise writing Chinese characters with a brush
Paint pictures of the mountains
Put out salt for deer
Bake coffee cake and biscuit in the iron oven,
Hours off hunting twisty firewood, packing it all back up and chopping.
Rice out for the ptarmigan and the conies
Mark well sunrise and sunset—drink lapsang soochong.
Rolling smokes
The Flower book and the Bird book and the Star book
Old Reader's Digests left behind
Bullshitting on the radio with a distant pinnacle, like you, hid in clouds;

Drawing little sexy sketches of bare girls.
Reading maps, checking on the weather, airing out musty Forest
    Service sleeping bags and blankets
Oil the saws, sharpen axes,
Learn the names of all the peaks you see
                and which is highest
learn by heart the drainages between.
Go find a shallow pool of snowmelt on a good day, bathe in the
    lukewarm water.
Take off in foggy weather and go climbing all alone
The Rock book,—strata, dip, and strike
Get ready for the snow, get ready
To go down.

Myths & Texts (Logging)

14

The groves are down
                cut down
Groves of Ahab, of Cybele
Pine trees, knobbed twigs
        thick cone and seed
        Cybele's tree this, sacred in groves
Pine of Seami, cedar of Haida
Cut down by the prophets of Israel
        the fairies of Athens
        the thugs of Rome
                both ancient and modern;
Cut down to make room for the suburbs
Bulldozed by Luther and Weyerhaeuser
Crosscut and chainsaw
        squareheads and finns
        high-lead and cat-skidding
Trees down
Creeks choked, trout killed, roads.

Sawmill temples of Jehovah.

Squat black burners 100 feet high
Sending the smoke of our burnt
Live sap and leaf
To his eager nose.
   15

Lodgepole
        cone/seed waits for fire
And then thin forests of silver-gray.
      in the void
       a pine cone falls
Pursued by squirrels
What mad pursuit! What struggle to escape!

Her body a seedpod
Open to the wind
"A seed pod void of seed
We had no meeting together"
         so you and I must wait
Until the next blaze
Of the world, the universe,
Millions of worlds, burning
         —oh let it lie.

Shiva at the end of the kalpa:
Rock-fat, hill-flesh, gone in a whiff.
Men who hire men to cut groves
Kill snakes, build cities, pave fields,
Believe in god, but can't
Believe their own senses
Let alone Gautama. Let them lie.

Pine sleeps, cedar splits straight
Flowers crack the pavement.
      Pa-ta Shan-jen
(A painter who watched Ming fall)
       lived in a tree:
"The brush
May paint the mountains and streams
Though the territory is lost."

Myths & Texts (Hunting)

3

this poem is for the birds

Birds in a whirl, drift to the rooftops
Kite dip, swing to the seabank fogroll
Form: dots in air changing line from line,
          the future defined.

Brush back smoke from the eyes,
               dust from the mind,
With the wing-feather fan of an eagle.
A hawk drifts into the far sky.
A marmot whistles across huge rocks.
Rain on the California hills.
Mussels clamp to sea-boulders
Sucking the Spring tides

Rain soaks the tan stubble
Fields full of ducks

Rain sweeps the Eucalyptus
Strange pines on the coast
          needles two to the bunch
The whole sky whips in the wind
Vaux Swifts
Flying before the storm
Arcing close hear sharp wing-whistle
Sickle-bird
               pale gray
               sheets of rain slowly shifting
               down from the clouds,
Black Swifts.
               —the swifts cry
As they shoot by, See or go blind!

4

The swallow-shell that eases birth
    brought from the south by Hummingbird.
"We pull out the seagrass, the seagrass,
    the seagrass, and it drifts away"
—song of the geese.
"My children
    their father was a log"
—song of the pheasant.
The white gulls south of Victoria
    catch tossed crumbs in midair.
When anyone hears the Catbird
    he gets lonesome.

San Francisco, "Mulberry Harbor"
    eating the speckled sea-bird eggs
    of the Farallones.
Driving sand sends swallows flying,
    warm mud puts the ducks to sleep.
Magical birds: Phoenix, hawk, and crane
    owl and gander, wren,
Bright eyes aglow: Polishing clawfoot
    with talons spread, subtle birds
Wheel and go, leaving air in shreds
    black beaks shine in gray haze.
Brushed by the hawk's wing
    of vision.

—They were arguing about the noise
Made by the Golden-eye Duck.
Some said the whistling sound
Was made by its nose, some said
No, by the wings.
        "Have it your way.
We will leave you forever."
They went upriver:
The Flathead tribe.

        Raven
    on a roost of furs
No bird in a bird-book,
    black as the sun.

Myths & Text (Burning)

17

the text

Sourdough mountain called a fire in:
Up Thunder Creek, high on a ridge.
Hiked eighteen hours, finally found
A snag and a hundred feet around on fire:
All afternoon and into night
Digging the fire line
Falling the burning snag
It fanned sparks down like shooting stars
Over the dry woods, starting spot-fires
Flaring in wind up Skagit valley

From the Sound.
Toward morning it rained.
We slept in mud and ashes,
Woke at dawn, the fire was out,
The sky was clear, we saw
The last glimmer of the morning star.

the myth

Fire up Thunder Creek and the mountain—
                    troy's burning
The cloud mutters
The mountains are your mind.
The woods bristle there,
Dogs barking and children shrieking
Rise from below.

Rain falls for centuries
Soaking the loose rocks in space
Sweet rain, the fire's out
The black snag glistens in the rain
& the last wisp of smoke floats up

Into the absolute cold
Into the spiral whorls of fire
The storms of the Milky Way
"Buddha incense in an empty world"
Black pit cold and light-year
Flame tongue of the dragon
Licks the sun

The sun is but a morning star

Affluence

under damp layers of pine needle
still-hard limbs and twigs
tangled as they lay,
two sixteen foot good butt logs took
all the rest, top, left

and this from logging twenty years ago
(figured from core-ring reading on a tree
still stands, hard by a stump)
they didn't pile the slash and burn then—

fire hazard, every summer day.

it was the logger's cost
at lumber's going rate then

now burn the tangles dowsing
pokey heaps with diesel oil.
paying the price somebody didn't pay.

Bedrock
for Masa

Snowmelt pond   warm granite
we make camp,
no thought of finding more.
and nap
and leave our minds to the wind.

on the bedrock, gently tilting,
sky and stone,

teach me to be tender.

the touch that nearly misses—
brush of glances—
tiny steps—
that finally cover worlds
        of hard terrain.
cloud wisps and mists
gathered into slate blue
bolts of summer rain.

tea together in the purple starry eve;
new moon soon to set,
why does it take so
long to learn to
love,
        we laugh
                and grieve.

The Late Snow & Lumber Strike
of The Summer of Fifty-Four

Whole towns shut down
        hitching the Coast road, only gypos
Running their beat trucks, no logs on
Gave me rides. Loggers all gone fishing
Chainsaws in a pool of cold oil
On back porches of ten thousand
Split-shake houses, quiet in summer rain.
Hitched north all of Washington
Crossing and re-crossing the passes
Blown like dust, no place to work.

Climbing the steep ridge below Shuksan
       clumps of pine
       float out the fog
No place to think or work
       drifting.

On Mt. Baker, alone
In a gully of blazing snow:
Cities down the long valleys west
Thinking of work, but here,

Burning in sun-glare
Below a wet cliff, above a frozen lake,
The whole Northwest on strike
Black burners cold,
The green-chain still,
I must turn and go back:
      caught on a snowpeak
      between heaven and earth
And stand in lines in Seattle.
Looking for work.

Four Poems for Robin

Siwashing It Out Once in Siuslaw Forest

I slept under   rhododendron
All night   blossoms fell
Shivering on   on a sheet of cardboard
Feet stuck   in my pack
Hands deep   in my pockets
Barely   able   to   sleep.
I remembered   when we were in school
Sleeping together   in a big warm bed
We were   the youngest lovers
When we broke up   we were still nineteen.
Now our   friends are married
You teach   school back east
I don't mind   living this way
Green hills   the long blue beach
But sometimes   sleeping in the open
I think back   when I had you.

A Spring Night in Shokoku-ji

Eight years ago this May
We walked under cherry blossoms
At night in an orchard in Oregon.
All that I wanted then
Is forgotten now, but you.
Here in the night
In a garden of the old capital
I feel the trembling ghost of Yugao
I remember your cool body
Naked under a summer cotton dress.

An Autumn Morning in Shokoku-ji

Last night watching the Pleiades,
Breath smoking in the moonlight,
Bitter memory like vomit
Choked my throat.

I unrolled a sleeping bag
On mats on the porch
Under thick autumn stars.
In dream you appeared
(Three times in nine years)
Wild, cold, and accusing.
I woke shamed and angry:
The pointless wars of the heart.
Almost dawn. Venus and Jupiter.
The first time I have
Ever seen them close.

December at Yase

You said, that October,
In the tall dry grass by the orchard
When you chose to be free,
"Again someday, maybe ten years."

After college I saw you
One time. You were strange.
And I was obsessed with a plan.

Now ten years and more have
Gone by: I've always known
               where you were—
I might have gone to you
Hoping to win your love back.
You still are single.

I didn't.
I thought I must make it alone. I
Have done that.

Only in dream, like this dawn,
Does the grave, awed intensity
Of our young love
Return to my mind, to my flesh.

We had what the others
All crave and seek for;
We left it behind at nineteen.

I feel ancient, as though I had
Lived many lives.

And may never now know
If I am a fool
Or have done what my
                karma demands.

GEORGE STARBUCK [Born 1931]

George Starbuck was born on June 15 in Columbus, Ohio. His childhood was spent in California and Illinois. He received his education at the California Institute of Technology, the University of California at Berkeley, the University of Chicago, and at Harvard. For two years he lived in Germany where he served in the United States Army as a corporal in the Military Police. He was the fiction editor for Houghton Mifflin in Boston before becoming a member of the English department at the State University of New York at Buffalo where he stayed from 1963 until 1967. He then directed the Writers Workshop at the University of Iowa for three years. Since 1971 he has been a professor of English at Boston University.

His first book of poetry, *Bone Thoughts*, was published in 1960, and he received the Yale Series of Younger Poets Award that same year. A Guggenheim Fellowship was awarded to him in 1961. Though his poems are often irreverent

> Mellifluous as bees, these brittle men
> droning of Honeyed Homer give me hives

they are not without serious intentions as can be seen in the poem, "Of Late." *Takin' B.A. Blues* (1980) and *The Argot Merchant Disaster* (1982) are among his recent works.

Of Late

"Stephen Smith, University of Iowa sophomore, burned
   what he said was his draft card"
and Norman Morrison, Quaker, of Baltimore Maryland,
   burned what he said was himself.
You, Robert McNamara, burned what you said was a
   concentration of the Enemy Aggressor.
No news medium troubled to put it in quotes.

And Norman Morrison, Quaker, of Baltimore Maryland,
   burned what he said was himself.
He said it with simple materials such as would be found
   in your kitchen.
In your office you were informed.
Reporters got cracking frantically on the mental dis-
   turbance angle.
So far nothing turns up.

Norman Morrison, Quaker, of Baltimore Maryland, burned,
   and while burning, screamed.
No tip-off. No release.
Nothing to quote, to manage to put in quotes.
Pity the unaccustomed hesitance of the newspaper edito-
   rialists.
Pity the press photographers, not called.

Norman Morrison, Quaker, of Baltimore Maryland, burned
   and was burned and said.
all that there is to say in that language.
Twice what is said in yours.
It is a strange sect, Mr. McNamara, under advice to try
the whole of a thought in silence, and to oneself.

Cora Punctuated with Strawberries

Sandra and that boy that's going to get her in trouble
one of these days were out in the garden where anyone in
Mother's sickroom could see them out the upperleft corner of the
window sitting behind the garage feeding each other
blueberries and Cherry was helping with the dishes alone in the
kitchen and
um good strawberries if we did grow them just can't can without
popping one in every so often Henry was at it again in the
attic with that whatchamacallit of his when the Big
Bomb fell smack in the MacDonalds' yard you know over on
Elm and they got into Life and the papers and all all very
well but they might have been in when it hit and it would have
been a very different story for Lucy MacDonald then I'll tell
you well they say it was right in the Geographic Center of the
country the Geographic
woody Center you could hear it just as plain I thought the
elevator had bown up and I guess you read yourself the awful
things it would have
ak another one woody I tell you I don't know what's got
into these strawberries used to be so juicy they
say they only had the one and it's all it would have took well I
always knew we could beat the enemy they made such
shoddy tricks and spring-toys and puzzles and fuses and
things and besides, it wouldn't have been right.

Outbreak of Spring

Stirring porchpots up with green-fingered witchcraft,
insinuating cats in proper outskirts,
hag Spring in a wink blacks the prim white magic
of winter-wimpled Boston's every matesick
splinter of spinster landscape.
                    Under the matchstick
march of her bridgework, melting, old lady Mystic
twitches her sequins coyly, but the calls
of her small tugs entice no geese. Canals
take freight; the roads throw up stiff hands, and the Charles
arches. Spring's ón us: a life raft wakes the waters
of Walden like a butt-slap.
                    And yet she loiters.
Where is song while the lark in winter quarters
lolls? What's so solace Scollay's hashhouse floaters
and sing them to their dolls? and yet—
                    strange musics,
migrant melodies of exotic ozarks,
twitter and throb where the bubble-throated jukebox
lurks iridescent by these lurid newsracks.
Browser leafing here, withhold your wisecracks:
tonight, in public, straight from overseas,
her garish chiaroscuro turned to please
you and her other newsstand devotees,
the quarter-lit Diana takes her ease.

So watch your pockets, cats, hang onto your hearts,
for when you've drunk her glitter till it hurts—
Curtain.
                    Winds frisk you to the bone.

                                        Full-feasted
Spring, like an ill bird, settles to the masthead
of here and there an elm. The streets are misted.
A Boston rain, archaic and monastic,
cobbles the blacktop waters, brings mosaic
to dusty windshields; to the waking, music.

On First Looking in on Blodgett's Keats's "Chapman's Homer"
(Sum. ½C. M9-II)

Mellifluous as bees, these brittle men
droning of Honeyed Homer give me hives.
I scratch, yawn like a bear, my arm arrives
at yours—oh, Honey, and we're back again,
me the Balboa, you the Darien,
lording the loud Pacific sands, our lives
as hazarded as when a petrel dives
to yank the dull sea's coverlet, or when,

breaking from me across the sand that's rink
and record of our weekend boning up
on *The romantic Agony,* you sink
John Keats a good surf-fisher's cast out—plump
in the sun's wake—and the parched pages drink
that great whales' blanket party hump and hump.

Bone Thoughts on a Dry Day

*Walking to the museum
over the Outer Drive,
I think, before I see them
dead, of the bones alive.*

How perfectly the snake smoothes over the fact
he strings sharp beads around that charmer's neck.

Bird bone may be breakable, but
have you ever held a cat's jaw shut?
Brittle as ice.

Take mice:
the mouse is a berry, his bones mere seeds:
step on him once and see.

You mustn't think that the fish
choke on those bones, or that chickens wish.

The wise old bat
hangs his bones in a bag.

Two chicks ride,
unlike
that legless swinger of crutches, the ostrich.

Only the skull of a man is much of an ashtray.

Each owl
turns on a dowel.

When all the other tents are struck, an old
elephant pitches himself on his own poles.

But as for my bones—
tug of a toe, blunt-bowed barge of a thighbone,
gondola-squadron of ribs, and the jaw scow—
they weather the swing and storm of the flesh they plow,
out of conjecture of shore, one jolt from land.

I climb the museum steps like a beach.
There, on squared stone, some cast-up keels bleach.
Here, a dark sea speaks with white hands.

Unfriendly Witness

I never played the Moor,
I never looked to see,
I don't know what my hands are for,
I know they're not for me:

I lent them to my Mother,
She yanked them into rules
and put them with my pencilbox
as fit to take to school;

I lent them to my Teacher,
she ruled them into pens
and sent them home to Fatherdear
who beat them straight again;

I lent them to my Judge,
he penned them into line,
since when they clasp and hold I swear
nothing of yours, or mine;

I lent them to my Sergeant,
he lined them into squads
and marched them off to sudden death
like little piston rods;

Death sent them back unused,
I squandered them on love:
they took the world for comrade then
as easy as a glove.

And yet the world is heavy
and filled with men like me —
with tired men, with heavy men
that slip my memory
if that be perjury.

Communication to the City Fathers
of Boston

Dear Sirs: Is it not time we formed a Boston
Committee to enact a Dirge for Boston?

When New York mushrooms into view, when Boston's
townspeople, gathered solemnly in basements,
feel on their necks the spiderwebs of bombsights,
when subway stations clot and fill like beesnests
making a honey-heavy moan, whose business
will it be then to mourn, to take a busman's
holiday from his death, to weep for Boston's?

Though dust is scattered to her bones, though grieving
thunderheads add hot tears, though copper grapevines
clickety-clack their telegraphic ragtime
tongues at the pit of it, how in God's name
will Boston in the thick of Armageddon
summon composure to compose a grave-song
grave and austere enough for such a grieving?

Move we commit some song, now, to the HOLD files
of papers in exotic places. Helpful
of course to cram our scholars with hogs' headfuls
of Lowells, khaki-cap them, ship them wholesale
to Wake or Thule—some safe base, where heartfelt
terror may milk them of a tear; but Hell's fire,
what'll they have on us in all those HOLD files?

You want some rewrite man to wrap up Boston
like garbage in old newsprint for the dustbin?
The Statehouse men convivial at Blinstrub's,
the textile men, the men of subtler substanced
squiring ledaean daughters to the swan-boats,
the dockers, truckers, teen-age hotrod-bandits—
what could he make of them, to make them Boston?

Or even make of me, perched in these Park Street
offices playing Jonah like an upstart
pipsqueak in raven's clothing—First Mate Starbuck
who thinks too much? Thinking of kids in bookstores
digging for dirty footnotes to their Shakespeares,
while by my window the Archbishop's upstairs
loudspeaker booms redemption over Park Street.

Thinking of up the hill the gilded Statehouse
where just last night the plaster-of-paris faces
of Sacco and Vanzetti craned on flannel
arms at the conscientiously empaneled
pain of a state's relentlessly belated
questioning of itself. (Last year the Salem
Witches; next year, if next year finds a Statehouse...?)

thinking of Thor, Zeus, Atlas. Thinking Boston.
Thinking there must be words her weathered brownstone
could still re-whisper—words to blast the brassbound
brandishers on their pads—words John Jay Chapman
scored on her singlehanded—words Sam Adams,
Garrison, Mott, Thoreau blazed in this has-been
Braintree-Jamaica-Concord-Cambridge-Boston.

There were such men. Or why remember Boston?
Strange how not one prepared a dirge for Boston.

SYLVIA PLATH [1932-1963]

Sylvia Plath was born on October 27 in Boston, Massachusetts. Her father, Otto Plath, was of German descent. Born in Grabow, Poland, he emigrated to America while in his teens. His health began to fail while Plath was a small child, so the family moved to Winthrop, a seaside town north of Boston. Although Otto Plath was in need of rest and quiet, he is not remembered by his daughter as a frail or weak man but as a strong, authoritative husband and father. A professor of German and biology at Boston University, Otto Plath was a noted scholar in the field of entomology. During the first four years of the poet's life, her father single-mindedly pursued the writing of his academic works. However, in 1936 when he became ill, he misdiagnosed himself as having lung cancer and refused medical treatment. In 1940 Otto Plath died of diabetes. Strong as his iron will appears to have been, the effect it had on his daughter was equally so as is evident in the poem "Daddy," Plath's best known poem.

The disturbances that manifest in her poems, especially those found in the posthumously published books *Ariel* and *Winter Trees*, are difficult to reconcile with a life that seems to have been so filled with success. Two years after her father's death, the Plath family returned inland, relocating in Wellesley. She excelled in public school there and received three scholarships to Smith College. An honors student in college, she was chosen along with nineteen other young women to spend a summer in New York City, guest-editing the annual college issue of Mademoiselle. Later that summer, when she returned to Massachusetts, she suffered a mental breakdown which resulted in a near-fatal suicide attempt. Written ten years later, her novel, *The Bell Jar*, reveals much about that period of her life. "Patched," just as the main character of that book describes herself, Plath returned to Smith and, graduating with high distinction, received a Fulbright fellowship to Cambridge. At Cambridge, she continued to achieve scholastically; and while there, she met and married British poet Ted Hughes. Within the next three years of her life, her husband had two books of poetry published and she had published her first. Also during this time she had given birth to her first child, Frieda Rebecca. Her life, however, was not completely untouched by sadness; she had a miscarriage and in the fall of 1962, not a year after their second child, Nicholas Farrar, was born, the Hugheses agreed to a legal separation. At this point Plath entered the most prolific period of her career, completing the poems which would comprise the book, *Ariel*. Then on February 11, 1963, she again attempted suicide, and this time was successful. This last "success" became her final solution to the pain that is so vividly voiced in the poems she had been writing at a feverish pace right up until the last week of her life.

Daddy

You do not do, you do not do
Any more, black shoe
In which I have lived like a foot
For thirty years, poor and white,
Barely daring to breathe or Achoo.

Daddy, I have had to kill you.
You died before I had time—
Marble-heavy, a bag full of God,
Ghastly statue with one grey toe
Big as a Frisco seal

And a head in the freakish Atlantic
Where it pours bean green over blue
In the waters off beautiful Nauset.
I used to pray to recover you.
Ach, du.

In the German tongue, in the Polish town
Scraped flat by the roller
Of wars, wars, wars.
But the name of the town is common.
My Polack friend

Says there are a dozen or two.
So I never could tell where you
Put your foot, your root,
I never could talk to you.
The tongue stuck in my jaw.

It stuck in a barb wire snare.
Ich, ich, ich, ich,
I could hardly speak.
I thought every German was you.
And the language obscene

An engine, an engine
Chuffing me off like a Jew.
A Jew to Dachau, Auschwitz, Belsen.
I began to talk like a Jew.
I think I may well be a Jew.

The snows of the Tyrol, the clear beer of Vienna
Are not very pure or true.
With my gypsy ancestress and my weird luck
And my Taroc pack and my Taroc pack
I may be a bit of a Jew.

I have always been scared of *you*,
With your Luftwaffe, your gobbledygoo.
And your neat moustache
And your Aryan eye, bright blue.
Panzer-man, panzer-man, O You—

Not God but a swastika
So black no sky could squeak through.
Every woman adores a Fascist,
The boot in the face, the brute
Brute heart of a brute like you.

You stand at the blackboard, daddy,
In the picture I have of you,
A cleft in your chin instead of your foot
But no less a devil for that, no not
Any less the black man who

Bit my pretty red heart in two.
I was ten when they buried you.
At twenty I tried to die
And get back, back, back to you.
I thought even the bones would do.

But they pulled me out of the sack,
And they stuck me together with glue.
And then I knew what to do.
I made a model of you,
A man in black with a Meinkampf look

And a love of the rack and the screw.
And I said I do, I do.
So daddy, I'm finally through.
The black telephone's off at the root,
The voices just can't worm through.

If I've killed one man, I've killed two—
The vampire who said he was you
And drank my blood for a year,
Seven years, if you want to know.
Daddy, you can lie back now.

There's a stake in your fat black heart
And the villagers never liked you.
They are dancing and stamping on you.
They always *knew* it was you.
Daddy, daddy, you bastard, I'm through.

Nick and the Candlestick

I am a miner. The light burns blue.
Waxy stalactites
Drip and thicken, tears

The earthen womb
Exudes from its dead boredom.
Black bat airs

Wrap me, raggy shawls,
Cold homicides.
They weld to me like plums.

Old cave of calcium
Icicles, old echoer.
Even the newts are white,

Those holy Joes.
And the fish, the fish—
Christ! They are panes of ice,

A vice of knives,
A piranha
Religion, drinking

Its first communion out of my live toes.
The candle
Gulps and recovers its small altitude,

Its yellows hearten.
O love, how did you get here?
O embryo

Remembering, even in sleep,
Your crossed position.
The blood blooms clean

In you, ruby.
The pain
You wake to is not yours.

Love, love,
I have hung our cave with roses.
With soft rugs—

The last of Victoriana.
Let the stars
Plummet to their dark address,

Let the mercuric
Atoms that cripple drip
Into the terrible well,

You are the one
Solid the spaces lean on, envious.
You are the baby in the barn.

A Birthday Present

What is this, behind this veil, is it ugly, is it beautiful?
It is shimmering, has it breasts, has it edges?

I am sure it is unique, I am sure it is just what I want.
When I am quiet at my cooking I feel it looking, I feel it thinking

"Is this the one I am to appear for,
Is this the elect one, the one with black eye-pits and a scar?

Measuring the flour, cutting off the surplus,
Adhering to rules, to rules, to rules.

Is this the one for the annunciation?
My god, what a laugh!"

But it shimmers, it does not stop, and I think it wants me.
I would not mind if it was bones, or a pearl button.

I do not want much of a present, anyway, this year.
After all I am alive only by accident.

I would have killed myself gladly that time any possible way.
Now there are these veils, shimmering like curtains,

The diaphanous satins of a January window
White as babies' bedding and glittering with dead breath. O ivory!

It must be a tusk there, a ghost-column.
Can you not see I do not mind what it is?

Can you not give it to me?
Do not be ashamed—I do not mind if it is small.

Do not be mean, I am ready for enormity.
Let us sit down to it, one on either side, admiring the gleam,

The glaze, the mirrory variety of it.
Let us eat our last supper at it, like a hospital plate.

I know why you will not give it to me,
You are terrified

The world will go up in a shriek, and your head with it,
Bossed, brazen, an antique shield,

A marvel to your great-grandchildren.
Do not be afraid, it is not so.

I will only take it and go aside quietly.
You will not even hear me opening it, no paper crackle,

No falling ribbons, no scream at the end.
I do not think you credit me with this discretion.

If you only knew how the veils were killing my days.
To you they are only transparencies, clear air.

But my god, the clouds are like cotton.
Armies of them. They are carbon monoxide.

Sweetly, sweetly I breathe in,
Filling my vein with invisible, with the million

Probable motes that tick the years off my life.
You are silver-suited for the occasion. O adding machine—

Is it impossible for you to let something go and have it go whole?
Must you stamp each piece in purple,

Must you kill what you can?
There is this one thing I want today, and only you can give it to me.

It stands at my window, big as the sky.
It breathes from my sheets, the cold dead centre

Where spilt lives congeal and stiffen to history.
Let it not come by the mail, finger by finger.

Let it not come by word of mouth, I should be sixty
By the time the whole of it was delivered, and too numb to use it.

Only let down the veil, the veil, the veil.
If it were death

I would admire the deep gravity of it, its timeless eyes.
I would know you were serious.

There would be a nobility then, there would be a birthday.
And the knife not carve, but enter

Pure and clean as the cry of a baby,
And the universe slide from my side.

The Bee Meeting

Who are these people at the bridge to meet me? They are the
    villagers—
The rector, the midwife, the sexton, the agent for bees.
In my sleeveless summery dress I have no protection,
And they are all gloved and covered, why did nobody tell me?
They are smiling and taking out veils tacked to ancient hats.

I am nude as a chicken neck, does nobody love me?
Yes, here is the secretary of bees with her white shop smock,
Buttoning the cuffs at my wrists and the slit from my neck to my
    knees.
Now I am milkweed silk, the bees will not notice.
They will not smell my fear, my fear, my fear.

Which is the rector now, is it that man in black?
Which is the midwife, is that her blue coat?
Everybody is nodding a square black head, they are knights in
    visors,
Breastplates of cheesecloth knotted under the armpits.
Their smiles and their voices are changing. I am led through a bean-
    field.

Strips of tinfoil winking like people,
Feather dusters fanning their hands in a sea of bean flowers,
Creamy bean flowers with black eyes and leaves like bored hearts.
Is it blood clots the tendrils are dragging up that string?
No, no, it is scarlet flowers that will one day be edible.

Now they are giving me a fashionable white straw Italian hat
And a black veil that moulds to my face, they are making me one
    of them.

They are leading me to the shorn grove, the circle of hives.
Is it the hawthorn that smells so sick?
The barren body of hawthorn, etherizing its children.

Is it some operation that is taking place?
It is the surgeon my neighbours are waiting for,
This apparition in a green helmet,
Shining gloves and white suit.
Is it the butcher, the grocer, the postman, someone I know?

I cannot run, I am rooted, and the gorse hurts me
With its yellow purses, its spiky armoury.
I could not run without having to run forever.
The white hive is snug as a virgin,
Sealing off her brood cells, her honey, and quietly humming.

Smoke rolls and scarves in the grove.
The mind of the hive thinks this is the end of everything.
Here they come, the outriders, on their hysterical elastics.
If I stand very still, they will think I am cow parsley,
A gullible head untouched by their animosity,

Not even nodding, a personage in a hedgerow.
The villagers open the chambers, they are hunting the queen.
Is she hiding, is she eating honey? She is very clever.
She is old, old, old, she must live another year, and she knows it.
While in their fingerjoint cells the new virgins

Dream of a duel they will win inevitably,
A curtain of wax dividing them from the bride flight,

The upflight of the murderess into a heaven that loves her.
The villagers are moving the virgins, there will be no killing.
The old queen does not show herself, is she so ungrateful?

I am exhausted, I am exhausted—
Pillar of white in a blackout of knives.
I am the magician's girl who does not flinch.
The villagers are untying their disguises, they are shaking hands.
Whose is that long white box in the grove, what have they accom-
    plished, why am I cold?

The Colossus

I shall never get you put together entirely,
Pieced, glued, and properly jointed.
Mule-bray, pig-grunt and bawdy cackles
Proceed form your great lips.
It's worse than a barnyard.

Perhaps you consider yourself an oracle,
Mouthpiece of the dead, or of some god or other.
Thirty years now I have labored
To dredge the silt from your throat.
I am none the wiser.

Scaling little ladders with gluepots and pails of lysol
I crawl like an ant in mourning
Over the weedy acres of your brow
To mend the immense skull plates and clear
The bald, white tumuli of your eyes.

A blue sky out of the Oresteia
Arches above us. O father, all by yourself
You are pithy and historical as the Roman Forum.
I open my lunch on a hill of black cypress.
Your fluted bones and acanthine hair are littered

In their old anarchy to the horizon-line.
It would take more than a lightning-stroke
To create such a ruin.
Nights, I squat in the cornucopia
Of your left ear, out of the wind,

Counting the red stars and those of plum-color.
The sun rises under the pillar of your tongue.
My hours are married to shadow.
No longer do I listen for the scrape of a keel
On the blank stones of the landing.

Words

Axes
After whose stroke the wood rings,
And the echoes!
Echoes travelling
Off from the centre like horses.

The sap
Wells like tears, like the
Water striving
to re-establish its mirror
Over the rock

That drops and turns,
A white skull,
Eaten by weedy greens.
Years later I
Encounter them on the road—

Words dry and riderless,
The indefatigable hoof-taps.
While
From the bottom of the pool, fixed stars
Govern a life.

LEROI JONES ("IMAMU AMIRI BARAKA") [Born 1934]

LeRoi Jones was born on October 7 in Newark, New Jersey. Graduating high school two years ahead of his peers, Jones had already obtained his B.A. from Howard University while not quite twenty years old. Before going on to graduate school, where he received two M.A. degrees: one from Columbia University in philosophy and the other from the New School for Social Research in German Literature, Jones spent two and a half years serving in the U.S. Air Force, stationed in Puerto Rico. Back in New York, he founded *Yugen* magazine and the Totem Press as well as coediting (with Diane DiPrima) the *Floating Bear*, a poetry newsletter. After teaching at the New School and at the State University of New York at Buffalo, he experienced some success with his one act play, *Dutchman*, which had an extended off-Broadway run and won an Obie award for the best American play of 1964.

The mid sixties became a turning point in Jones' life. In 1966 he fell away from his Bohemian, post-modern poet friends and, converting to the Kawaida branch of the Moslem faith, changed his name to Imamu Amiri Baraka. The focal point of his activities became increasingly political. He lived both in Harlem and then in Newark working within each community to improve living conditions. Over the years his involvement has expanded to national Black politics and relations between Black communities in the U.S. and the Black African nations. In addition to his interest in political activism which is reflected in his writing, he has had over a dozen books of poetry published and has written a prodigious amount of plays. Awards for his writing include a Whitney Fellowship, a National Endowment for the Arts grant, and a Guggenheim Fellowship.

A Guerrilla Handbook

In the palm
the seed
is burned up
in the wind.
      In their rightness
the tree trunks are socialists
leaves murder the silence and are brown
and old when they blow to the sea.
           Convinced
of the lyric. Convinced
of the man's image (since
he will not look at substance
other than his ego. Flowers, grapes
the shadows of weeds, as the weather
is colder, and women walk
with their heads down.
           Silent political rain
against the speech
of friends (We love them
trapped in life, knowing no way out
except description. Or black soil
floating in the arm.
           We must convince the living
           that the dead
           cannot sing.

Ka 'Ba

A closed window looks down
on a dirty courtyard, and black people
call aross or scream across or walk across
defying physics in the stream of their will

Our world is full of sound
Our world is more lovely than anyone's

tho we suffer, and kill each other
and sometimes fail to walk the air

We are beautiful people
with african imaginations
full of masks and dances and swelling chants
with african eyes, and noses, and arms,
though we sprawl in grey chains in a place
full of winters, when what we want is sun.

We have been captured,
brothers. And we labor
to make our getaway, into
the ancient image, into a new

correspondence with ourselves
and our black family. We need magic
now we need the spells, to raise up
return, destroy, and create. What will be

the sacred words?

Political Poem
(For Basil)

Luxury, then, is a way of
being ignorant, comfortably
An approach to the open market
of least information. Where theories
can thrive, under heavy tarpaulins
without being cracked by ideas.

(I have not seen the earth for years
and think now possibly "dirt" is
negative, positive, but clearly
social. I cannot plant a seed, cannot
recognize the root the clearer dent

than indiffernece. Though I eat
and shit as a natural man. (Getting up
from the desk to secure a turkey sandwich
and answer the phone: the poem undone
undone by my station, by my station,
and the bad words of Newark.) Raised up
to the breech, we seek to fill for this
crumbling century. The darkness of love,
in whose sweating memory all error is forced.

Undone by the logic of any specific death. (Old gentlemen
who still follow fires, tho are quieter
and less punctual. It is a polite truth
we are left with. Who are you? What are you
saying? Something to be dealt with, as easily.
The noxious game of reason, saying, "No, No,
you cannot feel," like my dead lecturer
lamenting thru gipsies his fast suicide.

In Memory of Radio

Who has ever stopped to think of the divinity of Lamont Cranston?
(Only Jack Kerouac, that I know of; & me.
The rest of you probably had on WCBS and Kate Smith,
Or something equally unattractive.)

What can I say?
It is better to have loved and lost
Than to put linoleum in your living rooms?

Am I a sage or something?
Mandrake's hypnotic gesture of the week?
(Remember, I do not have the healing powers of Oral Roberts...
I cannot, like F. J. Sheen, tell you how to get saved & *rich*!
I cannot even order you to gaschamber satori like Hitler or Goody
    Knight.

& Love is an evil word.
Turn it backward/see, see what I mean?
An evol word. & besides
who understands it?
I certainly wouldn't like to go out on that kind of limb.

Saturday mornings we listened to *Red Lantern* & his undersea folk.
At 11, *Let's Pretend*/& we did/& I, the poet, still do, Thank God!

What was it he used to say (after the transformation, when he
    was safe
& invisible, & the unbelievers couldn't throw strones?) "Heh, Heh,
    Heh,
Who knows what evil lurks in the hearts of men? The Shadow
    knows!"

O, yes he does
O, yes he does

An evil word it is,
This love.

Beautiful Black Women

Beautiful black women, fail, they act. Stop them, raining
They are so beautiful, we want them with us. Stop them, raining.
Beautiful, stop raining, they fail. We fail them and their lips
stick out perpetually, at our weakness. Raining. Stop them. Black
queens, Ruby Dee weeps at the window, raining, being lost in her
life, being what we all will be, sentimental bitter frustrated
deprived of her fullest light. Beautiful black women, it is
still raining in this terrible land. We need you. We flex our
muscles, turn to stare at our tormentor, we need you. Raining.
We need you, reigning, black queen. This/terrible black ladies
wander, Ruby Dee weeps, the window, raining, she calls, and her voice
is left to hurt us slowly. It hangs against the same wet glass, her
sadness and age, and the trip, and the lost heat, and the gray cold

buildings of our entrapment. Ladies. Women. We need you. We
are still;
trapped and weak, but we build and grow heavy with our
knowledge. Women.
Come to us. Help us get back what was always ours. Help us
women. Where
are you, women, where, and who, and where, and who, and
will you help
us, will you open your bodysouls, will you life me up mother, will you
let me help you, daughter, wife/lover, will you

*Preface to a Twenty Volume
Suicide Note*

Lately, I've become accustomed to the way
The ground opens up and envelops me
Each time I go out to walk the dog.
Or the broad edged silly music the wind
Makes when I run for a bus—

Things have come to that.

And now, each night I count the stars,
And each night I get the same number.
And when they will not come to be counted
I count the holes they leave.

Nobody sings anymore.

And then last night, I tiptoed up
To my daughter's room and heard her
Talking to someone, and when I opened
The door, there was no one there...
Only she on her knees,
Peeking into her own clasped hands.

An Agony. As Now.

I am inside someone
who hates me. I look
out from his eyes. Smell
what fouled tunes come in
to his breath. Love his
wretched women.

Slits in the metal, for sun. Where
my eyes sit turning, at the cool air
the glance of light, or hard flesh
rubbed against me, a woman, a man,
without shadow, or voice, or meaning.

This is the enclosure (flesh,
where innocence is a weapon. An
abstraction. Touch. (Not mine,
Or yours, if you are the soul I had
and abandoned when I was blind and had
my enemies carry me as a dead man
(if he is beautiful, or pitied.

It can be pain. (As now, as all his
flesh hurts me.) It can be that. Or
pain. As when she ran from me into
that forest.
          Or pain, the mind
silver spiraled whirled against the
sun, higher than even old men thought
God would be. Or pain. And the other. The
yes. (Inside his books, his fingers. They
are withered yellow flowers and were never
beautiful.) The yes. You will, lost soul, say
'beauty.' Beauty, practiced, as the tree. The
slow river. A white sun in its wet sentences.

Or, the cold men in their gale. Ecstasy. Flesh
or soul. The yes. (Their robes blown. Their bowls
empty. They chant at my heels, not at yours) Flesh
or soul, as corrupt. Where the answer moves too quickly.
Where the God is a self, after all.)

Cold air blown through narrow blind eyes. Flesh,
white hot metal. Glows as the day with its sun.
It is a human love, I live inside. A bony skeleton
you recognize as words or simple feeling.

But it has no feeling. As the metal, is hot, it is not,
given to love.

It burns the thing
inside it. And that thing
screams

> *Goodbye!*

                If we call
                to ourselves
                if we want to feel
                who we are if
                we want to love
                what we can
                be
                come
                into
                a wide space
                of heart
                and hearts
                meaning
                we love (love love
(these are soft cries of feeling
can you help me, who are here w/me can
you walk into my deep senses

I want you to understand the world
as I have come to understand it
I'll wait here a few seconds, please come

N. SCOTT MOMADAY [Born 1934]

N. Scott Momaday was born in Lawton, Oklahoma. A native American of the Kiowa tribe, he grew up on various reservations in the southwest. He received his education from the University of New Mexico and Stanford University. He taught English and comparative literature at Stanford University and at the University of California at Berkeley before accepting his present position at the University of Arizona. Best known for his Pulitizer Prize winning novel, *The House Made of Dawn* (1969), he has also published a collection of his poems in the book, *The Gourd Dancer* (1976).

The Gourd Dancer
Mammedaty, 1880-1932

I. The Omen

Another season centers on this place.
Like memory the blood congeals in it;
And like memory, too, the sun recedes
Into the hazy, southern distances.

A vagrant heat hangs on the dark river,
And shadows turn like smoke. An owl ascends
Among the branches, clattering, remote
Within its motion, intricate with age.

II. The Dream

Mammedaty saw to the building of this house.
Just there, but the arbor, he made a camp in the
old way. And in the evening when the hammers had
fallen silent and there were frogs and crickets
in the black grass—and a low, hectic wind upon
the pale, slanting plane of the moon's light—
he settled deep down in his mind to dream. He
dreamed of dreaming, and of the summer breaking
upon his spirit, as drums break upon the intervals
of the dance, and of the gleaming gourds.

III. The Dance

Dancing,
He dreams, he dreams—
The long wind glances, moves
Forever as a music to the mind;
The gourds are flashes of the sun.
He takes the inward, mincing steps
Describing old processions and refrains.

Dancing,
His moccasins,

His sash and bandolier
Contain him in insignia;
His fan is powerful, concise
According to his agile hand,
And catches on the sacramental air.

IV. The Give-away

Someone spoke his name, Mammedaty, in which
his essence was and is. It was a serious matter
that his name should be spoken there in the circle,
among the many people, and he was thoughtful,
full of wonder, and aware of himself and of his name.
He walked slowly to the summons, looking into the
eyes of the man who summoned him. For a moment
they held each other in close regard, and all about
them there was excitement and suspense.

Then a boy came suddenly into the circle, leading
a black horse. The boy ran, and the horse after him.
He brought the horse up short in front of Mammedaty,
and the horse wheeled and threw its head and cut
its eyes in the wild way. And it blew hard and
quivered in its hide so that light ran, rippling,
upon its shoulders and its flanks—and then it
stood still and was calm. Its mane and tail were
fixed in braids and feathers, and a bright red chief's
blanket was draped in a roll over its withers. The
boy placed the reins in Mammedaty's hands. And all
of this was for Mammedaty, in his honor, as even now
it is in the telling, and will be, as long as there
are those who imagine him in his name.

The Delight Song of Tsoai-Talee

I am a feather on the bright sky
I am the blue horse that runs in the plain
I am the fish that rolls, shining, in the water
I am the shadow that follows a child
I am the evening light, the lustre of meadows
I am an eagle playing with the wind
I am a cluster of bright beads
I am the farthest star
I am the cold of the dawn
I am the roaring of the rain
I am the glitter on the crust of the snow
I am the long track of the moon in a lake
I am a flame of four colors
I am a deer standing away in the dusk
I am a field of sumac and the pomme blanche
I am an angle of geese in the winter sky
I am the hunger of a young wolf
I am the whole dream of these things

You see, I am alive, I am alive
I stand in good relation to the earth
I stand in good relation to the gods
I stand in good relation to all that is beautiful
I stand in good relation to the daughter of *Tsen-tainte*
You see, I am alive, I am alive

Krasnopresnenskaya Station

For Will Sutter

Their faces do not change at their mouths.
They read and look after themselves.
I mean them no harm,
but they are afraid of me.

I sit at the window. I wonder
that they keep so, to themselves,
in their trains, in the deep streets.
I have no prospects here.

One, a girl not yet disappointed, perhaps,
approaches close to me. I suppose
she does not remember herself;
she dreams of the lindens at Arkhangelskoe.

She would speak of ordinary things;
I would listen
for the hard resonances of the river,
the ice breaking apart in the afternoon.

DIANE WAKOSKI [Born 1937]

Diane Wakoski was born in Whittier, California, and received a B.A. from the University of California at Berkeley before moving to New York City. In New York she worked as a book clerk and English teacher, and she associated with poets called "deep imagists." These poets felt that a poem should be organized intuitively through its imagery. Though similar to surrealism, the "deep image" poem, as written by Wakoski, is more objective, accessible, and coherent. In 1962 her first book of verse, *Coins and Coffins*, was published, and she was included in a volume edited by Leroi Jones entitled *Four Young Lady Poets*. However, her impact as a poet would not be felt until later. In 1967 she produced one of her most important works, *The George Washington Poems*. The poems are talks with George Washington who appears in various roles as historical persona, friend, father, and lover.

Wakoski is an extremely prolific writer whose later works explore different emotions such as anger, jealousy, sexuality, greed, in addition to the experience of woman in a complex society. Though her vision is piercing and forceful at times, it is frequently offset by a sympathetic tone. Wakoski has been the recipient of many fellowships and grants including the Robert Frost Fellowship which enabled her to produce *Discrepancies and Apparitions* (1966), a Guggenheim Grant in 1972, and a National Endowment for the Arts grant.

Patriotic Poem

George Washington, your name is on my lips.
You had a lot of slaves.
I don't like the idea of slaves. I know I am
a slave to
too many masters, already
a red cardinal flies out of the pine tree in my eye swooping
down to crack a nut and the bird feeds on a tray draped
    with
a thirteen-starred flag. Underneath my heart where the
    fat clings
like bits of wool
I want to feel a man slipping his hand inside my body
massaging the heart, bathing
it in stripes, streams of new blood with stars floating in it
must pass through my arteries, each star pricking
the walls of veins with the prickly sensation of life.
The blood is old,
perhaps was shipped from Mt. Vernon
which was once a blood factory.
Mr. Washington, the pseudo aristocrat with two large
    fish instead of
feet, slapping around the plantation,
managing the country with surveyor's tools,
writing documents with sweet potatoes, yams, ham hocks,
    and black-eyed
peas,
oh I hate southern gentlemen, too bad he was one;
somehow I've always hated the men who ran my country
but I was a loyal citizen. "Take me to your leader,"
and I'll give him a transfusion of my AB negative blood
    and stars
floating in it. I often said this
in a spirit of devotion, chauvinistic passion,
pining secretly for the beautiful Alexander Hamilton but
    making do with
George who, after all, was the first president

and I need those firsts. On my wall, yes the wall of my
   stomach;
on my money, yes play money and real money, money I
   spend and money
I save, in and out of pocket; on documents, and deeds,
   statuary, monu-
ments, books, pictures, trains, old houses, whiskey bottles,
   and even
sewing machine shuttles there is his name
and my commitment, after all, is to names, how else, to
   what else
do we commit ourselves but names
and George I have committed myself to you. No Western
   sheriffs for me;
they only really like men and horses and sometimes gun
   play.
I guess I'm stuck with you, George, despite your absolute
   inability
to feel anything personal, or communicate it,
or at least share it with me.
That you at least for being first in your white linen
   and black coat.
My body, the old story, is my country, the only territory
   I control
and it certainly has been torn by wars. I'd like to think the
Revolution is over and that at last I am going to have my
   first pres-
ident, at last I can have an inaugural ball;
the white house of my corpuscle
asks for new blood; I have give so many transfusions to
   others.
When will you make me your first lady, George?
When will I finally become the first president's wife?

Sestina from the Home Gardener

These dried-out paint brushes which fell from my lips have been
    removed
with your departure; they are such minute losses
compared with the light bulb gone from my brain, the sections
of chicken wire from my liver, the precise
silver hammers in my ankles which delicately banged and pointed
magnetically to you. Love has become unfamiliar

and plenty of time to tend the paint brushes now. Once unfamiliar
with my processes. Once removed
from that sizzling sun, the ego, to burn my poet shadow to the wall, I
    pointed,
I suppose, only to your own losses
which made you hate that 200 pound fish called marriage. Precise
ly, I hate my life, hate its freedom, hate the sections

of fence stripped away, hate the time for endless painting, hate the
    sections
of my darkened brain that wait for children to snap on the light, the
    unfamiliar
corridors of my heart with strangers running in them, shouting. The
    precise
incisions in my hip to extract an image, a dripping pickaxe or palmtree
    removed
and each day my paint brushes get softer and cleaner—better tools,
    and losses
cease to mean loss. Beauty, to each eye, differently pointed.

I admire sign painters and carpenters. I like that black hand pointed
up a drive-way whispering to me, "The Washingtons live in those
    sections"
and I explain autobiographically that George Washington is sympa-
    thetic to my losses;
His face or name is everywhere. No one is unfamiliar
with the American dollar, and since you've been removed
from my life I can think of nothing else. A precise
replacement for love can't be found. But art and money are precise
ly for distraction. The stars popping out of my blood are pointed

nowhere. I have removed
my ankles so that I cannot travel. There are sections
of my brain growing teeth and unfamiliar
hands tie strings through my eyes. But there are losses

Of the spirit like vanished bicycle tires and losses
of the body, like the whole bike, every precise
bearing, spoke, gear, even the unfamiliar
handbrakes vanished. I have pointed
myself in every direction, tried sections
of every map. It's no use. The real body has been removed.

Removed by the ice tongs. If a puddle remains what losses
can those sections of glacier be/ Perhaps a precise
count of drops will substitute the pointed mountain, far away, un-
    familiar?

An Apology

Past exchanges have left orbits of rain around my face,
Words used-up as the empty shell of the beetle.
        I did not mean to insult you,
        but perhaps wanted to scorch you with that steamy teakettle
        of my 2700 years,
        to tell you youth shouldn't be humble as the tablecloth,
        but arrogant and fierce/
        we get toothless with age;
        should bite hard when we're young.
        To tell you not to follow masters whose egos are sponges,
        To tell you not that you had nothing to say
        but that you need to pour it out at your own speed,
        in an empty space where it will knock against you.
        I saw the dream of tongue floating in a bowl of water
        as a desperate sacrifice. You,
        giving up your own words,
        You, giving up identity to float safely on display in
        another man's ocean;
        I saw everything that made me weep spools of rotten thread

for my own disconnected life—
drop cement trowels from my knees and
broken clocks from my elbows.
Wanting to discard the past; renege my own life, the pain
of recognition and hate mingles with the identity.
I apologize for lack of grace—
not passing you with a zen stance.
Elders should be lacquered in their place.
And women commit their words
to the dream code; toads & shooting stars in the blood,
icy milk pails,
snow,
oranges,
diamonds, eyes to the ground. Women should be
silently riding their zebras.

From a Girl in a Mental Institution

The morning wakes me as a broken door vibrating on its
hinges.
We are drifting out to sea this morning. I
can barely feel the motion of the boat as it rocks me.
I must be a gull, sitting on the mast,
else why would I be so high above the world?
Yes.
I see everything down there—
children tucked, sleeping, into the waves,
their heads nestled in foam
        AND I DON'T LIKE THE WAVES THEY
        DISTINCTLY SAY THINGS
        AGAINST ME.
The wind is blowing my feathers. How good
that feels. If the wind
had always blown my feathers, I would
never have cried
when the waves spoke
that way—

taking my brother away, when he dove in and never came
back.
                    it was because he loved the seashells
                    too much
                    I know
                    and broken water foams in my hair
                    in its new color—the color of my wing
Why don't we hear the fog-horns today?
                    IF I AM TO SIT HERE ALL DAY I MUST
                    HAVE SOMETHING TO LISTEN TO.
The waves have torn the sleeping children to bits. I
see them scattered on the crests now.
There—an arm floating by.
                    leave me alone, I have not hurt you
                    Stop pulling my wings,
                    my beak, DON'T YOU HEAR STOP IT.
There is nothing more horrible than hands
like ancient crabs, pulling at one. And they cannot
hear because they have no ears.
                    I have no ears.
I am a gull. Birds have no ears. I cannot hear
Them
or anyone
The fingers on the dismembered arm, floating
in the waves,
can point and make signs,
but I will not hear
the waves
telling the fingers odious things about me.
I will not watch their obscenities
pointing to the bottom where the children are buried;
where he is buried;
where I am buried.

Slam the door as often as you like—you will
not wake me.
I am a gull
sitting on the mast, and I feel the ocean rocking
because I can hear nothing
but silent voices the wind carries from the past—

                    gently rocking.
The ocean is as still as a newly made bed,
rocking.

                        Belly Dancer

Can these movements which move themselves
be the substance of my attraction?
Where does this thin green silk come from that covers my body?
Surely any woman wearing such fabrics
would move her body just to feel them touching every part of her.

Yet most of the women frown, or look away, or laugh stiffly.
They are afraid of these materials and these movements
in some way.
The psychologists would say they are afraid of themselves,
    somehow.
Perhaps awakening too much desire—
that their men could never satisfy?
So they keep themselves laced and buttoned and made up
in hopes that the framework will keep them stiff enough not to feel
the whole register.
In hopes that they will not have to experience that unquenchable
desire for rhythm and contact.

If a snake glided across this floor
most of them would faint or shrink away.
Yet that movement could be their own.
That smooth movement frightens them—
awakening ancestors and relatives to the tips of the arms and toes.

So my bare feet
and my thin green silks
my bells and finger cymbals
offend them—frighten their old-young bodies.
While the men simper and leer—

glad for the vicarious experience and exercise.
They do not realize how I scorn them;
or how I dance for their frightened,
unawakened, sweet
women.

Picture of a Girl Drawn in Black and White

A girl sits in a black room.
She is so fair
the plums have fallen off the trees outside.
Icy winds blow geese
into her hair.
The room is black,
but geese are wandering there,
breaking into her mind
and closing the room off
into its own black secret.
She is not alone, for there is the sound
of a hundred flapping wings,
and from fruit rotting in the dark earth
the smell of passing time.

A girl sits in an unreal room
combing her unreal hair.
The flapping wings of the geese have
broken plums
from the trees outside,
and the wind has frozen them all
to keep the girl in the black room
there, combing her
unreal wintry hair.

A girl sits in a picture
with the background painted solid black
and combs her hair.
She is so fair the wind has broken

plums and scattered geese.
Winter has come.
The sound of flapping wings is so loud I hear
nothing
but must only stare out of the picture
and continue combing my black
unreal hair.

AL YOUNG [Born 1939]

Al Young was born in Ocean Springs, Mississippi, and attended the University of Michigan, Stanford University, and the University of California at Berkeley. He has won a National Endowment for the Arts grant three times and a Guggenheim Fellowship in 1974. Some notable influences in Young's poetry are Black culture, jazz, American Indian poetry, and poets such as T.S. Eliot, Rimbauld, LeRoi Jones, Denise Levertov, and Diane Wakoski. His books of verse include *Dancing, The Song Turning Back into Itself,* and *Geography of the Near Past*.

One West Coast
For Gordon Lapides

Green is the color of everything
that isn't brown, the tones ranging
like mountains, the colors changing.

You look up toward the hills & fog—
the familiarity of it after so many years
            a resident tourist.
                        A young man walks
toward you in vague streetcrossing denims
& pronounced boots. From the pallor of
    his gait, the orange splotch twin gobs of sunset
    in his shades, from the way he vibrates
    his surrounding air, you can tell, you can tell
        he's friendly, circulating,

                he's a Californian: comes to visit,
            stays for years, marries, moves a wife in,
        kids, wears out TV sets, gets stranded on
                        loneliness,
                    afternoon pharmaceutica,
            so that the sky's got moon in it by
            3 o'clock, is blooo, is blown—

                The girls: they're all
            winners reared by grandmothers & CBS.
        Luckier ones get in a few dances with
        mom, a few hours, before dad goes back
    in the slam, before "G'bye I'm off
    to be a singer!" & another runaway
            Miss American future drifts
                over the mountain &
                into the clouds.

            Still
                there's a beautifulness about California.
It's based on the way each eyeblink toward

the palms & into the orange grove leads backstage
  into the onionfields.

Unreachable, winter happens inside you.

Your unshaded eyes dilate at the spectacle.

You take trips to contain the mystery.

Identities

So youre playing
Macbeth in Singapore
1937 before you were
even born perhaps

The lady is warm,
your lines are waiting
in your stomach
to be heard.

An old seacoast drunk
in pullover blue cap
stomps up one-legged
onto the stage to
tell you youve got no
business playing this

bloody Macbeth,
not a lonely black boy
like you, lost like
himself in a new world
where it's no longer
a matter of whom
thou knowest so much
as it is who you know.

(Say the lady warming
is a career bohemian
with OK looks & a
Vassar education)

Say the future seems
fractured in view of
the worsening wars
in Europe & Asia &
the old man's just
shattered your last
chance illusion.

Well, do you go on
& Shakespeare anyway
or reach for the sky
for the 500th time?

Sweet Sixteen Lines

You bet it would've made a tender movie!
If only someone had been flighty enough
to capture the shape of what turned out to be
our last days alone, the end of a rough
journey that dulled every sense but touch.
Heroically juvenile, lighter than light,
we talked what we felt, but never thought much.
We were Romeo and Juliet night after night.
It was like we'd sailed from heaven in a jet,
copilots, cool but glorious, and landed
our sullen craft too artfully—poets yet;
runaways on life's slick runway of expanded
unconsciousness. Maybe. Who knows for sure?
But Ruby and the Romantics came out that year
with a sweet-nothing single: hot, airy and pure
enough to hold us aloft by heart and by ear.

Birthday Poem

First light of day in Mississippi
son of laborer & of house wife
it says so on the official photostat
not son of fisherman & child fugitive
from cottonfields & potato patches
from sugarcane chickens & well-water
from kerosene lamps & watermelons
mules named jack or jenny & wagonwheels,

years of meaningless farm work
work Work WORK WORK WORK—
"PAPA pull you outta school bout March
to stay on the place & work the crop"
—her own earliest knowledge
of human hopelessness & waste

She carried me around nine months
inside her fifteen year old self
before here I sit numbering it all

How I got from then to now
is the myscry that could fill a whole library
much less an arbitrary stanza

But of course you already know about that
from your own random suffering
& sudden inexplicable bliss

NIKKI GIOVANNI [Born 1943]

Nikki Giovanni was born in Knoxville, Tennessee, but grew up in Lincoln Heights, Ohio—a Black suburb of Cincinnati. As she explains in "Nikki-Rosa" her childhood was "quite happy" in spite of the money shortages responsible for some domestic strife. At the age of sixteen, the precocious young poet, daughter of college graduates in the field of social work, began her higher education at Fisk University. However, not long after her admission, she was suspended for leaving the campus without permission. That rule remained unbent by the administration even under the circumstance that she had gone: to visit her sick grandmother. At that point she left school for three years of traveling. She was readmitted to Fisk where she entered a writing workshop which exposed her to the politics of the Black Movement, a subject charged with immediacy at that time. She graduated in 1967. Out of these early experiences came her first book, *Black Feeling, Black Talk, Black Judgement*. Since then, she has had various books published, taught at many universities, raised her son Thomas as a single parent, and received many awards for her poetry including grants from Ford and the National Endowment for the Arts. Her style, an unforced hybrid spanning the academic and the colloquial, is fused with such energy and compassion that she is a constant inspiration to young readers who, perhaps, are her favorite audience.

Nikki-Rosa

childhood remembrances are alway a drag
if you're Black
you always remember things like living in Woodlawn
with no inside toilet
and if you become famous or something
they never talk about how happy you were to have your mother
all to yourself and
how good the water felt when you got your bath from one of those
big tubs that folk in chicago barbecue in
and somehow when you talk about home
it never gets across how much you
understood their feelings
as the whole family attended meetings about Hollydale
and even though you remember
your biographers never understand
your father's pain as he sells his stock
and another dream goes
and though you're poor it isn't poverty that
concerns you
and though they fought a lot
it isn't your father's drinking that makes any difference
but only that everybody is together and you
and your sister have happy birthdays and very good christmasses
and I really hope no white person ever has cause to write about me
because they never understand Black love is Black wealth and they'll
probably talk about my hard childhood and never understand that
all the while I was quite happy

Kidnap Poem

ever been kidnapped
by a poet
if I were a poet
I'd kidnap you
put you in my phrases and meter
you to jones beach
or maybe coney island
or maybe just to my house
lyric you in lilacs
dash you in the rain
blend into the beach
to complement my see
play the lyre for you
ode you with my love song
anything to win you
wrap you in the red Black green
show you off to mama
yeah if I were a poet I'd kid
nap you

They Clapped

they clapped when we landed
thinking africa was just an extension
of the black world
they smiled as we taxied home to be met
black to black face not understanding africans lack
color prejudice
they rushed to declare
cigarettes, money, allegiance to the mother land
not knowing despite have read fanon and deavenport
hearing all of j.h. clarke's lectures, supporting
nkrumah in ghana and nigeria in the war that there was
    once

a tribe called afro-americans that populated the whole
of africa
they stopped running when they learned the packages
on the women's heads were heavy and that babies didn't
cry and disease is uncomfortable and that villages are
    fun
only because you knew the feel of good leather on good
pavement
they cried when they saw mercedes benz were as
    common
in lagos as volkswagens are in berlin
they shook their heads when they understood there was
    no
difference between the french and the english and the
    americans
and the afro-americans or the tribe next door or the
    country
across the border
they were exasperated when they heard sly and the
    family stone
in francophone africa and they finally smiled when
little boys
who spoke no western tongue said "james brown" with
    reverence
they brought out their cameras and bought out africa's
    drums
when they finally realized they are strangers all over
and love is only and always about the lover not the
    beloved
they marveled at the beauty of the people and the
    richness
of the land knowing they could never possess either

they clapped when they took off
for home despite the dead
dream they saw a free future

Knoxville, Tennessee

I always like summer
best
you can eat fresh corn
from daddy's garden
and okra
and greens
and cabbage
and lots of
barbecue
and buttermilk
and homemade ice-cream
at the church picnic
and listen to
gospel music
outside
at the church
homecoming
and go to the mountains with
your grandmother
and go barefooted
and be warm
all the time
not only when you go to bed
and sleep

The Funeral of Martin Luther King, Jr.

His headstone said
FREE AT LAST, FREE AT LAST
But death is a slave's freedom
We seek the freedom of free men
And the construction of a world
Where Martin Luther King could have lived and
    preached non-violence

The World Is Not
a Pleasant Place to Be

the world is not a pleasant place
to be without
someone to hold and be held by

a river would stop
its flow if only
a stream were there
to receive it

an ocean would never laugh
if clouds weren't there
to kiss her tears

the world is not
a pleasant place to be without
someone

Scrapbooks

it's funny that smells and sounds return
so all alone uncalled unneeded
on a sweaty night as I sit armed
with coffee and cigarettes waiting

sometimes it seems
my life is a scrapbook

I usta get 1.50 per week
for various duties unperformed
while I read *green dolphin street*
and *the sun is my undoing*
never understanding my exclusion
but knowing quite clearly the hero
is always misunderstood
though always right in the end

roy gave me a yellow carnation
that year for the junior prom

the red rose was from michael
who was the prettiest boy I'd ever known
he took me to the *jack and jill* dance
and left me sitting in the corner until
the slow drags came on then he danced
real tight and sweated out my bangs

I had a white leather monstrosity that passed
for taste in my adolescence pressed with dances
undanced though the songs were melodious

and somehow three or four books were filled
with proms and parties and programs that
my grandmother made me go to
for "culture" so that I could be
a lady
my favorite is the fisk book with clippings
of the *forum* and notes from the dean of women
saying "you are on social probation" and "you are
suspended from fisk"
and letters from my mother saying "behave yourself"
and letters from my grandmother reminding me
"your grandfather graduated fisk in 1905" and not
to try to run the school
but mostly notes from alvin asking when
was I coming over
again
I purchased a blue canvas notebook for the refrain

it's really something when you sit
watching dawn peep over apartment buildings
that seemed so ominous during the night and see
pages of smiling pictures   groups of girls throwing
pillows   couples staring nervously ahead as if they
think the kodak will eat them   someone with a ponytail

and a miles davis record   a lady with an afro pointing
joyously to a diploma   a girl in a brown tan and red
bathing suit holding a baby that looks like you
and now there is a black leather book filled
efficiently by a clipping service
and a pile of unanswered letters that remind
you to love those who love you
and I sit at dawn
all my defenses gone sometimes
listening to *something cool* sometimes
hearing *tears on my pillow*
and know there must be other books
filled with failures and family and friends
that perhaps one day I can unfold
for my grandchildren

LOUISE GLÜCK [Born 1943]

Louise Glück was born in New York City on April 22. She attended Sarah Lawrence College and then Columbia University where she studied under Stanley Kunitz. Her first book, published when she was twenty years old, is entitled *Firstborn*. Since that time she has published several other books and has received numerous awards. Among her achievements are grants from the Guggenheim Foundation, the Rockefeller Foundation, and from the National Endowment for the Arts. She also was the recipient of the Academy of American poets prize in 1966, and the Eunize Tietjens Memorial Prize in 1971. Most recently she received the 1985 National Book Critics Circle Award for her book, *The Triumph of Achilles*. Her teaching positions include Columbia University and the University of Virginia. She is now teaching at Williams College.

Portrait

A child draws the outline of a body.
She draws what she can, but it is white all through,
she cannot fill in what she knows is there.
Within the unsupported line, she knows
that life is missing; she has cut
one background from another. Like a child,
she turns to her mother.

And you draw the heart
against the emptiness she has created.

The Garden

1   The Fear of Birth

One sound. Then the hiss and whir
of houses gliding into their places.
And the wind
leafs through the bodies of animals—

But my body that could not content itself
with health—why should it be sprung back
into the chord of sunlight?

It will be the same again.
This fear, this inwardness,
until I am forced into a field
without immunity
even to the least shrub that walks
stiffly out of the dirt, trailing
the twisted signature of its root,
even to a tulip, a red claw.

And then the losses,
one after another,
all supportable.

2   The Garden

The garden admires you.
For your sake it smears itself with green pigment,
the ecstatic reds of the roses,
so that you will come to it with your lovers.

And the willows—
see how it has shaped these green
tents of silence. Yet
there is still something you need,

your body, so soft, so alive, among the stone
    animals.

Admit that it is terrible to be like them,
beyond harm.

3   The Fear of Love

That body lying beside me like obedient stone—
once its eyes seemed to be opening,
we could have spoken.

At that time it was winter already.
By day the sun rose in its helmet of fire
and at night also, mirrored in the moon.
Its light passed over us freely,
as though we had lain down
in order to leave no shadows,
only these two shallow dents in the snow.
And the past, as always, stretched before us,
still, complex, impenetrable.

How long did we lie there,
as, arm in arm in their cloaks of feathers,
the gods walked down
from the mountain we built for them.

4   Origins

As though a voice were saying
You should be asleep by now —
But there was no one. Nor
had the air darkened,
though the moon was there,
already filled in with marble.

As though, in a garden crowded with flowers,
a voice had said
How dull they are, these golds,
so sonorous, so repetitious
until you closed your eyes,
lying among them, all
stammering flame:

And yet you could not sleep,
poor body, the earth
still clinging to you—

5   The Fear of Burial

In the empty field, in the morning,
the body waits to be claimed.
The spirit sits beside it, on a small rock—
nothing comes to give it form again.

Think of the body's loneliness.
At night pacing the sheared field,
its shadow buckled tightly around.
Such a long journey.
And already the remote trembling lights
     of the village
not pausing for it as they scan the rows.
How far away they seem,
the wooden doors, the bread and milk
laid like weights on the table.

Gretel in Darkness

This is the world we wanted.
All who would have seen us dead
are dead. I hear the witch's cry
break in the moonlight through a sheet
of sugar: God rewards.
Her tongue shrivels into gas...
　　　　　　　　　Now, far from women's arms
and memory of women, in our father's hut
we sleep, are never hungry.
Why do I not forget?
My father bars the door, bars harm
from this house, and it is years.

No one remembers. Even you, my brother,
summer afternoons you look at me as though
you meant to leave,
as though it never happened.
But I killed for you. I see armed firs,
the spires of that gleaming kiln—

Nights I turn to you to hold me
but you are not there.
Am I alone? Spies
hiss in the stillness, Hansel,
we are there still and it is real, real,
that black forest and the fire in earnest.

World Breaking Apart

I look out over the sterile snow.
Under the white birch tree, a wheelbarrow.
The fence behind it mended. On the picnic table,
mounded snow, like the inverted contents of a bowl
whose dome the wind shapes. The wind,
with its impulse to build. And under my fingers,
the square white keys, each stamped
with its single character. I believed
a mind's shattering released
the objects of its scrutiny: trees, blue plums in a bowl,
a man reaching for his wife's hand
across a slatted table, and quietly covering it,
as though his will enclosed it in that gesture.
I saw them come apart, the glazed clay
begin dividing endlessly, dispersing
incoherent particles that went on
shining forever. I dreamed of watching that
the way we watched the stars on summer evenings,
my hand on your chest, the wine
holding the chill of the river. There is no such light.
And pain, the free hand, changes almost nothing.
Like the winter wind, it leaves
settled forms in the snow. Known, identifiable—
except there are no uses for them.

JAMES TATE [Born 1943]

James Tate was born on December 8 in Kansas City, Missouri. He studied at Kansas State College, the University of Missouri, and the University of Iowa. From the last, he received his Master of Fine Arts degree and taught creative writing there for one year. At the age of twenty-three, his first book, *Cages*, was published. One year later, his third book, *The Lost Pilot*, was chosen for the Yale Younger Poets Series. From that time until the early seventies, Tate consistently put out two books per year and in some cases more. For example, in 1970 he had a total of six books published. While writing at this furious pace, he also has taught at various universities and colleges. Since 1967 he has been at the University of Massachusetts at Amherst. He has edited the *Dickinson Review*, served as a consultant for the Coordinating Council of Literary Magazines, and acted as associate editior for Pym Randall Press and also for Dream Barn Press. Awards for an artist whose productivity seems tireless are understandably numerous; among them are a National Endowment for the Arts grant (1968, 1969) a National Institute of Arts and Letters Award (1974) and a Guggenheim Fellowship (1976). Given all of these serious accomplishments, his language remains playful and his subject material is often on the verge of the impossible. Logical absurdities are frequently found in his writing, yet his words never lack meaning:

This is the house of unwritten poems,
this is where I am unborn.

The Eagle Exterminating Company

There are birds larger than us, I know that.
There is a bird in the bedroom much larger than the bed.
There is a photograph of a dead bird somewhere, I can't remember.
There is a wingspan that would put us all in the shadows.

There is the birdcall I must anticipate each night.
There are feathers everywhere.
Everywhere you walk there are feathers, you can try
to hop over and between them but then
you look like a bird. You are too small to be one.

You look like a tiny one-winged bird.
If you are your mother will come and kill you.
If you are not you will probably beat yourself to death.

But what matters is that every room in the house is filled,
is filled with the cry of the eagle.
Exterminating the eagles is now all but impossible
for the house would fall down without them.

There is a photograph of a dead bird somewhere.
Everywhere you walk there are feathers.
You look like a tiny one-winged bird.
There is the birdcall. There is the wingspan.

The Lost Pilot
(for my father, 1922-1944)

Your face did not rot
like the others—the co-pilot,
for example, I saw him

yesterday. His face is corn-
mush: his wife and daughter,
the poor ignorant people, stare

as if he will compose soon.
He was more wronged than Job.
But your face did not rot

like the others—it grew dark,
and hard like ebony;
the features progressed in their

distinction. If I could cajole
you to come back for an evening,
down from your compulsive

orbiting, I would touch you,
read your face as Dallas,
your hoodlum gunner, now,

with the blistered eyes, reads
his braille editions. I would
touch your face as a disinterested

scholar touches an original page.
However frightening, I would
discover you, and I would not

turn you in; I would not make
you facè your wife, or Dallas,
or the co-pilot, Jim. You

could return to your crazy
orbiting, and I would not try
to fully understand what

it means to you. All I know
is this: when I see you,
as I have seen you at least

once every year of my life,
spin across the wilds of the sky
like a tiny, African god,

I feel dead, I feel as if I were
the residue of a stranger's life,
that I should pursue you.

My head cocked toward the sky,
I cannot get off the ground,
and, you, passing over again,

fast, perfect, and unwilling
to tell me that you are doing
well, or that it was mistake

that placed you in that world,
and me in this; or that misfortune
placed these worlds in us.

Pity Ascending with the Fog

He had no past and he certainly
had no future. All the important
events were ending shortly before
they began. He says he told mama

earth what he would not accept: and I
keep thinking it had something to do

with her world. Nights expanding into
enormous parachutes of fire, his

eyes were little more than mercury.
Or sky-diving in the rain when there
was obviously no land beneath,
half-dead fish surfacing all over

his body. He knew all this too well.
And she who might at any time be
saying the word that would embrace all
he had let go, he let go of course.

I think the pain for him will end in
May or January, though the weather
is far too clear for me to think of
anything but august comedy.

Stray Animals

This is the beauty of being alone
toward the end of summer:
a dozen stray animals asleep on the porch
in the shade of my feet,
and the smell of leaves burning
in another neighborhood.
It is late morning,
and my forehead is alive with shadows,
some bats rock back and forth
to the rhythm of my humming,
the mimosa flutters with bees.
This is a house of unwritten poems,
this is where I am unborn.

Read the Great Poets

What good is life without music.
But that's impossible,
one shuffle has always led to another.
One man hears it start on his lathe,
a mother beats her eggs.
There's a typewriter in the next room.
Two cars are angry at each other.
The baby downstairs is wet again.
I remember the voice of a dead friend.
Everything speaks at the same time.
Music will watch us drown.

I write letters to all those from whom I receive
and to many of those from whom I don't.
I read books, anything, useless piles of random
insufferable rubbish for which, in my torpid panic,
I fall through time and space each day
in my foolish way, remembering only the present feeling,
not the village with its face of death,
nothing to be carried secretly in a car.
I move from the stiff-backed chair
to the brown leather one
as the day wears on. And then finally
the couch, allowing the spirit to leave
the broken body and wander at will.
Lately it's a pasture of Holsteins she longs for.

There's a certain point in each evening when I have to put on
some really soul-shattering rock-and-roll music and comb my
hair into this special caveman fright-wig. I've done as much as
two or even three dollars worth of damage to my apartment in
one hour of all-stops-pulled Bacchic, Dionysian celebration
and revolution of this great dull life, so fascinating it hypno-
tizes you and then puts you to sleep, only to never know the
ending. It's strange though, no one ever complains. It is what I
feared all along? We are playing the same song and no one has
ever heard anything.

People read poems like newspapers, look at paintings as though they were excavations in the City Center, listen to music as if it were rush hour condensed. They don't even know who's invaded whom, what's going to be built there (when, if ever). They get home. That's all that matters to them. They get home. They get home alive.

So what it's been burgled. The heirlooms. Mother's rings, father's cufflinks. They go to a distant island and get robbed there. It's the same everywhere. Read the great poets, listen to the great composers. It's the same everywhere. The Masters. The Thieves.

Letting Him Go

A shiny arm from
the hoary firmament
without whose hand

our personal gloom
and joy is rocketing:
our own tongues

can furnish the room
and, see, nothing
much is loosening.

For eatage we have
the remembrance
of a bowl of fire,

and a dish of snow.
That's quite enough.
The whole galaxy

was weary of your
services—there were
messages, messages

everywhere: please
close the door
gently as you go.

Schizophrenic Kiss

And what a day it was!
This was the night we had been
in the jungle as well as in the city:
It was night everywhere,
with spiderbones beneath the costume in the cellar
and still no fountain of ink.
The suburbs as well,
what we could see of them.
Their personalities and pasts to a certain extent
are the most ancient and sacred:
when we finally decided to take the subway
with a tape-recorder for our summerhouse.
And during the days, what there was of them,
a little monkey woke me.
It was light enough to read
the handwriting of someone
who appeared to not care,
and stumble without regard
to collect the birds from apple trees
on secret hands and knees
night after night after.

ALICE WALKER [Born 1944]

Alice Walker was born in Eatonton, Georgia, and attended Spellman College and Sarah Lawrence College, where she received a B.A. She has worked in welfare rights, in voter registration in Georgia, and in the New York City Welfare Department. She has also lived with families in the Soviet Union and in Kenya. Ms. Walker has written a biography of Langston Hughes, has been awarded the American Book Award and the Pulitzer Prize for her novel, *The Color Purple*, and was a National Book Award nominee for her poetry collection, *Good Night, Willie Lee, I'll See You in the Morning*. Other poetry collections include *Once, Revolutionary Petunias*, and *Horses Make a Landscape Look More Beautiful*.

Facing the Way

the fundamental question about revolution
as lorraine hansberry was not afraid to know
is not simply whether I am willing to give up my life
but if I am prepared to give up my comfort:
clean sheets on my bed
the speed of the dishwasher
and my gas stove
gadgetless
but still preferable to cooking out of doors
over a fire of smouldering roots
my eyes raking the skies for planes
the hills for army tanks.
paintings I have revered stick against my walls
as unconcerned as saints
their perfection alone sufficient for their defense.
yet not one lifeline thrown by the artist
beyond the frame
reaches the boy whose eyes were target
for a soldier's careless aim
or the small girl whose body napalm
a hot bath after mass rape
transformed
or the old women who starve on muscatel
nightly
on the streets of New York.

it is shameful how hard it is for me to give
them up!
to cease this cowardly addiction
to art that transcends time
beauty that nourishes a ravenous spirit
but drags on the mind whose sale would patch
a roof
heat the cold rooms of children. replace an eye.
feed a life.

it does not comfort me now to hear
thepoorweshallhavewithusalways
(Christ should never have said this:
it makes it harder than ever to change)
just as it failed to comfort me
when I was poor.

Janie Crawford

I love the way Janie Crawford

left her husbands   the one who wanted
to change her into a mule
and the other who tried to interest her
in being a queen
a woman unless she submits is neither a mule
nor a queen
though like a mule she may suffer
and like a queen pace
the floor

Now That the Book Is Finished

Now that the book is finished,
now that I know my characters
will live,
I can love my child again.
She need sit no longer
at the back of my mind,
the lonely sucking of her thumb
a giant stopper in my throat.

"Good Night, Willie Lee,
I'll See You in the Morning"

Looking down into my father's
dead face
for the last time
my mother said without
tears, without smiles
without regrets
but with *civility*
"Good night, Willie Lee, I'll see you
in the morning."
And it was then I knew that the healing
of all our wounds
is forgiveness
that permits a promise
of our return
at the end.

GREGORY ORR [Born 1947]

Gregory Orr was born and raised in upstate New York. He attended Antioch College and Columbia University School of the Arts. While at Columbia he was a recipient of the Academy of American Poets Prize. His works include *Burning the Empty Nests* (1973) and *The Red House* (1980).

The Voyages

It's late when I try to sleep, resting
one hand on your hip, the other on my chest
where the rise and fall of breath
is a faint light that brightens and fades.
Today the doctor placed his stethoscope
against your belly and an amplifier
filled the tiny room with a scene
from old war movies—the submarine,
the churning of a destroyer's engines
fathoms above rapt, terrified sailors.
Child's heart, whose thrumming the doctor
pronounced as perfect as such things
can be guessed across such gulfs.

Here, deep in the night, I calm my fears
by choosing a place among Homer's crew,
lolling on Hades' shore. Inland, Odysseus
brims a trench with blood, extorts predictions
from the thirsty dead. But common sailors
already know that launching and wrecks
make the same sounds: scrape of keel on rock,
loud cries. As for the rest,
we need our ignorance to keep us brave.

A Shelf Is a Ledge

I don't understand by what perversity
Darwin and St. Paul are kissing cousins
on my shelf. And how they both lean against
an encyclopedia of history...
It must give them bad dreams.
I watch Saul topple from his horse, but
Paul's all right. Darwin in the underbrush

glimpses a finch. And then there's that damned
history book ticking all night
like a cheap clock while it adds
the day's events to its late blank pages
and erases the early ones so it has
more space...
            It's true a sane man
would resist the temptation to animate
dead things of the object world, and
such a shunning proves he's sane. Myself,
I hear a blessed humming in my head
and I'm its glad amanuensis.
Paul's taught me this: Love passes
understanding. And Darwin's on my side
as he screams in the dark: Survive! Survive!

Gathering the Bones Together

I   A Night in the Barn

The deer carcass hangs from a rafter.
Wrapped in blankets, a boy keeps watch
from a pile of loose hay. Then he sleeps

and dreams about a death that is coming:
Inside him, there are small bones
scattered in a field
among burdocks and dead grass.
He will spend his life walking there,
gathering the bones together.

Pigeons rustle in the eaves.
At his feet, the German shepherd
snaps its jaws in its sleep.

II

A father and his four sons
run down a slope toward
a deer they just killed.
The father and two sons carry
rifles. They laugh, jostle,
and chatter together.
A gun goes off,
and the youngest brother
falls to the ground.
A boy with a rifle
stands beside him, screaming.

III

I crouch in the corner of my room,
staring into the glass well
of my hands; far down
I see him drowning in air.

Outside, leaves shaped like mouths
make a black pool
under a tree. Snails glide
there, little death-swans.

IV   Smoke

Something has covered the chimney
and the whole house fills with smoke.
I go outside and look up at the roof,
but I can't see anything.
I go back inside. Everyone weeps,
walking from room to room.
Their eyes ache. This smoke
turns people into shadows.
Even after it is gone, and the tears are gone,
we will smell it in pillows
when we lie down to sleep.

V

He lives in a house of black glass.
Sometimes I visit him, and we talk.
My father says he is dead,
but what does that mean?
Last night I found a child
sleeping on a nest of bones.
He had a red, leaf-shaped
scar on his cheek. I lifted him up
and carried him with me, even though
I didn't know where I was going.

VI   The Journey

Each night, I knelt on a marble slab
and scrubbed at the blood.
I scrubbed for years and still it was there.
But tonight the bones in my feet
began to burn. I stood up
and started walking, and the slab
appeared under my feet with each step,
a white road only as long as your body.

VII   The Distance

The winter I was eight, a horse
slipped on the ice, breaking its leg.
Father took a rifle, a can of gasoline.
I stood by the road at dusk and watched
the carcass burning in the far pasture.

I was twelve when I killed him;
I felt my own bones wrench from my body.
Now I am twenty-seven and walk
beside this river, looking for them.
They have become a bridge
that arches toward the other shore.

Making Beasts

for Daniel Young

When I was about ten
I glued together an old
white turtle shell,
a woodchuck's skull,
and a red sqirrel's tail
to make my first
mythical beast.
What has been created
is never lost. It crawls
up through my thoughts now
on the feet I never gave it.

MARK JARMAN [Born 1952]

Mark Jarman grew up in Southern California and Scotland. He attended the University of Iowa Writer's Workshop where he earned a Master of Fine Arts degree. He received the Joseph Henry Jackson Award for his poetry in 1974 and has taught at Indiana University; he presently teaches at Vanderbilt University. His works include *North Sea* and *The Rote Walker*.

Writing for Nora

I should be pleasing myself, you know,
old woman, though I owe
myself to you. Through the hospital window
edged with ferns, the trucks and birds appear,
gearing up hill, up air.
Should they be included?
They have not been informed you are here.
Or that I, waiting with you
for your last seizure, can't
stand to listen again
as your dictaphone winds through
the summer of the first:
the buckets of sweet water,
the sponges stroking and stroking,
your wrists and ankles cinched
because your prone dancing tore
too many sheets...Each time I've almost
got it, the red
recording tape ticks off
and again you accuse me,
thinking me one of the brothers who sent you to fetch
foxfire in the woods, and followed, and watched,
laughing when you fell down.
I can't convince you they are gone.
Bold as the girl
you think you are you twirl
around in bed and thrust your knees
in my face,
pointing to scars as fresh cuts,
to the shine of the loose skin.
Desperate story-teller,
those words of yours that wore me out
sworn on tapes crammed in a box
will be lost.
You know I owe you them.
And you will twist
me everywhere to find, at least,

one way to tell how you died
the way you would tell it, digressions turning
and twisting till I fall
as you fell in your fit,
Grandmother, ghost, epileptic,
caught, sick of it.

Lullaby for Amy

We are here, in another provisional city,
talking of places we will live.
Our bed is another world inside
the blocks of Midwestern houses,
the windows each showing the moon
of a streetlight through Chinese blinds,
watery reflections on the walls,
tropical and bland.
The way birds follow weather
we followed circumstance
and wait for it to change.

The earth is a wave that will not set us down.

Last summer our nerves lay down
to sleep a month in the mountains.
One night in two hours of rain
the river, far below us, rose
around its islands of motels.
A man on the road was picked up
off his feet, an old couple
was torn with him fanned out
with others thirty miles away.
Cars bobbed with headlights on,
shuddered and ducked under.

The earth is a wave that will not set us down.

There is a town in Scotland
on the edge of the North Sea. In fall
the carnival unbolts its haywire rides
along the strand. Night sweeps in
from Norway with the breath of cod;
candles are set afloat in wash tubs.

With a leaky water gun you snuff three wicks
and win a coconut. I hear the screams
of prizewinners, smell the cod
on slabs in the High Street markets.
Sixteen years. I have never been back.

The earth is a wave that will not set us down.

Or does wherever we sleep become our home?
I see us walking among castles
that are great mounds and windings
of wet sand, in the mist of waves
breaking out of sight.
Like the horn of a lost boat,
a voice says, "Live here
as you used to live."
And it surprises us, so that we stop
and look back at our scar of footprints,
for we have always lived here, in this way.

Greensleeves

So much comes to mind
from the side, like the dust
down blades of sunlight.
Memory shows a morning
of all the family together,
palpable through the years—
but only as elbows and cups.

So much comes to pieces
like the dust, seeking attachments,
leaning obliquely forward
to get the whole picture
when the edge says, "Not there,
not there anymore." We haunt
our own lives, posing,

or scan our portraits
squinting into the glare
of the background, hoping
a guardian secret attends us.
Everyone out, I touch
the piano and find five notes
still cling to my right hand.

A scrap of melody,
it is the one piece
I ever played well; my heart
is still in it, too.
It is possibly this
that I mean. So much meant
to be lost is saved.

LORNA DEE CERVANTES [Born 1954]

Lorna Dee Cervantes was born in San Francisco and raised in San Jose. She was educated at San Jose City College (1972-1975) and at San Jose State University (1975-1977). In 1978 she was a Hudson D. Walker fellow at the Fine Art Work Center in Provincetown, Massachusetts. That same year she was also awarded a National Endowment for the Arts fellowship. This recipient of the Pushcart Prize has given over one hundred readings and workshops in the United States and Mexico. She is currently active in both Chicano community affairs and a Chicano theater group.

*Poem for the Young White Man Who Asked Me How
I, an Intelligent, Well-Read Person, Could Believe in
the War Between Races*

In my land there are no distinctions.
The barbed wire politics of oppression
have been torn down long ago.
There are no boundaries. The only reminders
of past battles, lost or won, is the slight
rutting in the fertile fields.

In my land people write poems about love.
They dance on the rooftops, all
of their babies are fat, everyone reads
Russian short stories and weeps;
there are no colors; there is no race;

there are only hands
softly stroking thighs, only words
full of nothing but contented childlike syllables,
and the only hunger is a real hunger,
none of this complicated starving
of the soul from oppression.

I am not a revolutionary.
I don't even like political poems.
Do you think I can believe in a war between races?
I can deny it. I can forget about it
when I'm safe,
living on my own continent of harmony
and home, but I am not
there...

I believe in the revolution
because everywhere there is an enemy waiting,
sharp-shooting diplomats round every corner,
there are snipers in the schools...
(I know you don't believe this,

you think this is nothing
but faddish exaggeration, but
they are not shooting
at you!)
Their bullets are discrete and designed to kill slowly.
They are aimed at my children.
These are facts.
Let me show you my wounds: my stumbling mind, my
"excuse me" tongue, and this
nagging preoccupation
with the feeling of not being good enough.

These bullets bury deeper than logic.
Racism is not intelligence.
I can not reason these scars away.

Outside my door
there is a real enemy
who hates me.

I am a poet who yearns to dance on rooftops,
to whisper delicate lines about joy
and the blessings of human understanding.

I try. I go to my land, my tower of words and
shut the door, but the typewriter doesn't fade out
the sound of the blasting,
the screams, the muffled outrage...
My own days bring me slaps on the face.
Every day I am deluged with reminders
that this is not
my land.
I do not believe in a war between races

but in this country
there is war.

JANICE MIRIKITANI

Janice Mirikitani is a third generation Japanese-American. Working as an editor for various magazines and anthologies, she was responsible for the publication of a bilingual anthology showcasing the talents of Japanese-American writers and artists. *Awake in the River* is a collection of her own writings; she has been published in many anthologies and magazines as well. She now resides in San Francisco, where she is the Program Director at Glide Church/Urban Center encouraging community participation in the arts.

Sing with Your Body
—for my daughter, Tianne Tsukiko

We love with great difficulty
spinning in one place
afraid to create
        spaces
            new rhythm

the beat of a child
dangled by her own inner ear
takes Aretha with her

            upstairs, somewhere
go quickly, Tsukiko,

                into your circled dance
    go quickly

                before your steps are
                halted by who you are not

    go quickly

                to learn the mixed
                sounds of your tongue,

    go quickly

                to who you are

                before

                    your mother swallows
                    what she has lost

Breaking Silence

For my mother's testimony
before the Commission on Wartime Relocation
and Internment of Japanese-American Civilians

There are miracles that happen
she said.
From the silences
in the glass caves of our ears,
from the crippled tongue,
from the mute, wet eyelash,
testimonies waiting like winter.
    We were told
that silence was better
golden like our skin,
    useful like
go quietly,
    easier like
don't make waves,
    expedient like
horsestalls and deserts.
        "Mr. Commissioner...
        ...the U.S. Army Signal Corps confiscated
        our property...it was subjected to vandalism
        and ravage. All improvements we had made
        before our incarceration was stolen
        or destroyed...
        I was coerced into signing documents
        giving you authority to take..."
        ...to take
        ...to take.

My mother,
soft like tallow,
words peeling from her
like slivers of yellow flame.
Her testimony,
a vat of boiling water

surging through the coldest
bluest vein.
    She had come to her land
as shovel, hoe and sickle searing
reed and rock and dead brush,
labored to sinew the ground
to soften gardens pregnant with seed.
awaiting each silent morning
birthing
        fields of flowers,
mustard greens
and tomatoes
throbbing like the sea.
    And then
All was hushed for announcements:
    "Take only what you can carry..."
We were made to believe our faces
betrayed us. Our bodies
were loud with yellow screaming flesh
needing to be silenced
behind barbed wire.

        "Mr. Commissioner...
    ...it seems we were singled out
    from others who were under suspicion.
    Our neighbors were of German and Italian
    descent, some of whom were not citizens...
    It seems we were singled out.."

She had worn her work
like lemon leaves,
shining in her sweat,
driven by her dreams that honed
the blade of her plow.
The land she built
like hope
grew quietly
irises, roses, sweet peas
opening, opening.

And then
all was hushed for announcements
    "...to be incarcerated for your own good"
The sounds of her work
bolted in barracks...
silenced.
        Mr. Commissioner...
        So when you tell me I must limit testimony,
        when you tell me my time is up,
        I tell you this:
        Pride has kept my lips
        pinned by nails
        my rage coffined.
        But I exhume my past
        to claim this time.
        My youth is buried in Rohwer,
        Obachan's ghost visits Amache Gate,
        My niece haunts Tule Lake.
        Words are better than tears,
        so I spill them.
        I kill this, the silence...

There are miracles that happen,
she said,
and everything is made visible.
        We see the cracks and fissures in our soil:
        We speak of suicides and intimacies,
        of longings lush like wet furrows,
        of oceans bearing us toward imagined riches,
        of burning humiliation and
        crimes by the government.
        Of self hate and of love that breaks
        through silences.
        We are lightening and justice.
        Our souls become transparent like grass
revealing tears for war-dead sons
red ashes of Hiroshima
jagged wounds from barbed wire.
        We must recognize ourselves at last
        We are a rainforest of color

and noise.
> We hear everything.
> We are unafraid.

> Our language is beautiful.

(Quoted excerpts from my mother's testimony modified with her permission)

INDEX

Poet names are in bold face; poem titles are in italics; and poem first lines are enclosed in quotation marks.

About Thirty Jews Were Taken to Chelmno. VIII, 156.
"Above the fresh ruffles of the surf." VIII, 177.
Abraham Davenport. V, 7.
Abraham Lincoln Walks at Midnight. VII, 105.
Acquainted with the Night. VII, 65.
An Acrostick on Mrs. Winifret Griffin. I, 62.
Address to Della Crusca. III, 4.
Address to Miss Phillis Wheatley. II, 2.
Advice to a Blue-Bird. VII, 292.
The Aeolian Harp. V, 38.
Affluence. X, 213.
Africa. VII, 277.
African Distress. II, 166.
The African Chief. II, 160.
After Apple-Picking. VII, 50.
After Experience Taught Me... X, 137.
"After malted, licking his lips." IX, 247.
After the Pleasure Party. V, 49.
After the Surprising Conversions. IX, 218.
"The afternoon turned dark early." IX, 113.
"Again last night I dreamed the dream called laundry." X, 106.
"Again the infant flowers of Spring." III, 248.
Against Time. VII, 224.
Age in Prospect. VIII, 36.
Age in Youth. VI, 243.
The Ages. III, 181.
An Agony. As Now. X, 246.
"Ah why, when all the scene around." III, 12.
"Ah, broken is the golden bowl!—the spirit flown." IV, 188.
Aiken, Conrad. VII, 259-270.
Airs of Palestine. III, 46.
"Airy traveller, queen of song." II, 171.
Al Araaf. IV, 171.
Alcott, Amos Bronson. IV, 7-9
Aldrich, Thomas Bailey. V, 254-262.
"Alembics turn to stranger things." VII, 184.
"Aleta mentions in her tender letters." VII, 274.
"All day long I have been working." VII, 44.
"All day subdued, polite." VIII, 207.
"All endeavor to be beautiful." IX, 203.
"All hail! thou noble land." III, 24.
"All out-of-doors looked darkly in at him." VII, 52.
"All the sights are fair to the recover'd." III, 262.
All Things Are Current Found. IV, 238.
all which isn't singing is mere talking. VIII, 145.
"All/wrong." X, 13.

Allen, Elizabeth Akers. V, 236-241.
Allston, Washington. III, 17-26.
Alnwick Castle. III, 99.
Alone I Cannot Be. V, 206.
"Alone on Lykaion since man hath been." VI, 266.
"Along the shore the tall, thin grass." VIII, 214.
"Aloof as aged kings." VII, 175.
"Aloof upon the day's immeasured dome." VI, 147.
Alsop, Richard. II, 162-164.
Always, from My First Boyhood. VIII, 115.
Amaze. VI, 279.
"Ambassador Pusser the ambassador." VIII, 119.
Ambition. III, 155.
America. V, 44.
America to Great Britain. III, 24.
American Farm, 1934. VIII, 135.
The American Flag. III, 227.
American Poetry. X, 53.
American Rhapsody. VIII, 200.
The American Times. II, 19.
Among Shadows. VII, 133.
Among the Redwoods. V, 268.
"Among twenty snowy mountains." VIII, 14.
And Did the Animals? VIII, 149.
"And God stepped out on space." VIII, 3.
"And here face down beneath the sun." VIII, 122.
And So the Day Drops By. IV, 280.
"'and something that...that is theirs—no longer...'" IX, 176.
"And still her gray rocks tower above..." III, 107.
And the Physician? VII, 166.
And the Sins of the Fathers. VI, 198.
"And then went down to the ship." VII, 209.
"And there the stranger stays." III, 145.
"And this reft house that the which he built." III, 6.
"And turning to me, the young poet." IX, 234.
"And what a day it was!" X, 289.
And You Love Me? VI, 210.
Andree Rexroth. IX, 2.
Anecdote of the Jar. VIII, 18.
The Angelus. VI, 55.
"Angry men and furious machines." VIII, 24.
The Anguish. VII, 289.
Annabel Lee. IV, 205.
Anne. VI, 85.
Anne Rutledge. VII, 7.
"Announced by all the trumpets of the sky." IV, 21.
Anonymous. II, 177.
Anonymous. VI, 38.
"Anonymous—nor needs a name." VI, 38.
"Another armored animal-scale." VIII, 56.
"Another four I've left yet to bring on." I, 49.
"Another season centers on this place." X, 349.
Ante Mortem. VIII, 36.

Antique Harvesters. VIII, 107.
anyone lived in a pretty how town. VIII, 141.
Apology for Bad Dreams. VIII, 38.
Apology of Genius. VII, 123.
An Apology. X, 257.
"The apparition of these faces in the crowd." VII, 197.
Appointment in Doctor's Office. IX, 64.
Appreciation. V, 255.
April Inventory. X, 130.
"April is the cruellest month." VIII, 74.
Archibald Higbie. VII, 9.
"Are your rocks shelter for ships?" VII, 242.
Ariel in the Cloven Pine. IV, 290.
Arlo Will. VII, 12.
Ars Poetica. VIII, 121.
Art. V, 49.
"As a twig trembles, which a bird." IV, 265.
"As I sit looking out of a window of the building." X, 145.
"As I was walking." X, 84.
As in the Midst of Battle There Is Room. VI, 108.
"As Jove The Olympian." II, 103.
"As landscapes richen after rain, the eye." X, 112.
"As long as we looked lay the low country." IX, 91.
"As the cat/climbed over." VII, 147,
"As the melting park." X, 129.
As You Leave the Room. VIII, 33.
Ashbery, John. X, 143-152.
The Asians Dying. X, 169.
Ask No Return. VIII, 166.
"Asking what, asking what?—all a boy's afternoon." VIII, 236.
Aspects of Robinson. IX, 156.
"At Eutaw springs the valiant died." II, 98.
"At evening when I go to bed." V, 315.
At Magnolia Cemetery. V, 173.
At Mass. VII, 112.
At Melville's Tomb. VIII, 175.
"At midnight, in the month of June." IV, 189.
"At midnight, in his guarded tent." III, 102.
At Midsummer. V, 253.
At Sainte-Marguerite. VI, 263.
"At Shelley's birth." VI, 37.
"At some point in the pageant there is a moment." X, 144.
"At ten A.M. the young housewife." VII, 140.
"At the dun cloud, that, slowly rising..." III, 46.
At the Grave of Walker. VI, 25.
At the Indian Killer's Grave. IX, 245.
At the Park Dance. X, 129.
"At the Poem Society a black-haired man stands up..." X, 69.
"At Woodlawn I heard the dead cry." IX, 18.
Athassel Abbey. VI, 97.
An Athenian Garden. VI, 265.
"Atoms as old as stars." VII, 173.
"Attend my lays, ye ever honour'd nine." II, 134.

Aubade: Lake Erie. IX, 224.
The Auction. IX, 11.
August. VII, 179.
The Author to Her Book. I, 39.
Auto Wreck. IX, 135.
Autobiographia Literaria. X, 127
An Autumn Morning in Shokoku-ji. X, 216.
Autumn Woods. III, 196.
The Autumnal Flower. III, 12.
Ave Caesar. VIII, 46.
Awake yee Westerne Nymphs, Arise and Sing. I, 58.
Awakening. VI, 21.
"Axes/After whose stroke the wood rings." X, 239.
"Ay, tear her tattered ensign down!" IV, 147.
"Ay! Unto thee belong." V, 244.
"Aye, thou art welcome, heaven's...breath." III, 220.

Bacchus. IV, 26.
"Backward, turn backward, O time, in your flight." V, 238.
The Backwoodsman. III, 28.
Bacon's Epitaph, Made By His Man. I, 94.
"Bah! I have sung women in three cities." VII, 188.
The Ballad of Davy Crockett. IV, 305.
The Ballad of Sue Ellen Westerfield. IX, 118.
The Ballad of the Oysterman. IV, 146.
Baptism. VII, 275.
Baraka, Imamu Amiri. See Jones, Leroi
Barlow, Joel. II, 140-158.
Barter. VII, 172.
Bates, Arlo. VI, 48-50.
The Battle of Bunkers-Hill. II, 22.
Battle of Niagara. III, 145.
The Battle of the Kegs. II, 14.
"The battle rent a cobweb diamond-strung." VII, 59.
"Be natural/wise." X, 83.
Be Still, The Hanging Gardens Were a Dream. VI, 258.
The Bear. X, 154.
Bearded Oaks. VIII, 235.
The Bearer of Evil Tidings. VII, 69.
Beat! Beat! Drums!. V, 67.
The Beauties of Santa Cruz. II, 92.
Beautiful Black Women. X, 244.
The Beautiful Changes. IX, 291.
"Beautifully Janet slept." VIII, 105.
Beauty. VII, 179.
"Beauty calls and gives no warning." VI, 274.
"Because he was a butcher and thereby." VI, 154.
Because I Could Not Stop for Death. V, 209.
"Because I feel that, in the Heavens above." IV, 214.
"Because they could not give it too much ground." IX, 287.
Bedouin Song. IV, 293.
Bedrock. X, 214.

The Bee Meeting. X, 236.
Before Sunrise In Winter. V, 265.
"Before the solemn bronze Saint Gauden made." VI, 138.
"Behind him lay the gray Azores." VI, 23.
"Behind King's Chapel what the earth has kept." IX, 245.
Behind Me Dips Eternity. V, 208.
"Behind the house the upland falls." V, 49.
"'Behold another singer!' Criton said." V, 247.
"Behold where Beauty walks with Peace!" VI, 27.
Behold, from the Land of the Farther Suns. VI, 205.
Behold, the Grave of a Wicked Man. VI, 203.
"The bell-rope that gathers God at dawn." VIII, 176.
Bells for John Whiteside's Daughter. VIII, 99.
The Bells. IV, 206.
Belly Dancer. X, 260.
Belsen, Day of Liberation. IX, 118.
Ben Bolt. IV, 250.
Ben Jonson Entertains a Man from Stratford. VI, 172.
"Bend low, O dusky Night." V, 249
Bending the Bow. IX, 278.
Beowulf. IX, 293.
The Berg. V, 55.
Berryman, John. IX, 174-191.
"Beside the ungathered rice he lay." IV, 61.
"Between me and the sunset, like a dome." VI, 182.
Between the Sunken Sun and the New Moon. V, 225.
Big Wind. IX, 14.
The Bigelow Papers. IV, 257.
The Birth of a Poet. III, 154.
Birthday Poem. X, 267.
A Birthday Present. X, 234.
A Birthday Song. II, 18.
Bishop, Elizabeth. IX, 47-60.
Bishop, John Peale. VIII, 114-117.
Black Majesty. VIII, 219.
Black Riders. VI, 194.
The Black Vulture. VI, 147.
Bleecker, Anna Eliza. II, 127-128.
Blind William's Song. X, 179.
Blue Girls. VIII, 100.
Blue Island Intersection. VII, 80.
Blue Squills. VII, 172.
The Blue Symphony. VII, 228.
"Blue, brown, blue: sky, sand, sea." VII, 228.
Blustering God. VI, 216.
The Bobolinks. IV, 226.
Bodenheim, Maxwell. VII, 290-296.
The Body is Like Roots Stretching Down into the Earth. VIII, 155.
Bogan, Louise. VIII, 159-162.
Bone Thoughts on a Dry Day. X, 223.
Bonny Barbara Allen. IV, 307.
"Booth led boldly with his big bass drum." VII, 95.
"Bowed by the weight of centuries he leans." VI, 52.

Bowery. IX, 216.
A Boy. X, 151.
The Boys. IV, 155.
Brackenridge, Hugh Henry. II, 21-24.
"A brackish reach of shoal off Madaket." IX, 239.
Bradford, William. I, 9-12.
Bradstreet, Anne Dudley. I, 38-56.
Brahma. IV, 40.
The Brain Is Wider Than the Sky. V, 202.
Brainard, John Gardiner Calkins. III, 259-266.
Bread and Music. VII, 260.
"Break forth, break forth, O Sudbury town." VI, 85.
Breaking Silence. X, 308.
"The breath of air that stirs the...string." III, 261.
"Breathe-in experience, breathe-out poetry." IX, 126.
"The breezes went steadily through the tall pines." II, 178.
Bridal Ballad. IV, 193.
The Bridge, sels. VIII, 182.
"The bright sea washed beneath her feet." V, 246.
Bring Me the Sunset in a Cup. V, 214.
"Bring me wine, but wine which never grew." IV, 26.
The British Prison Ship. II, 96.
The Broken Home. X, 103.
Broken Music. V, 261.
"The broken pillar of the wing jags..." VIII, 44.
The Broken Tower. VIII, 176.
The Broncho That Would Not Be Broken. VII, 108.
Bronx. III, 228.
Bronze Trumpets and Sea Water—on Turning Latin into English. VII, 184.
Brooks, Gwendolyn. IX, 257-269.
Brooks, Mary (Gowen). III, 252-258.
Brother Ass and St. Francis. VI, 39.
The Brothers. IV, 2.
Brown, Phoebe (Hinsdale). III, 38-40.
Bryant. IV, 268.
Bryant, William Cullen. III, 172-225.
The Buccaneer. III, 74.
The Bucket. III, 42.
"Buildings above the leafless trees." VII, 169.
"Bums are the spirit of us parked in ratty old hotels." IX, 216.
Bunner, Henry Cuyler. V, 302-308.
Burial of the Young. III, 124.
Buried Love. VII, 168.
"The burned and dusty garden said." VI, 265.
Burning the Christmas Greens. VII, 151.
Burning the Letters. IX, 171.
Burnt Norton. VIII, 91.
The Bustle in a House. V, 211.
But I Do Not Need Kindness. X, 200.
"But may a rural pen try to set forth." I, 158.
"The buzzards over Pondy Woods." VIII, 233.
"By a route obscure and lonely." IV, 195.
"By dark severance the apparition head." VIII, 112.

"By ear, he sd." X, 9.
"By some sad means, when Reason holds no sway." II, 84.
"By the fire that loves to tint her." V, 314.
"By the North Gate, the wind blows full of sand." VII, 200.
By the Pacific Ocean. VI, 24.
"By the road to the contagious hospital." VII, 143.
"By the rude bridge that arched the flood." IV, 22.
Byles, Mather. I, 161-165.

"Caesar, the amplifier voice, announces." IX, 102.
Caliban in the Coal Mines. VII, 220.
A California Christmas. VI, 27.
"Call the roller of big cigars." VIII, 19.
"Calm as that second summer which precedes." V, 170.
"Calm was the sea to which your course you kept." VI, 106.
Calmly We Walk Through This April's Day. IX, 108.
Calumny. IV, 221.
The Campus on the Hill. X, 132.
"Can nobody/answer..." VII, 166.
"Can these movements which move themselves." X, 260.
Cancion. X, 43.
Canto I. VII, 209.
Canto LXXXI. VII, 213.
Canto XIII. VII, 211.
Captain Carpenter. VIII, 102.
The Captain, sels. III, 262.
Carl Hamblin. VII, 6.
Carleton, Will. V, 271-277.
Cassandra. VI, 151.
Cat. IX, 64.
Cataract. IX, 233.
Cavalry Crossing a Ford. V, 68.
Cawein, Madison. VI, 127-131.
"Celestial choir! enthron'd in realms of light." II, 138.
The Celestial Passion. VI, 33.
Cells breathe in the Emptiness. X, 157.
Central Park at Dusk. VII, 169.
Ceremony. IX, 296.
A Certain Village. IX, 236.
Cervantes, Lorna Dee. X, 305-309.
Channing II, William Ellery. IV, 246-248.
Chaplinesque. VIII, 169.
Charity, Thou Art a Lie. VI, 199.
Charleston. V, 170.
The Chatter of a Death Demon. VI, 228.
"Chatter of birds two by two raises a night song..." VII, 79.
Chicago. VII, 75.
"Chickens a-crowin' on Sourwood Mountain." IV, 311.
"A child draws the outline of a body." X, 277.
"Childhood remembrances are always a drag." X, 269.
Children of the Sun. VII, 253.
Chocolates. X, 58.

A Choice of Weapons. VIII, 230.
Chopin. V, 279.
Christian Endeavor. VII, 165.
"The churches go on." VII, 165.
Cino. VII, 188.
The City in the Sea. IV, 185.
Claudius Gilbert. I, 7.
"Clear smoke." X, 89.
"Clearing in the forest." VII, 115.
"Clearly my ruined garden as it stood." VII, 287.
The Clerks. VI, 154.
Cliffton, William. II, 170-173.
"Climbing from the Lethal dead." VIII, 192.
Climbing Milestone Mountain, August 22, 1937. IX, 4.
The Close of Autumn. III, 197.
"A closed window looks down." X, 241.
Cloud. IX, 67.
Clouds of Evening. VIII, 38.
Clover. VI, 39.
"Cock-a-doodle-doo the brass-lined rooster says." VIII, 109.
A Cold Spring. IX, 57.
Cole's Island. X, 20.
The Coliseum. IV, 190.
Colonization Society. III, 262.
"Colored pictures/of all things to eat: dirty." X, 12.
The Colossus. X, 238.
Columbia. II, 119.
Columbus. VI, 23.
Come into Animal Presence. X, 50.
"Come join hand in hand..." II, 11.
"Come listen all you gals and boys." IV, 317.
"Come to me, angel of the weary hearted". IV, 224.
"Come you, cartoonists." VII, 77.
"Come, all you sailors of the southern waters." VI, 15.
The Comfort of Darkness. X, 165.
The Coming of the Cold. IX, 10.
Communication to the City Fathers of Boston. X, 225.
"Complacencies of the peignoir, and late." VIII, 10.
Comradery. VI, 128.
The Conflagration. I, 162.
The Conflict of Convictions. V, 41.
The Congo. VII, 100.
The Conjunction of Jupiter and Venus. III, 218.
Connecticut. III, 107.
Connecticut River. III, 132.
Conscience. IV, 239.
"Conscience is instinct bred in the house." IV, 239.
The Conscientious Objector. IX, 150.
Constantly Risking Absurdity. X, 29.
Consumption. III, 241.
Contemplations. I, 39.
Cook, Ebenezer. I, 169-172.
Cool Tombs. VII, 79.

Cooper. IV, 272.
"Cooper, whose name is with his country." III, 113.
A Copy of Verses. I, 7.
Cora Punctuated with Strawberries. X, 221.
The Coral Grove. III, 239.
The Coral Insect. III, 119.
Corso, Gregory. X, 193-203.
The Cotton Boll. V, 164.
Cotton [of Queens Creek], John. I, 93-95.
Cotton, John. I, 4-5.
Counting. VII, 258.
Country Ode for the Fourth of July. III, 2.
"The Courteous pagan...condemne Uncourteous Englishmen." I, 27.
"Cowhorn-crowned, shockheaded, cornshuck-bearded." IX, 161.
Cranch, Christopher Pearse. IV, 225-228.
Crane, Hart. VIII, 167-183.
Crane, Stephen. VI, 193-233.
Crapsey, Adelaide. VI, 276-279.
Crapshooters. VII, 82.
The Creation. VIII, 3.
Credo. VI, 155.
The Creedless Man. V, 312.
Creeley, Robert. X, 78-93.
Critics and Connoiseurs. VIII, 50.
The Cross. VIII, 187.
Crossing Brooklyn Ferry. V, 77.
"Crossing the street." X, 103.
Crossing the Plains. VI, 28.
"Crowning a bluff where gleams the lake below." V, 57.
Crystal Night, fr. During the Eichmann Trial. X, 41.
Cullen, Countee. VIII, 213-220.
Cultural Exchange. VIII, 209.
Cummings, Edward Estlin. VIII, 140-145.

Daddy. X, 230.
Daffodils. VI, 87.
The Daily Grind. VII, 256.
Daisies. V, 315.
Daisy Fraser. VII, 3.
"The dam Bellona." VII, 124.
"Damn it all! all this our South stinks peace." VII, 191.
Dana, Richard Henry. III, 73-96.
A Dancing Girl. IV, 221.
Danforth, John. I, 152-155.
Danforth, Samuel. I, 57-60.
Danse Russe. VII, 140.
Dark Confusion. VII, 163.
"The darkness rolls upward." VII, 228.
"Darkness swept the earth in my dream." X, 165.
"Daughters of Time, the Hypocritic days." IV, 41.
Davis Matlock. VII, 11.
"Dawn; and the jew's-harp's sawing seesaw song." IX, 169.

Day and Dark. VI, 238.
The Day of Doom, sels. I, 70.
"Day of glory! welcome day!" III, 70.
Day of the Dead. IX, 121.
The Day Undressed Herself. V, 203.
Day's Ending. VII, 175.
Days. IV, 41.
De Blue-Tail Fly. IV, 313.
"De railroad bridge's." VIII, 204.
The Deacon's Masterpiece. IV, 151.
Dead Boy. VIII, 99.
The Dead. IV, 230.
"Dear boy, you will not hear me speak." IX, 297.
"Dear common flower, that grow'st beside the way." IV, 256.
"Dear Jo, Margaret has been taken." IX, 65.
"Dear Kitty, while you rove through sylvan bowers." II, 128.
"Dear Sirs: Is it not time we formed a Boston." X, 225.
"Dear wife, last midnight, whilst I read." VI, 46.
"The dearest Lord of heaven gave." I, 157.
Death. VII, 148, 291.
Death and Love. VI, 49.
"Death found strange beauty on that cherub brow." III, 120.
Death of an Infant. III, 120.
The Death of the Ball Turret Gunner. IX, 165.
"Death's but one more to-morrow..." V, 185.
"Death, why so cruel? What! no other way." I, 94.
Debate: Question, Quarry, Dream. VIII, 236.
A Decanter of Madeira, Aged 86, to George Bancroft, Aged 86... V, 188.
December in Yase. X, 217.
"Deep in the bosom of old Time there stood." II, 5.
"Deep in the wave is a coral grove." III, 239.
The Deep. III, 263.
"The deer carcass hangs from a rafter." X, 296.
Defence of Fort M'Henry. III, 16.
The Delight Song of Tsoai-Talee. X, 251.
"Delivers papers to the doors of sleep." IX, 62.
Der Blinde Junge. VII, 124.
Dere's No Hidin' Place Down Dere. IV, 314.
Desert Places. VII, 67.
The Deserted Wife. III, 238.
Design. VII, 68.
The Desolate City. III, 249.
"The dew, the rain and moonlight." VII, 99.
Dibdin's Ghost. VI, 46.
Dickinson, Emily. V. 191-220.
Dickinson, John. II, 10-12.
"Did the skies." VII, 164.
"Did you ever hear tell of Sweet Betsy from Pike." IV, 302.
"Did you ever hear of Editor Whedon." VII, 3.
"Did you ever see an alligator." VII, 12.
Dilemma of the Elm. VIII, 138.
"Dim vales—and shadowy floods." IV, 183.
Dirge. VI, 129.

"Dis world was made in jis' six days." IV, 304.
Disillusionment of Ten O'Clock. VIII, 14.
The Dispossessed. IX, 176.
The Distant Runners. VIII, 147.
Divine Compassion. V, 10.
"Divinely shapen cup, thy lip." V, 316.
Diving into the Wreck. X, 182.
Dixie. IV, 304.
Do Not Weep, Maiden. VI, 224.
"Do you think, my boy, when I put my arms around..." VII, 114.
Doane, George Washington. IV, 10-12.
Doc Hill. VII, 4.
Doctor Meyers. VII, 4.
The Doctor. IX, 217.
Dodge, Mary Mapes. V, 230-235.
Dodson, Owen. IX, 192-199.
Dog. VII, 109.
A Dog Named Ego, the Snowflakes as Kisses. IX, 112.
"Dog-tired, suisired, will now my body down." IX, 177.
"The dog stops barking after Robinson has gone." IX, 157.
Dogs Are Shakespearean, Children Are Strangers. IX, 109.
"Don't believe/that nothing lies." VII, 165.
"Don't forget the crablike/hands, slithering." X, 44.
"Don't you remember sweet Alice, Ben." IV, 250.
Doolittle ("H.D."), Hilda. VII, 238-249.
Doves. IX, 275.
"Down the goldenest of streams." V, 281.
"Down the world with Marna!" VI, 117.
Drake, Joseph Rodman. III, 226-234.
"A dream of interlinking hands, of feet." V, 279.
Dream-Land. IV, 195.
The Dream Songs, sels. IX, 184.
A Dream Within a Dream. IV, 215.
The Dream. VIII, 162.
Dreams. IV, 163.
Driftwood. VI, 255.
"'Driver, what stream is it?' I asked..." IX, 37.
"Droning a drowsy syncopated tune." VIII, 203.
Drug Store. VII, 298.
The Drunk in the Furnace. X, 168.
The Drunken Fisherman. IX, 243.
"A dryad's home was once the tree." IV, 223.
Duncan, Robert. IX, 270-281.
During December's Death. IX, 113.
A Dutch Courtyard. IX, 288.
Dutch Graves in Bucks County. VIII, 24.
A Dutch Lullaby. VI, 42.
The Dutch Patrol. VI, 7.
Dwight, Theodore. II, 165-169.
Dwight, Timothy. II, 118-126.

Each and All. IV, 23.

"Each shift you make in the sunlight somewhere." IX, 289.
The Eagle Exterminating Company. X, 283.
The Eagle That Is Forgotten. VII, 98.
The Eagle, sels. III, 143.
"Earth, bind us close, and time; nor sky, deride." IX, 130.
The Earth-Spirit. IV, 247.
Earth Felicities, Heavens' Allowances. I, 129.
Eastward the Armies. IX, 92.
The Ebb and the Flow. I, 97.
"The ebb slips from the rock, the sunken." VIII, 42.
Eberhart, Richard. VIII, 221-225.
Editor Whedon. VII, 8.
Effigy of a Nun. VII, 176.
"Eight years ago this May."
"Either you will/go through this door." X, 192.
Eldorado. IV, 210.
Electrical Storm. IX, 116.
An Elegie upon the death of... Thomas Shepard, sels. I, 66.
Elegy Before Death. VII, 284.
Elegy for a Dead Soldier. IX, 146.
An Elegy to Dispel Gloom. X, 33.
Elegy to the Memory of Mr. Thomas Godfrey. I, 188.
Eliot, Thomas Sterns, VIII, 65-96.
Elizabeth. V, 292.
Elsa Wertman. VII, 6.
Emerson. IV, 266.
Emerson, Ralph Waldo. IV, 17-41.
The Emperor of Ice-Cream. VIII, 19.
End of Summer. IX, 94.
The End of the World. VIII, 123.
Endless Variation. X, 144.
England. VIII, 52.
"England's done the right thing." VII, 164.
English, Thomas Dunn. IV, 249-251.
"Enormous cloud-mountains that form..." VIII, 38.
"Entering his office, he looks at his nurse." IX, 217.
"The entire country is overrun...private property..." IX, 68.
Envious Satan. VII, 165.
Envoy. VI, 124.
Epilogue. VIII, 207.
Epilogue for FDR. IX, 212.
Epistle to be Left in the Earth. VIII, 123.
Epitaphium Meum. I, 10.
Epithalamium. III, 260.
The Equilibrists. VIII, 110.
"Ere, in the northern gale." III, 196.
The Escape. VIII, 149.
Ethnogenesis. V, 174.
Euclid Alone Has Looked on Beauty Bare. VII, 285.
Eulalie—a Song. IV, 197.
Eurydice. VII, 245.
Evanescence. VI, 17.
Evangeline. IV, 63.

Evans, Nathaniel. I, 187-195.
Eve's Daughter. V, 266.
"Even in the moment of our earliest kiss." VII, 288.
Evening. IV, 11.
The Evening Wind. III, 223.
Evening Without Angels. VIII, 21.
Evensong. VI, 274.
"The event stands clear of history." VII, 224.
"Ever been kidnapped." X, 270.
Everett, David. III, 9-10.
Everson ("Brother Antoninus"), William. IX, 85-95.
"Everyone cries/the good Lord Christ." VII, 165.
Evolution. VI, 37.
"Evolution fall foul of." VII, 128.
An Examination into Life and Death. IX, 79.
Excuse for Not Fulfilling an Engagement. III, 118.
"The exhortation of the Lord." I, 158.
"The eyelids glowing, some chill morning." X, 134.

A Fable for Critics, sels. IV, 266.
Faces. VII, 28.
Facing the Way. X, 291.
Faded Pictures. VI, 136.
"Fair Ellen was long the delight of the young." III, 18.
"Fair flower, that dost so comely grow." II, 108.
"Fair river! not unknown to classic song." III, 132.
"Fair Verna, loveliest village of the west." II, 120.
Fairy-land. IV, 183.
Faith. VI, 105.
Faith Is a Fine Invention. V, 195.
The Fall of Niagara. III, 260.
False Country of the Zoo. IX, 204.
Fame of Myself to Justify. V, 200.
Family Prime. VIII, 148.
"Famine hath worn them pale, that noble band." III, 121.
"Far back when I went zig-zagging." X, 191.
"Far down, down through the city's great gaunt gut." VII, 280.
The Far field. IX, 31.
"Far through the lilac sky the Angelus bell." VI, 55.
"Far, far from hence be satire's aspect rude." II, 167.
"Farewell to such a world! Too long I press." V, 268.
"Farewell, Dear Daughter Sara; Now Thour't gone." I, 5.
Fast Rode the Knight. VI, 225.
"Fat black bucks in a wine-barrel room." VII, 100.
Fatal Interview, sels. VII, 287.
Father and Son. IX, 98.
Father's Bedroom. IX, 255.
"Fathered by March, the daffodils are here." VI, 87.
Fear of Death. X, 149.
Fearing, Kenneth. VIII, 197-201.
"Feeling/the enemy's." VII, 163.
Fenollosa, Ernest Francisco. V, 299-301.

"Ferdinand De Soto lies." VIII, 147.
Ferlinghetti, Lawrence. X, 24-39.
A Few Lines to Fill Up a Vacant Page. I, 153.
Ficke, Arthur Davidson. VII, 132-135.
Fidelity. VI, 262.
Field, Eugene. VI, 41-47.
Fields, Annie Adams. V, 242-247.
Fire. X.
Fire and Ice. VII, 64.
"First having read the book of myths." X, 182.
"First light of day in Mississippi." X, 267.
"First you bite your fingernails..." VIII, 200.
The Fish. IX, 55.
The Fisher's Boy. IV, 240.
Fiske, John. I, 34-37.
Five Groups of Verse, sels. VIII, 152.
Five Lives. V, 266.
"Five mites of momads dwelt in a round drop." V, 266.
Five Women Bathing in Moonlight. IX, 292.
Flame-Heart. VII, 272.
Flash Crimson. VII, 81.
The Flesh and the Spirit. I, 46.
Fletcher, John Gould. VII, 225-237.
"Flood-tide below me! I see you face to face!" V, 77.
Flora's Party. III, 135.
Florida. IX, 53.
Florida road Workers. VIII, 206.
"The flower-born Blodueda." VI, 116.
Flux. VIII, 224.
The Fly. IX, 136.
Fog-Horn. X, 170.
Fog. VII, 77.
Foliage of Vision. X, 112.
"Folly and Time have fashioned." VI, 97.
Food and Drink. VII, 221.
The Fool's Prayer. V, 264.
Footprints on the Glacier. X, 174.
"For a good decade." X, 168.
For a Lady's Album. III, 71.
"For a month now, wandering over the Sierras." IX, 4.
For Annie. IV, 210.
For Fear. X, 92.
"For her these lines are penned, whose luminous..." IV, 201.
For James Dean. X, 123.
For My Birthday, 1939. IX, 36.
For My Daughter. IX, 156.
For My Mother: Genevieve Jules Creeley. X, 79.
For Robert Frost. X, 160.
For Sally, with a Piano. IX, 36.
"For sixty days and upwards." V, 223.
For the Marriage of Faustus and Helen. VIII, 171.
"For three years, out of key with his time." VII, 201.
"For twenty years and more surviving after." VII, 21.

For You. X, 79.
Forerunners. IV, 29.
Forest. IX, 202.
A Forest Hymn. III, 210.
The Forgotten Man. VI, 57.
"Forlorn and white." VII, 232.
Foss, Sam Walter. V, 309-312.
Foster, Stephen Collins. IV, 294-299.
A Fountain, a Bottle, a Donkey's Ears and Some Books. VII, 53.
Four Epitaphs. VIII, 214.
Four Poems for Robin. X, 216.
Four Preludes on Playthings of the Wind. VII, 88.
Four Quartets, sels. VIII, 91.
The Four Seasons of the Year. I, 49.
Four Sides to a House. VII, 37.
"Four straight brick walls, severely plain." V, 186.
Frau Bauman, Frau Schmidt, and Frau Schwartze. IX, 16.
Freedom for the Mind. IV, 43.
Freneau, Philip. II, 77-117.
Fresh Air. X, 69.
Friend, Your White Beard Sweeps the Ground. VI, 221.
"From a deserted graveyard." VIII, 195.
From a Girl in a Mental Institution. X, 258.
"From a junto that labor with absolute power." II, 82.
"From a vision red with war I awoke..." VII, 254.
"From blacked-out streets." X, 41.
"From far she's come, and very old." VI, 243.
"From my mother's sleep I fell into the state." IX, 165.
"From my years young in dayes of Youth." I, 10.
"From near the sea, like Whitman...great predecessor." X, 117.
"From silent night, true Register of moans." I, 25.
"From Susquehanna's farthest springs." II, 112.
"From the Desert I come to thee." IV, 293.
"From the hilltop we could overlook." X, 166.
"From the vast caverns of old ocean's bed." II, 92.
From Venice Was That Afternoon. IX, 201.
"From winter so dreary and long." II, 171.
Frost, Robert. VII, 46-72.
The Fuhrer Bunker, sels. X, 139.
Full Moon. IX, 117.
"Full of her long white arms and milky skin." VIII, 110.
"The fundamental question about revolution." X, 291.
The Funeral of Martin Luther King, Jr. X, 272.
The Fury of Aerial Bombardment. VIII, 224.

"Gaily bedlight." IV, 210.
"The gale was propitious, all canvas was spread." III, 42.
"Gallants attend and hear..." II, 14.
The Gamblers. VII, 97.
The Garden. X, 277.
Gargoyle. VII, 80.
Garrigue, Jean. IX, 200-209.

Garrison, William Lloyd. IV, 42-44.
"The gates clanged and they walked you into jail." IX, 150.
Gathering Leaves. VII, 58.
"Gathering the echoes of forgotten wisdom." VI, 110.
Gathering the Bones Together. X, 296.
"Gay, guiltless pair." IV, 3.
"Genealogists, geologists, and experts in flaconry." IX, 69.
General Self-Satisfied. VII, 164.
General Washington. IX, 44.
General William Booth Enters into Heaven. VII, 95.
George the Third's Soliloquy. II, 93.
"George Washington, your name is on my lips." X, 254.
Ghetto Funeral. VIII, 153.
The Ghetto, sels. VII, 27.
The Ghosts of the Buffaloes. VII, 109.
A Gift of Great Value. X, 87.
A Gift. VII, 33.
Gilder, Richard Watson. VI, 30-35.
Ginsberg, Allen. X, 94-101.
Giovanni, Nikki. X, 268-275.
"A girl sits in a black room." X, 261.
"Give a rouse, then, in the Maytime." VI, 125.
"Glory and honor and fame and everlasting laudation." VI, 35.
Glory Is That Bright Tragic Thing. V, 203.
Gloucester Moors. VI, 133.
Gluck, Louise. X, 276-281.
"Go count the stars!" VII, 258.
Go Down Death. VIII, 6.
Go Down, Moses. IV, 315.
"Go to the western gate, Luke Havergal. VI, 152.
A God Came to a Man. VI, 232.
God Complex. VII, 164.
God Fashioned the Ship. VI, 195.
A God in Wrath. VI, 200.
"God is the Old Repair Man." VII, 258.
God Lay Dead in Heaven. VI, 222.
"God's angry with the world again." IX, 116.
God's Controversy with New-England. I, 78.
God's World. VII, 282.
"God, though this life is but a wraith." VII, 220.
"God, we don't like to complain." VII, 220.
The Goddess. X, 43.
Godfrey, Thomas. I, 181-186.
Gods Determinations: The Preface. I, 97.
"Going from us at last." VIII, 149.
Goldau. III, 151.
The Golden Age. V, 300.
"The golden spider of the sky." VIII, 132.
"Gone the three ancient ladies." IX, 16.
"Good Christian Reader, judge me not." I, 79.
"Good Master, you and I were born." V, 188.
Good News from New-England, sels. I, 14.
Good Night, Willie Lee, I'll See You in the Morning. X, 293.

"Good oars, for Arnold's sake." VI, 94.
Goodbye! X, 247.
Goodman, Paul. IX, 34-46.
The Gourd Dancer. X, 299.
"The grackles have come." VII, 40.
"The grail broken/the light gone from the glass." IX, 279.
Grass. VII, 79.
A Grave. VIII, 55.
Gravepiece. IX, 206.
The Graves of the Patriots. III, 246.
"Gray-robed Wanderer in sleep...Wanderer." VII, 133.
"Gray swept the angry waves." V, 189.
"The gray tide flows and flounders in the rocks." VI, 263.
"Great Alexander sailing was from his true course..." IX, 132.
"Great God! I ask thee for no meaner pelf." IV, 235.
"The great Jehova's working word effecting wondrously." I, 14.
"Green be the turf above thee." III, 98.
"The green catalpa tree has turned." X, 130.
Green Fields and Running Brooks. V, 296.
"Green is the color of everything." X, 264.
Green River. III, 198.
"Green things grow." VII, 131.
Green, Joseph. I, 166-168.
Greenfield Hill, sels. II, 120.
Greensleeves. X, 303.
Gregory, Horace. VIII, 163-166.
Gretel in Darkness. X, 280.
A Grey Day. VI, 135.
"Grey drizzling mists the moorlands drape." VI, 135.
"Grief is fatiguing. He is out of it." IX, 189.
The Groundhog. VIII, 222.
"The groves are down" X, 208.
"The groves were God's first temples..." III, 210.
The Guarded Wounded. VI, 279.
A Guerrilla Handbook. X, 291.
Guiney, Louise Imogen. VI, 91-102.
"A gull rides on the ripples of a dream." IX, 30.
Gulls. VII, 139.
The Gun. IX, 140.
"Guns carried/up and up." VII, 162.
"The gusty morns are here." VI, 100.
"Guvener NB. is a sensible man." IV, 262.
Gypsy. IX, 68.

"Had we two gone down the world together." VI, 66.
"Hail and beware the dead who will talk life..." X, 19.
"Hail beauteous and inconstant!" III, 126.
Halleck, Fitz-Greene. III, 97-116.
Halsted Street Car. VII, 77.
Hamatreya. IV, 30.
Hamilton Greene. VII, 7.
Hammond, Jupiter. II, 1-3.

"The hand that swept the sounding lyre." IV, 222.
A Hand-Mirror. V, 68.
The Hands. X, 44.
"Hanging from the beam." V, 40.
The Happiness of America, sels. II, 130.
"Happy people die whole, that are all dissolved..." VIII, 37.
Harlem Shadows. VII, 277.
"Has not altered—." VIII, 60.
"Has there any old fellow...mixed up with/the boys?" IV, 155.
The Hasty Pudding. II, 147.
"Hath God, who freely gave you his own son." I, 151.
"Hath not the morning dawned with added light?" V, 174.
The Haunted Palace. IV, 194.
"Have you ever heard the rain at night." X, 49.
"Have you heard of the wonderful one hoss shay." IV, 151.
"Have you seen walking through the village." VII, 3.
"Having no father anymore, having got up." X, 163.
Hawthorne. IV, 8, 272.
Hayden, Robert. IX, 115-124.
Hayne, Paul Hamilton. V, 221-229.
He. X, 25.
"He climbs the stair." X, 202.
"He comes not—I have watch'd the moon go down." III, 238.
"He comes, Arsaces comes! my gallant Brother." I, 182.
"He fed them generously who were his flocks." X, 129.
"He had no past and he certainly." X, 285.
"He is one of the prophets come back." X, 25.
"He lies low in the levelled sand." VI, 25.
"He protested all his life long." VII, 5.
"He woke at five and, unable." X, 59.
"He's dead." VII, 148.
Headless. IX, 70.
A Health. III, 269.
"Hear the sledges with the bells." IV, 206.
"Hear thy indictment, Washington..." II, 19.
"Hearing your words, and not a word among them." VII, 288.
The Heart Asks for Pleasure First. V, 197.
Heat. VII, 239.
"Heaven is lovelier than the stars." VI, 255.
"Heaven's Mercy shines, Wonders and Glory meet." I, 154.
Hebrews. VII, 120.
"Helen, thy beauty is to me." IV, 187.
Hell in Texas. IV, 309.
Hello. X, 202.
"Help! oh, help! thou God of Christians." II, 166.
"Henry sats in de bar & was odd." IX, 185.
"Henry shuddered: a war which has no war." IX, 191.
Henry's Confession. IX, 189.
"Her body is not as white as." VII, 146.
"Her eyes be like the violets." VI, 85.
Her Guitar. V, 314.
"Her parents and her dolls destroyed." IX, 118.
Herald. IX, 62.

"Here falls no light of sun nor stars." VI, 121.
"Here from the field's edge we survey." IX, 13.
"Here in my head, the home that is left for you." IX, 171.
"Here lies a fool flat on his back." II, 26.
Here Lies a Lady. VIII, 102.
"Here rest the great and good—here they repose." III, 246.
"Here room and kingly silence keep." VI, 24.
"Here's Cooper, who's written six volumes to show." IV, 272.
"Here, above/cracks in the buildings are filled..." IX, 50.
"Here, in the withered arbor, like the arrested win." VIII, 161.
Heredity. V, 258.
Heritage. VIII, 215.
"A hermit's house beside a stream." II, 108.
Hic Jacet. V. 252.
"High walls and huge the body may confine." IV, 43.
A High-Toned Old Christian Woman. VIII, 18.
Highway: Michigan. IX, 13.
Hill-Side Tree. VII, 292.
The Hill. VII, 2.
Hillcrest. VI, 170.
"'Hiram, I think the sump is backing-up.'" X, 69.
"His brother's wife can't stand Clayton." IX, 65.
His Excellency, George Washington. II, 138.
"His fourscore years and five." VI, 20.
"His headstone said/Free at last..." X, 272.
"His Spirit in smoke ascended to high heaven." VII, 276.
"History is a dialogue between." IX, 222.
Histrion. VII, 188.
"Ho! green fields and running/brooks!" V, 296.
Hoffman, Charles Fenno. IV, 45-47.
"Hog Butcher for the World." VII, 75.
"Hold high the woof, dear friends, that we may see." VI, 104.
"Hold it up sternly—see this it sends back..." V, 68.
A Holiday. VI, 88.
The Hollow Men. VIII, 87.
Holmes, Oliver Wendell. IV, 145-158.
"Holy of England! since my light is short." VI, 95.
Homage to Mistress Bradstreet, sels. IX, 178.
"Home of the Percys' high-born race." III, 99.
The Homecoming of Emma Lazarus. X, 163.
Homesick Blues. VIII, 204.
The Hook. IX, 231.
Hope Is the Thing with Feathers. V, 193.
Hopkins, Lemuel. II, 25-27.
Hopkinson, Francis. II, 13-16.
"The horns in the harbor booming, vaguely." IX, 102.
Hot Night on Water Street. X, 56.
"Hot-headed patriots, many of them bigoted." IX, 44.
"A hot midsummer night on Water Street." X, 56.
Hotel Transylvanie. X, 121.
The House by the Side of the Road. V, 310.
The House of a Hundred Lights, sels. VI, 271.
The House of Night, sels. II, 84.

"The houses are haunted." VIII, 14.
Hovey, Richard. VI, 115-126.
"How can you do the things you know you'll do?" X, 139.
"How dear to this heart are the scenes...my childhood." III, 42.
"How funny you are today New York." X, 115.
"How many dawns, chill from his rippling rest." VIII, 182.
"How many million Aprils came." VII, 172.
"How shall we forget your smile." IX, 212.
"How strange it seems! These Hebrews in their graves." IV, 108.
"How strange that here is nothing as it was!" VI, 267.
How the Cumberland Went Down. V, 189.
"Huffy Henry hid the day." IX, 184.
Hugh Selwyn Mauberley. VII, 201.
Hughes, Langston. VIII, 202-212.
"Humankind can indeed bear." X, 433.
The Humble Springs of Stately Sandwich Beach. I, 151.
Humphreys, David. II, 129-131.
Hurt Hawks. VIII, 44.
Huswifery. I, 99.
Hymn of the City. III, 225.
Hymn of the Earth. IV, 248.
Hymn of Trust. IV, 158.
Hymn to Death. III, 200.
An Hymn to the Evening. II, 134.
An Hymn to the Morning. II, 134.
Hymn to the Night. IV, 55.
Hymn to the North Star. III, 193.
Hymn: Sung at the Completion of the Concord Monument. IV, 22.
"I always like summer." X, 272.
"I am a feather on the bright sky." X, 251.
"—I am a gentleman in a dustcoat trying." VIII, 105.
"I am a miner. The light burns blue." X, 232.
I Am a Parcel of Vain Strivings Tied. IV, 241.
"I am fevered with the sunset." VI, 119.
"I am in love with the laughing sickness." X, 197.
"I am inside someone." X, 246.
"I am not a painter, I am a poet." X, 118.
I Am Not Yours. VII, 171.
"I am the little man who smokes & smokes." IX, 187.
"I am the spirit of the morning sea." VI, 31.
"I am Thy grass, O Lord!" VI, 88.
"I am tired of work..." VII, 255.
I Am to My Own Heart Merely a Serf. IX, 110.
I Am Waiting. X, 36.
"I am watching them churn the last milk." X, 199.
I Am Weary of Being Bitter. VII, 135.
"I asked the heaven of stars." VII, 171.
I Break the Sky. IX, 199.
I Broke the Spell That Held Me Long. III, 206.
"I burn no incense, hang no wreath." III, 272.
"I came to the crowded Inn of Earth." VII, 170.
"I can't believe there's not." X, 127.
"I cannot find my way: there is no star." VI, 155.

I Cannot Forget with What Fervid Devotion. III, 217.
I Cannot Live with You. V, 219.
"I caught a tremendous fish." IX, 55.
"I celebrate myself and sing myself." V, 84.
"I come from Alabama." IV, 296.
"I come of a mighty race..." VII, 120.
"I could believe that I am here alone." VI, 108.
"I could love her with a love so warm." VII, 257.
I Count My Time by Times That I Meet Thee. VI, 34.
"I count the sidewalk slits." Interior dialogue. IX, 211.
"I did not dream, and yet untiring thought." III, 139.
"I did not think that I should find them there." VI, 154.
"I do not say to you, Be rich." VI, 52.
"I don't understand by what perversity." X, 295.
"I dream of journeys repeatedly." IX, 31.
"I dwelt alone." IV, 197.
I Felt a Funeral in My Brain. V. 216.
"I fill this cup to one made up of loveliness alone." III, 269.
"I found a dimpled spider, fat and white." VII, 68.
"I gazed upon the glorious sky." III, 214.
"I had a vision." III, 249.
"I had come to the house, in a cave of trees." VIII, 161.
"I had over-prepared the event." VII, 199.
"I had to kick their law into their teeth..." IX, 265.
"I have a bookcase, which is what." V, 307.
"I have a river in my mind." IX, 193.
"I have been acquainted with the night." VII, 65.
"I have had to learn the simplest things." X, 16.
"I have known the silence of the stars..." VII, 23.
"I have known the strange nurses of kindness." X, 200.
"I have never seen him, this invisible member..." VIII, 199.
"I have seen faces of want." X, 15.
I Have Seen the Spring. VII, 176.
"I have three simple eyes." IX, 207.
"I have to bury Love." VII, 168.
"I have woven shrouds of air." IV, 247.
"I hear the halting footsteps of a lass." VII, 277.
"I heard one who said: 'Verily.'" VI, 151.
"I heard the trailing garments of the Night." IV, 55.
The Heavy Bear Who Goes with Me. IX, 111.
"I hereby swear that to uphold your house." VII, 182.
"I hoped that he would love me." VII, 168.
"I know a house made of mud & wattles." X, 15.
I Know Moonrise. IV, 315.
"I know not in what fashion she was made." V, 261.
I Know Some Lonely Houses Off the Road. V, 201.
"I know where the timid fawn abides." III, 190.
"I know/Not these my hands." VI, 279.
"I leave behind me the elm-shadowed square." V, 262.
"I like a church; I like a cowl." IV, 24.
"I like to find." X, 42.
I Like to See It Lap the Miles. V, 210.
"I loathed you, Spoon River, I tried to rise above..." VII, 9.

"I look out over the sterile snow." X, 281.
I Looked Here. VI, 196.
"I love the way Janie Crawford." X, 292.
"I love you first because your face is fair." IX, 144.
"I loved to hear the war-horn cry." III, 155.
"I make a pact with you, Walt Whitman." VII, 197.
"I make my shroud, but no one knows." VI, 279.
I Meant to Have but Modest Needs. V, 218.
I Met a Seer. VI, 208.
"I met death—he was a sportsman—on Cole's." X, 20.
"I must be mad, or very tired." VII, 45.
"I must have passed the crest a while ago." VII, 174.
I Never Felt at Home Below. V, 205.
"I never played the Moor." X, 220.
I Never Saw a Moor. V, 210.
"I picked up a leaf." X, 123.
"I placed a jar in Tennessee." VIII, 18.
"I promise you these days and an understanding." VIII, 128.
"I said." VIII, 220.
"I sat me down upon a green bank-side." III, 228.
I Saw a Man. VI, 202.
"I saw a mouth jeering..." VII, 80.
"I saw a ship of martial build." V, 55.
"I saw him once before." IV, 148.
"I saw the first pear." VII, 239.
"I saw the sky descending, black and white." IX, 248.
"I saw thee once—once only—years ago." IV, 218.
"I saw them kissing in the shade and knew." VI, 271.
"I saw two clouds at morning." III, 260.
"I see them—crowd on crowd they walk the earth." IV, 230.
"I shall cry God to give me a broken foot." VII, 81.
"I shall never get you put together entirely." X, 238.
I Shall Not Care. VII, 170.
"I shall walk down the road." VII, 291.
"I should be pleasing myself, you know." X, 301.
"I slept under rhododendron." X, 216.
"I speak this poem now with grave and level voice." VIII, 127. 111.
"I speak to the unbeautiful of this bird." X, 111.
"I stayed the night for shelter at a farm." VII, 59.
"I stole along through the dark." VI, 49.
"I stood above the sea, I heard the roar." III, 156.
I Stood Musing in a Black World. VI, 214.
I Stood Upon a High Place. VI, 197.
I Stood Upon a Highway. VI, 207.
I Taste a Liquor Never Brewed. V, 213.
"I think I should have loved you presently." VII, 283.
"I think of Amundsen, enormously bit." IX, 286.
"I thought it proper to provide." I, 170.
"I touch you in the night, whose gift was you." VIII, 228.
"I try to knead and spin, but my life is low..." VI, 97.
"I waited in the little sunny room." V, 266.
"I waked; the sun was in the sky." V, 243.
"I walk down the garden-paths." VII, 34.

I Walked in a Desert. VI, 211.
"I walking on my birthday met a young." IX, 36.
"I wander all night in my vision." V, 145.
"I wanted so ably." X, 87.
"I was a peasant girl from Germany." VII, 6.
"I was far forward on the plain, the burning swamp." VIII, 136.
I Was in the Darkness. VI, 212.
"I was the only child of Francis Harris of Virginia." VII, 7.
"I watch the Indians dancing to help the young corn..." VIII, 45.
"I went to the dances at Chandlerville." VII, 11.
"I went to turn the grass once after one." VII, 47.
"I went up and down the streets." VII, 4.
I Will Go into the Ghetto. VIII, 154.
"I will teach you townspeople." VII, 149.
"I won't go with you. I want to stay with Grandpa!" IX, 251.
"I would not always reason..." III, 218.
"I would to God I were quenched and fed." VII, 289.
I Years Had Been from Home. V, 195.
"I'll do what the raids suggest" X, 151.
I'll Tell You How the Sun Rose. V, 199.
"I'm makin' a road." VIII, 206.
"I've heard in old times a sage used to say." II, 75.
"I've known rivers." VIII, 208.
I, Maximus of Gloucester, to You. X, 9.
"I, too, dislike it. there are things..." VIII, 54.
"I, too, sing America." VIII, 207.
The Ice Cream Parlor Romance. IX, 218.
Ichabod. V, 2.
The Idea of Order at Key West. VIII, 19.
Identities. X, 265.
Idleness. V, 187.
"If any have a stone to shy." VII, 180.
If Anybody's Friend Be Dead. V, 194.
"If ever I am old, and all alone." VI, 155.
If I Could Only Live at the Pitch That Is Near Madness. VIII, 223.
"If I must die." VI, 237.
If I Should Cast Off This Tattered Coat. VI, 222.
"If it/Were lighter touch." VI, 279.
"If knowledge and the thing known are one." VIII, 28.
If Love Loves. VI, 211.
"If Nature says to you." VII, 256.
"If the red slayer thinks he slays." IV, 40.
If There Is a Witness. VI, 198.
"If we call/to ourselves." X, 247.
If We Must Die. VII, 275.
"If when my wife is sleeping." VII, 140.
"If with light head erect I sing." IV, 237.
Ignatow, David. IX, 210-218.
The Illusion. IX, 88.
The Imaginary Iceberg. IX, 49.
Immortal Autumn. VIII, 127.
The Impact of a Dollar. VI, 228.
The Impossible Choices. IX, 89.

Impulsive Dialogue. VII, 294.
In a Bird Sanctuary. IX, 287.
In a City Garden. VI, 267.
"In a dark hour, tasting the Earth." VII, 119.
"In a dream I returned to the river of bees." X, 173.
In a Lonely Place. VI, 197.
In a Station of the Metro. VII, 197.
In Ampezzo. VI, 247.
In Bed, sels. X, 64.
In Distrust of Merits. VIII, 62.
In Fields of Summer. X, 157.
"In halls of sleep you wandered by." VII, 133.
In Heaven. VI, 200.
"In Heaven a spirit doth dwell." IV, 216.
"In June, amid the golden fields." VIII, 222.
"In late winter." X, 154.
"In May, when sea-winds pierced our solitudes." IV, 21.
"In me is a little painted square." VII, 291.
In Memory of Colonel Charles Young. VIII, 214.
In Memory of Radio. X, 243.
"In mothers womb thy fingers did me mak." I, 5.
"In my father's bedroom" IX, 255.
"In my grandmother's house there was always chicken." X, 53.
"In my land there are no distinctions." X, 306.
"In nineteenfourteen." VII, 161.
"In November, in the days to remember the dead." IX, 226.
"In placid hours well-pleased we dream." V, 49.
In Saram. I, 5.
"In secret place where once I stood." I, 46.
"In some calm midnight, when no whispering breeze." I, 162.
"In some/Prenatal plagiarism." VII, 130.
"In spite of all the learned have said." II, 109.
In Summer. VI, 245.
"In summer elms are made for me." VIII, 138.
"In the cold I will rise, I will bathe." VI, 278.
In the Desert. VI, 194.
In the Dordogne. VIII, 116.
In the Dream's Recess. IX, 95.
"In the falls, music-woven." IX, 233.
"In the golden reign of Charlemaign the king." IV, 282.
"In the greenest of our valleys." IV, 194.
In the Naked Bed, in Plato's Cave. IX, 97.
In the Night. VI, 227.
"In the old days (a custom laid aside/...)" V, 7.
"In the palm." 241.
"In the purple light, heavy with redwood..." VIII, 38.
"In the Quarter of the negroes." VIII, 209.
"In the rustling shelter of Japanese peach." IX, 271.
"In the turret's great glass dome, the apparition." IX, 167.
In the Ward: the Sacred Wood. IX, 163.
In This Age of Hard Trying, Nonchalance Is Good And. VIII, 49.
In Winter, in My Room. V, 217.
Incident. VIII, 219.

Independence. III, 70.
The Indian Burying Ground. II, 109.
Indian Sky. VII, 160.
An Indian Story. III, 190.
The Indian Student. II, 112.
The Indian Summer. III, 264.
"Infinite gentleness, infinite irony." VII, 176.
"Infinity, when all things it beheld." I, 97.
The Inn of Earth. VII, 170.
Inquest. X, 135.
Inscription for the Entrance to a Wood. III, 180.
Inspiration, sels. IV, 237.
The Instruction Manual. X, 145.
"The instructor said." VIII, 210.
Interior Dialogue. IX, 211.
"Into the furnace let me go alone." VII, 275.
Invocation to the Social Muse. VIII, 129.
Irish Peasant Song. VI, 97.
Ironica. VII, 163.
Irridations, sels. VII, 226.
"Is a monstrance." X,122.
Isaac and Archibald. VI, 156.
"The island lies nine leagues away." III, 74.
Israfel. IV, 216.
"It comes to pass." VI, 39.
"...It is colder now." VIII, 123.
"It is disasterous to be a wounded deer." X, 202.
"It is likely enough that lions and scorpions." VIII, 36.
"It is morning, Senlin says, and in the morning." VII, 260.
"It is portentous, and a thing of state." VII, 105.
"It is the first day of the world." IX, 162.
"It is there where the worm has egress." IX, 206.
"It stops the town we come through. Workers raise." IX, 139.
"It was a tall young oysterman live..." IV, 146.
"It was many and many a year ago." IV, 205.
"It was not dying: everybody died." IX, 165.
"It was nothing but a rose I gave her." VI, 18.
"It was the west wind caught her up, as." X, 17.
"It was upon a high, high hill." IV, 307.
It Was Wrong to Do This. VI, 217.
"It's autumn in the country I remember." VI, 249.
"It's funny that smells and sounds return." X, 273.
"It's growing evening in my soul." VI, 245.
"It's late when I try to sleep, resting. X, 295.
"It's not difficult." X, 51.
"Italia's vales in verdune slept." III, 127.
Italy. III, 268.
"Its quick soft silver bell beating, beating." IX, 135.

Janet Waking. VIII, 105.
Janie Crawford. X, 292.
January. IX, 158.

Jarman, Mark. X, 301-304.
Jarrell, Randall. IX, 160-173.
Jazz Band in a Parisian Cabaret. VIII, 205.
Jeffers, Robinson. VIII, 35-46.
Jew. IX, 141.
The Jewish Cemetery at Newport. IV, 108.
"John Brown in Kansas settled, like a steadfast." VI, 2.
John Brown of Osawatomie. VI, 2.
John Brown's Body. IV, 310.
Johnson, Edward. I, 13-25.
Johnson, Fenton. VII, 250-258.
Johnson, James Weldon. VIII, 1-8.
Jones ["Imamu Amiri Baraka"], Leroi. X, 240-247.
Joshua Fit de Battle ob Jericho. IV, 316.
Judas Against the World. VI, 60.
Jump, Jim Crow. IV, 317.
June. III, 214.
Just Friends. X, 91.
"Just now/Out of the strange." VI, 279.
"Just where the Treasury's marble front." VI, 11.

Ka'Ba. X, 241.
Kalypso. VI, 240.
Kees, Weldon. IX, 155-159.
A Key into the Language of America, sels. I, 27.
Key, Francis Scott. III, 15-16.
Kidnap Poem. X, 270.
"Kind solace in a dying hour!" IV, 164.
Kindred. VI, 147.
"A King—estranged from his loving Queen." V, 286.
King Haydn of Miami Beach. IX, 271.
The Kingfishers. X, 3.
Kings River Canyon. IX, 3.
Kinnell, Galway. X, 153-166.
The Kiss. VII, 168.
"A kitten can/Bite with his feet." IX, 27.
The Klondike. VI, 166.
The Knight, Death, and the Devil. IX, 161.
"Knives/may still aid." VII, 164.
"Know'st thou the land which lovers ought to choose." III, 268.
Knoxville, Tennessee. X, 272.
Koch, Kenneth. X, 63-77.
Kore. X, 84.
Krasnopresnenskaya Station. X, 252.
Kreymborg, Alfred. VII, 158-166.
"Kung walked/by the dynastic temple." VII, 211.
Kunitz, Stanley. VIII, 226-231.

L'Envoi. V, 37.
"Lady Flora gave cards for a party at tea." III, 135.
"Lady in the leopard skin." IX, 64.

"The lady put off her fur, it was so warm..." IX, 64.
Lakeward. VI, 259.
"Lament of Anastasius." IV, 14.
Lament of the Frontier Guard. VII, 200.
A Lamentation on My dear Son Simon Who Dyed... I, 62.
"Lana Turner has collapsed!" X, 116.
"Land lies in water; it is shadowed green." IX, 48.
"The land was overmuch like scenery." IX, 293.
The Landsend. III, 42.
The Language. X, 85.
Languages. VII, 78.
The Last Days. VI, 148.
The Last Leaf. IV, 148.
"Last night at black midnight I woke with a cry." VII, 109.
The Last Night That She Lived. V, 196.
"Last night watching the Pleiades." X, 216.
Last Words. X, 107.
The late peach yields a subtle musk." IX, 10.
The Late Show & lumber Strike of the Summer of Fifty-Four. X, 215.
"A late snow beats." VII, 28.
"Lately, I've become accustomed to the way." X, 245.
Laus Veneris. V, 251.
"Lay down these words," X, 205.
Lazarus, Emma. V, 278-283.
The Leaden-Eyed, VII, 104.
A Learned Man. VI, 201.
Leviathan. X, 175.
Lemuel's Blessing. X, 176.
Lenore. IV, 188.
Lent in a Year of War. IX, 223.
Les Etiquettes Jaunes. X, 123.
"Let ardent heroes seek reknown in arms." I, 174.
"Let cowards and laggards fall back!..." VI, 96.
"Let Cowley soft in armorous verse." III, 3.
"Let Joy go solace-winged." VII, 129.
Let No Charitable Hope. VII, 184.
"Let not young souls be smothered out before." VII, 104.
Let Other People Come as Streams. VIII, 155.
"Let such pure hate still underprop." IV, 243.
"Let the crows go by hawking their caw and caw." VII, 82.
Let Us Be Happy as Long as We Can. II, 75.
"Let us go then, you and I." VIII, 68.
"Let us not sit upon the ground." X, 33.
"Let us suppose, valleys & such ago." IX, 186.
A Letter on the Use of Machine Guns at Weddings. IX, 77.
The Letter. VII, 34.
Letting him go. X, 288.
Levertov, Denise. X, 40-51.
Liberty for All. IV, 44.
The Liberty Song. II, 11.
"Life has loveliness to sell." VII, 172.
"Life is a print-shop where the eye may trace." II, 175.
"Life's a jail where men have common lot." VII, 97.

"Life, friends, is boring. We must not say so." IX, 185.
"Light-winged Smoke! Icarian bird" IV, 237.
"The light will never open sightless eyes." IV, 230.
Lightly like Music Running. IX, 207.
"Like a drowsy, rain-browned saint." VII, 292.
"Like battered old millhands, they stand in...orchard." X, 133.
Like Him Whose Spirit. VII, 135.
"Like the soldier, like the sailor..." IX, 77.
"Like watching rings extend in water." X, 79.
The Lily Confidante. V, 178.
"Lily, lady of the garden." V, 178.
The Lincoln Child. VII, 115.
Lincoln, the Man of the People. VI, 58.
Lindsay, Vachel. VII, 93-112.
"A Line in long array where they wind betwext green." V, 68.
Lines on the Death of Washington. II, 167.
Lines Spoken By a Boy of Seven Years. III, 10.
"List the harp in window wailing." V, 38.
"Listen.../With faint dry sound." VI, 278.
Little Birds of the Night. VI, 231.
Little Boy Blue. VI, 44.
"A little colt—broncho, loaned to the farm." VII, 108.
"The little cousin is dead, by foul subtraction." VIII, 99.
"Little cramped words scrawling all over the paper." VII, 34.
Little Guinever. V, 245.
"Little masters, hat in hand." VI, 39.
"Little thinks, in the field, yon red-cloaked clown." IV, 23.
"The little toy dog is covered with dust." VI, 44.
A Little While I Fain Would Linger Yet. V, 228.
The Livid Lightnings Flashed in the Clouds. VI, 210.
Livingstone, William. I, 173-180.
"Lo! Death has reared himself a throne." IV, 185.
"Locate I/love you some-." X, 85.
Lodge, George Cabot. VI, 234-238.
Lodovico Martelli. VI, 250.
Loneliness. VI, 262.
The Lonely Child. VII, 114.
The Lonely Death. VI, 278.
The Lonely Mother. VII, 252.
"Long buried, ancient men-at-arms." IX, 220.
"Long had the sage, the first who dar'd to brave." II, 141.
The Long Hill. VII, 174.
"Long I followed happy guides." IV, 29.
"Long since, a dream of heaven I had." V, 10.
Longfellow, Henry Wadsworth. IV, 51-142.
"Look out upon the stars, my love." III, 271.
"Looking as I've looked before, straight down..." X, 190.
"Looking down into my father's." X, 293.
"Looking into my daughter's eyes I read." IX, 156.
Lord, I Have Seen Too Much. IX, 141.
The Lordly Hudson. IX, 37.
The Lords of the Main. II, 74.
Losses. IX, 165.

The Lost Love. VII, 251.
The Lost Pilot. X, 284.
The Lost Pleiad. III, 276.
The Lost Son. IX, 18.
Lost Youth: The Last War, sels. VII, 161.
Love. III, 106.
Love and Doubt. VI, 82.
Love in Labrador. VII, 87.
"Love is not all: it is not meat or drink." VII, 287.
Love Poem. I, 63.
The Love Song of J. Alfred Prufrock. VIII, 68.
Love Songs. VII, 127.
Love Walked Alone. VI, 211.
Love's Eyes. III, 43.
The Lovers of the Poor. IX, 267.
Loving You Less than Life, a Little Less. VII, 285.
"The low wind talks on the boards of the house." IX, 88.
Lowell, Amy. VII, 32-45.
Lowell, James Russell. IV, 252-277.
Lowell, Robert, IX, 238-256.
Lower the Standard. IX, 151.
Loy, Mina. VII, 122-131.
Lucifer Alone. IX, 69.
Lucinda Matlock. VII, 11.
Luke Havergal. VI, 152.
Lull. IX, 12.
Lullaby for Amy. X, 302.
Lunar Baedeker. VII, 125.
"Lurching from gloomy limousines we slip." IX, 152.
"Luxury, then, is a way of." X, 242.
Lydia, VI, 85.
"Lying by the summer sea." V, 258.
The Lynching. VII, 276.

M'Fingal, sels. II, 59.
MacLeish, Archibald. VIII, 118-130.
The Mad Scene. X, 106.
The Mad Yak. X, 199.
Madonna of the Evening Flowers. VII, 44.
Magda Goebbals, fr. The Fuhrer Bunker. X, 129.
The Maimed Grasshopper Speaks Up. IX, 207.
"Make me, O Lord, thy Spin[n]ing Wheele compleate." I, 99.
Making Beasts. X, 299.
Malvern Hill. V, 48.
"Man looking into the sea." VIII, 55.
"The man sits in a timelessness." X, 86.
"The man who fiercest charged in fight." V, 37.
"The man who sold his lawn to standard oil." VIII, 227.
"The man with no ears." IX, 70.
The Man-Moth. IX, 50.
A Man Adrift on a Slim Spar. VI, 230.
The Man Against the Sky. VI, 182.

A Man Feared. VI, 218.
The Man Hunt. VI, 130.
A Man Said to the Universe. VI, 229.
A Man Saw a Ball of Gold. VI, 208.
A Man Toiled on a Burning Road. VI, 217.
A Man Went Before a Strange God. VI, 215.
The Man with the Hoe. VI, 52.
"Many prophets have failed, their voices silent." X, 96.
Many Red Devils Ran from My Heart. VI, 213.
Many Workmen, VI, 206
The Map. IX, 48.
Marco Bozzaris. III, 102.
Margaret Fuller. IV, 8.
Marie. VII, 30.
Market. IX, 122.
Markham, Edwin. VI, 51-78.
Marriage. IX, 211.
Marriage. X, 194.
"Martha/Mary passed this morning." IX, 193.
Martial Ditty. VII, 161.
Mary Passed This Morning. IX, 193.
Mass Graves, sels. VIII, 156.
Massa's in the Cold, Cold Ground. IV, 297.
"Master, this very hour." VI, 90.
Masters, Edgar Lee. VII, 1-25.
Mater Amabilis. V, 281.
Mather, Cotton. I, 156-160.
Maximus, to Himself. X, 16.
"May I, for my own self, song's truth reckon." VII, 194.
McKay, Claude. VII, 271-280.
Mea Culpa. VII, 166.
Medusa. VIII, 161.
Meeting-House Hill. VII, 45.
Meeting. VII, 133.
"The melancholy days are come, the saddest of the year." III, 197.
"Mellifluous as bees, these brittle men." X, 223.
Melville, Herman. V, 35-59.
Memorial Rain. VIII, 119.
Men Loved Wholly Beyond Wisdom. VIII, 160.
"Men of this passing age!" II, 117.
Men Say They Know Many Things. IV, 244.
"The men the/machine guns." VII, 162.
"Men with picked voices chant the names." VII, 137.
Mending Sump. X, 69.
A Mendocino Memory. VI, 69.
The Mercies of the Year, Commemorated. I, 154.
"Mercury shew'd Apollos, Bartas book." I, 2.
Merlin: I. IV, 32.
Merlin: II. IV, 35.
Merrill, James. X, 102-113.
Merton, Thomas. IX, 219-229.
Merwin, W.S. X, 167-180.
Metaphors of a Magnifico. VIII, 17.

Mhtis Outis. X, 129.
"Midnight empties the street." VII, 130.
"A mile behind is Gloucester town." VI, 133.
Miles, Josephine. IX, 61-75.
"The mill goes toiling slowly around." VI, 45.
Millay, Edna St. Vincent. VII, 281-289.
Miller, Cincinnatus Heine ("Joaquin" Miller). VI, 22-29.
Milton by Firelight. X, 206.
"The mind has shown itself at times." VIII, 171.
Mine by the Right of the White Election. V, 214.
Miniver Cheevy. VI, 169.
"Minott, Lee, Willard, Hosmer, Meriam, Flint." IV, 30.
Mirikitani, Janice. X, 308-313.
Missolonghi. III, 121.
Mitchell, Silas Weir. V, 183-190.
Mnemosyne. VI, 249.
The Mocking-Birds. V, 226.
Molly McGee. VII, 3.
Momaday, N. Scott. X, 248-252.
"Moment to/moment the." X, 90.
"Monet never knew." X, 30.
Monet's Lilies Shuddering. X, 30.
Monet: "Les Nympheas". X, 134.
"Money and fame break in the room." IX, 221.
The Monkeys. VIII, 151.
Monochrome. VI, 102.
Monterey. IV, 46.
Monument Mountain. III, 207.
The Monument. IX, 51.
A Monumental Memorial of Marine Mercy. I, 143.
Moody, William Vaughn. VI, 132-144.
The Moon and the Night and the Men. IX, 175.
The Moon is the Number 18. X, 22.
Moon Shadows. VI, 278.
Moore, Clement Clarke. III, 34-37.
Moore, Marianne. VIII, 47-64.
Morning. IV, 230.
"The Morning is clean and blue..." VII, 227.
Morning Song from 'Senlin'. VII, 260.
"The morning wakes me as a broken door vibrating..." X, 258.
"Morning: blue, cold, and still." IX, 158.
"Mornings in bed." X, 64.
Morton, Sarah Wentworth. II, 159-160.
Moss-Gathering. IX, 14.
"Most men know love but as a part of life." V, 170.
Mother and Son. VIII, 185.
"The mother of Judas Iscariot." VI, 60.
"Mother of mouthings." IX, 275.
Moulton, Louise Chandler. V, 248-253.
The Mountain Passes. VII, 162.
Mowing. VII, 47.
Mr. Flood's Party. VI, 190.
Mr. Pope. VIII, 185.

Mr. Ward of Anagrams Thus. I, 2.
Mrs. Alfred Uruguay. VIII, 23.
Mrs. Meyers. VII, 5.
Mt. Lykaion. VI, 266.
Mt. Tamalpais. IX, 2.
The Murdered Traveller. III, 177.
"Music I heard with you was more than music." VII, 260.
Music in the Night. VI, 17.
Music of the Night. III, 170.
Musing Thoughts. III, 139.
"Musing, between the sunset and the dark." VI, 147.
Mutability. VII, 226.
My Aunt. IV, 149.
"My bands of silk and miniver." VII, 180.
"My books I'd fain cast off, I cannot read." IV, 235.
My Dearling. V, 237.
"My dog lay dead five days without a grave." IX, 295.
My Father in the Night Commanding No. X, 57.
My Father Moved Through Dooms of Love. VIII, 142.
My Father Paints the Summer. IX, 288.
My Father's Funeral. IX, 152.
"My friend, I gave a glad assent." III, 118.
My Grandmother's Love Letters. VIII, 168.
"My heart rebels against my generation." VI, 110.
"My highway is unfeatured air." IV, 248.
My Last Afternoon with Uncle Devereux Winslow. IX, 251.
My Life Closed Twice Before Its Close. V, 213.
"My life is like a stroll upon the beach." IV, 240.
"My life more civil is and free." IV, 242.
"My life, your light green eyes." X, 107.
"My long two-pointed ladder's sticking through." VII, 50.
My Lost Youth. IV, 110.
"My mind i th' mines of rich Philosophy." I, 155.
My Mistresses. III, 3.
My Mother. VII, 273.
My Old Kentucky Home, Good-Night! IV, 295.
My Papa's Waltz. IX, 17.
My Playmate. V, 12.
My Sad Self. X, 100.
"My songs to sell, good sir!" VI, 277.
"My sorrow is so wide." IX, 3.
"My spirit is a pestilential city." VII, 278.
"My thanks, friends of the County Scientific Assoc." VII, 9.
"My towers at last! These rovings end." V, 37.
"My townspeople, beyond in the great world." VII, 139.
"My wedding-ring lies in a basket." X, 46.
Mystic Shadow, Bending Near Me. VI, 196.
"Mysticism, but let us have no words." VII, 270.
Myths & Texts, sels. X, 208.
"The name is immortal but only the name..." IX, 141.
The Name. X, 83.
A Narrow Fellow in the Grass. V, 215.
Nathan Hale. II, 178.

Nature's First Green Is Gold, VII, 58.
Neal, John. III, 142-171.
Near Helikon. VI, 266.
Negro Hero. IX, 265.
Negro Servant. VIII, 207.
The Negro Speaks of Rivers. VIII, 208.
"Neither love, the subtlety of refinement." IX, 90.
"Neither on horseback nor seated." X, 54.
Neither Out Far Nor in Deep. VII, 68.
Neo Catholicism. VII, 165.
A Net to Snare the Moonlight. VII, 99.
Never May the Fruit Be Plucked. VII, 286.
"Never mind the day we left..." VI, 166.
Never Said a Mumbalin' Word. IV, 318.
"Never the nightingale." VI, 277.
"Never yet was a springtime." VI, 21.
New-Englands Crisis. I, 117.
The New Church Organ. V, 274.
The New Collossus. V, 279.
The New Day. VII, 254.
New Mexican Mountain. VIII, 45.
The New World. IV, 231.
A Newly Discovered 'Homeric' Hymn. X, 19.
A Newspaper Is a Collection. VI, 225.
From "Curiosity", The News IV, 5.
"News! our morning, noon, and evening/cry." IV, 5.
1926. IX, 158.
Nick and the Candlestick. X, 232.
Night. VIII, 42.
Night Has Been as Beautiful as Virginia. IX, 77.
Night Light. X, 35.
Night Song. VI, 49.
Night Song at Amalfi. VII, 171.
"The night that has no star lit up by God." IV, 231.
Night Watching. III, 236.
Night, Death, Mississippi. IX, 120.
"Night, night/Death's true self, death's second self." X, 35.
Nightfall in Dordrecht. VI, 45.
Nikki-Rosa. X, 269.
Nine Below Zero. IX, 6.
"No bitterness: our ancestors did it." VIII, 46.
"No doubt to-morrow I will hide." VII, 112.
"No fawn-tinged hospital pajamas..." VII, 293.
"No longer throne of a goddess to whom we pray." IX, 117.
"No man hath dared to write this thing as yet." VII, 188.
"No other man, unless it was Doc Hill." VII, 4.
"No sound of any storm that shakes." VI, 170.
No Swan So Fine. VIII, 48.
"No water so still as the." VIII, 48.
"No, not ever, in no time." IX, 89.
"Nobody planted roses, he recalls." IX, 124.
Nocturne. VII, 299.
A Noiseless Patient Spider. V, 70.

"Not by a Fiery Chariot as Elisha was." I, 7.
"Not from the scorpion, that arcs its poison..." IX, 95.
Not in a Silver Casket Cool with Pearls. VII, 289.
"Not in the sky." III, 276.
"Not in the solitude." III, 225.
"Not like the brazen giant of Greek fame." V, 279.
"Not lost or won but above all endeavour." VI, 262.
"Not noisily, but solemnly and pale." VII, 227.
"Not on our golden fortunes builded high." VI, 57.
Not Overlooked. VII, 115.
"Nothin' or everythin' it's got to be." VII, 299.
"Nothin' very bad happen to me lately." IX, 189.
Nothing Gold Can Stay. VII, 58.
"Nothing is new; I have seen the spring too often." VII, 176.
November Night. VI, 278.
November, 1939. IX, 12.
"Now all day long the man who is not dead." VIII, 185.
"Now can you see the monument? It is of wood." IX, 51.
"Now I am slow and placid, fond of sun." VIII, 132.
"Now I must betray myself." IX, 103.
"Now in the suburbs and the falling light." VIII, 229.
"Now let no charitable hope." VII, 184.
Now That the Book Is Finished. X, 292.
"Now the frosty stars are gone." IV, 290.
"Now the golden fields of sunset rose to me-ward..." VI, 238.
"Now toward the Hunter's gloomy sides we come." II, 96.
"Now, don't you want to know something concernin'." IV, 305.

"Of all the rides since the birth of time." V, 4.
O Black and Unknown Bards. VIII, 2.
"O Boston, though thou now art grown." I, 11.
O Captain! My Captain!. V, 66.
"O come you pious youth." II, 2.
"O death! thou victor of the human frame!" I, 188.
O Fairest of the Rural Maids. III, 205.
"O Gaddi, open the casement, open wide." VI, 250.
"O god, in the dream the terrible horse began." VIII, 162.
"'O hell, who do mine eyes.'" X, 206.
"O hideous little bat, the size of snot." IX, 136.
"O it was but a dream I had." V, 291.
"O lonesome sea-gull, floating far." V, 237.
"O Love Divine, that stooped to share." IV, 158.
"O Pour upon my soul again." III, 25.
"O seeded grass, you army of little men." VII, 226.
"O shaggy god of the ground, barbaric Pan!" VI, 76.
"O thou bright jewel in my aim I strive." II, 133.
"O Thou, who, with thy blue cerculean blaze." III, 4.
"O white and midnight sky! O starry bath!" VI, 33.
"O wind, rend open the heat." VII, 239.
"O world, I cannot hold thee close enough!" VII, 282.
"O World, thou choosest not the better part!" VI, 105.
"O! nothing earthly save the ray." IV, 171.

"O! say can you see, by the dawn's early light." III, 16.
"O'er the rough main with flowing sheet." II, 99.
O'Hara, Frank. X, 114-127.
"O, is not this a holy spot?" III, 69.
Oakes, Urian. I, 65-68.
"The oaks, how subtle and marine." VIII, 235.
Obituary. VIII, 198.
The Ocean Said to Me Once. VI, 209.
October. III, 220.
The Octopus. X, 110.
Ode. IV, 37.
Ode for a Master Mariner Ashore. VI, 92.
An Ode in Time of Hestitation. VI, 138.
Ode on the Prospect of Peace. I. 190.
Ode to Failure. X, 96.
Ode to Peace. III, 166.
Ode to the Confederate Dead. VIII, 187.
Ode: Salute to the French Negro Poets. X, 117.
Odell, Jonathan. II, 17-20.
Odes. VI, 109.
Of 1826. IX, 187.
Of Boston in New England.. I, 11.
"Of John Cabanis' wrath and of the strife." VII, 13.
Of Late. X, 220.
Of Mere Being. VIII, 34.
Of Modern Poetry. VIII, 22.
Of One Who Seemed to Have Failed. V, 185.
"Of thee the Northman by his beached galley." VI, 113.
"Often beneath the wave, wide from this ledge." VIII, 175.
"Often I think of the beautiful town." IV, 110.
"Oh that horse I see so high." X, 87.
"Oh that I were a Poet now in grain!" I, 66.
"Oh! could I hope the wise and pure in heart." III, 200.
"Oh! is it bale-fire in thy brazen hand." VI, 146.
Oh! Susanna. IV, 296.
"Oh! that my young life were a lasting dream!" IV, 163.
"Oh! the old swimmin'-hole! whare." V, 293.
"Oh, all day long they flood with song." V, 226.
"Oh, dey whupped him up the hill, up." IV, 318.
"Oh, my mother's moaning by the river." VII, 252.
"Oh, say not, wisest of all the kings." III, 71.
"Oh, the Devil in hell they say he was chained." IV, 309.
"Oh, what's the way to Arcady?" V, 303.
"Oh, where has my honey gone?" VII, 251.
The Old Adam. X, 47.
Old Age. VII, 291.
"Old age is/a flight of small." VII, 141.
Old Apple Trees. X, 133.
"Old Davis owned a solid mica mountain." VII, 53.
"Old Eben Flood, climbing alone one night." VI, 190.
Old Folks at Home. IV, 298.
Old Ironsides. IV, 147.
The Old Jew. VII, 293.

An Old Man's Winter Night. VII, 52.
Old Manuscript. VII, 159.
"The Old Penobscot Indian." VIII, 224.
The Old Repair Man. VII, 258.
"Old Sodos no longer makes saddles." VII, 27.
"The old squaw/Is one." VII, 160.
The Old Swimmin'-Hole. V, 293.
"The old watch: their." X, 158.
Olson, Charles. X, 1-23.
Omnia Exeunt in Mysterium. VI, 148.
"On a blue summer night." III, 154.
On a Boy's First Reading of "King Henry V". V, 183.
On a Dead Poet. IV, 222.
On a Greek Vase. V, 316.
On a Late Loss. III, 261.
On a Patient Killed by a Cancer Quack. II, 26.
On a Piece of Tapestry. VI, 104.
On a Ruined House in a Romantic Country. III, 6.
On Being Brought from Africa to America. II, 133.
On First Entering Westminster Abbey. VI, 95.
On First Looking in on Blodgett's Keat's "Chapman's Homer". X, 223.
On Imagination. II, 135.
On Laying the Corner Stone of the Bunker Hill Monument. III, 69.
On Mr. Paine's Rights of Man. II, 115.
On My Lord Bacon. I, 155.
On Sivori's Violin. IV, 223.
On Some Shells Found Inland. VI, 257.
On the Concert. VI, 258.
On the Death of a Metaphysician. VI, 104.
On the Death of His Daughter. I, 157.
On the Death of His Son. I, 158.
On the Death of Joseph Rodman Drake, III, 98.
On the Eyes of an SS Officer. IX, 286.
On the Horizon. VI, 209.
On the Life-Mask of Lincoln. VI, 34.
On the Memorable Victory. II, 99.
"On the night of the Belgian surrender the moon." IX, 175.
On the Night of a Friend's Wedding. VI, 155.
On the Slain Collegians. V, 46.
"On these occasions, the feelings surprise." IX, 98.
"On thy fair bosom, silver lake!" III, 240.
On Virtue. II, 133.
On Waking from a Dreamless Sleep. V, 243.
Once and for All. IX, 113.
Once Before. V, 231.
"Once death in malice cruel sought to slay." VI, 49.
Once I Knew a Fine Song. VI, 222.
"Once I loved a spider." VII, 106.
Once I Saw Mountains Angry. VI, 202.
"Once I was good like the Virgin Mary..." VII, 256.
"Once in a messanino." VII, 129.
"Once in late summer." IX, 236.
"Once in my lonely, eager youth I rode." VI, 69.

"Once on returning home, purse-proud and hale." IX, 11.
"Once riding in old Baltimore." VIII, 219.
"Once some people were visiting Chekhov." X, 58.
Once There Came a Man. VI, 195.
Once There Was a Man. VI, 213.
"Once upon a midnight dreary, while I pondered..." IV, 198.
Once, a Man, Clambering to the House-Tops. VI, 227.
"Once, on a golden afternoon." V, 240.
"Once, when I was a boy." IX, 113.
"One arch of the sky." VII, 87.
"One of you is a major, made of cord and catskin." IX, 223.
"One rat across the floor and quick to floor's..." IX, 69.
"One sound. then the hiss and whir." X, 277.
"One wadding a Fall meadow finds on all sides." IX, 291.
One West Coast. X, 264..
"Only once more and not again—the larches." VI, 247.
"Only the deep well." IX, 199.
"Only two patient eyes to stares." VI, 136.
Open, Time. VI, 98.
Oppenheim, James. VII, 113-121.
Opportunity. V, 270.
"Oppress'd with grief, in heavy strains I mourn." I, 167.
Orchard. VII, 239.
Orchids. IX, 13.
Oread. VII, 239.
Orion, IX, 86. 191.
Orpheus. VIII, 192.
Orr, Gregory. X, 294-299.
Osgood, Francis Sargent. IV, 220-224.
"Ostracized as we are with God." VII, 123.
"Our golden age was then, when lamp and rug." VIII, 148.
Our Israfel. VI, 72.
"Our Tom has grown a sturdy boy." II, 29.
"Out for a walk, after a week in bed." X, 108.
"Out of me unworthy and unknown." VII, 7.
Out of the Cradle Endlessly Rocking. V, 70.
"Out of the dusk a shadow." VI, 37.
"Out of the mud two strangers came." VII, 65.
Out of the Old House, Nancy. V, 272.
"Out of the table endlessly rocking." X, 91.
"Out walking in the frozen swamp one gray day." VII, 49.
Outbreak of Spring. X, 222.
The Outlaw. IX, 217.
Outward Bound. V, 262.
"Over the roof-tops race the shadows of clouds." VII, 226.
The Oven-Bird. VII, 52.
"Overhead at sunset all heard the choir." VI, 275.
Overture to a Dance of Locomotives. VII, 137.

Pacifist. VII, 165.
A Pact. VII, 197.
Paine, Robert Treat. II, 174-176.

The Paint King. III, 18.
A Painted Fan. V, 249.
Painted Head. VIII, 112.
Palimpsest: A Deceitful Portrait. VII, 262
"Pallid with too much longing." V, 251.
"The palm at the end of the mind." VIII, 34.
Pampinea. V, 258.
Pan in Wall Street. VI, 11.
Pangloss's Song. IX, 297.
The Pangolin. VIII, 56.
"Pardon me lady, but I wanta ast you." VII, 298.
The Pardon. IX, 295.
"The park is filled with night and fog." VII, 169.
Parlez-Vous Francais? IX, 102.
The Parnassians. X, 107.
"Past exchanges have left orbits of rain around my." X, 257.
The Past. III, 221.
Patchen, Kenneth. IX, 76-84.
The Patent of a Lord. VI, 233.
Patriotic Poem. X, 254.
Patterns. VII, 34.
Paulding, James Kirke. III, 27-33.
Pax Pagnanica. VI, 94.
Peabody, William Oliver Bourne. IV, 13-16.
The Peace of Cities. IX, 286.
The Peacock. X, 111.
The Pebble. VII, 180.
Pebbles. V, 53.
Peck, Harry Thurston. VI, 79-83.
The Pennycandystore Beyond the El. X, 30.
"The people along the sand." VII, 68.
The People vs. the People. VIII, 199.
The People Will Live On. VII, 90.
"The peppertrees, the peppertrees!" X, 45.
Percival, James Gates. III, 235-251.
Perry Zoll. VII, 9.
Personification. IX, 63.
"Peter, Peter, along the ground." VII, 37.
Petit, the Poet. VII, 5.
Phantoms All. VI, 15.
Philosophic Solitude. I, 174.
"A photo of someone else's childhood." X, 47.
Physical Universe. X, 59.
Piazza Piece. VIII, 105.
Picture of a Girl Drawn in Black and White. X, 261.
A Picture Song. III, 270.
Pierpont, John. III, 45-72.
"Pile the bodies high at Austerlitz and Waterloo." VII, 79.
"The pilgrim fathers—where are they?" III, 67.
The Pilgrim Fathers. III, 67.
Pilots, Man Your Planes. IX, 169.
"The pines were dark on Ramoth Hill." V, 12.
Pinkney, Edward Coate. III, 267-272.

Pinwheels, VII, 164.
A Pitcher of Mignonette. V, 306.
Pity Ascending with the Fog. X, 285.
Pity This Busy Monster, Manukind. VIII, 144.
Places Among the Stars. VI, 202.
Planetarium. X, 185.
Plath, Sylvia. X, 228-239.
"Play it once." VIII, 204.
"Play that thing." VIII, 205.
Pleasures. X, 42.
Poe and Longfellow. IV, 276.
Poe, Edgar Allan. IV, 159-219.
Poem. VII, 147.
*Poem for the Young White Man Who Asked Me How I...*X, 306.
"The poem of the mind in the act of finding." VIII, 22.
Poem Out of Childhood. IX, 126.
"A poem should be palpable and mute." VIII, 121.
Poems for my Daughter. VIII, 165.
The Poet Is a Hospital Clerk. IX, 214.
"Poet, will you, like other men." VII, 294.
The Poet's Final Instructions. IX, 177.
The Poet's Lamentation for the Loss of His Cat. I, 167.
Poetry. VIII, 54.
"Poetry is a projection across silence of cadences." VII, 76.
"Poetry is the supreme fiction, madame." VIII, 18.
"Poets make pets of pretty, docile words." VII, 185.
The Political Balance, sels. II, 103.
A Political Litany. II, 82.
Political Poem. X, 242.
Pondy Woods. VIII, 233.
Pontoosuce. V, 57.
"The porchlight coming on again." IX, 158.
The Portent. V, 40.
Portrait. X, 277.
Portrait d'une Femme. VII, 193.
Portrait of a Lady. VII, 138.
Portrait of an Old Woman. VII, 134.
Possessions. VIII, 170.
Post Mortem. VIII, 37.
Pound, Ezra. VII, 186-218.
The Power of Fancy. II, 78.
Prairie Waters by Night. VII, 79.
"Praise thou the Mighty Mother for what is wrought..." VI, 101.
"Praise youth's hot blood if you will..." VIII, 36.
Prayer. IV, 235; VII, 220.
Prayer after World War. VII, 86.
Preface. IX, 234.
Preface to a Twenty Volume Suicide Note. X, 245.
Preparatory Meditations...Approach to the Lords Supper, sels. I, 99.
The Presence. IX, 90.
"The press of the Spoon River Clarion was wrecked." VII, 6.
"Pressure of sun on the rockslide." X, 207.
Pretty Words. VII, 185.

Primer of Plato. IX, 203.
The Prince of Parthia, sels. I, 182.
Private Devotions. III, 39.
The Problem. IV, 24.
Poem: To Brooklyn Bridge. VIII, 182.
The Progress of Dulness. II, 29.
Prospective Immigrants Please Note. X, 192.
Prothalamion. IX, 103.
A Psalm. IX, 225.
A Psalm of Life. IV, 54.
"The pure products of America." VII, 144.
A Puritan Lady. VI, 89.
"A purple cloud hangs half way down." V, 265.
Purple Grackles. VII, 40.
The Quaker Graveyard. V, 186.
The Quaker Graveyard in Nantucket. IX, 239.
Quatorzain. V, 170.
Queen-Ann's-Lace. VII, 146.
Questions of Travel. IX, 58.
"Quite unexpectedly as Vasserot." VIII, 123.

"The rain is splashingon my sill." V, 177.
Rain Spirit Passing. X, 49.
Randall Jarrell. IX, 152.
Range-Finding. VII, 59.
Ransom, John Crowe. VIII, 97-113.
"Rats/running over." VII, 163.
The Raven. IV, 198.
Read the Great Poets. X, 387.
Reading Adonais. IX, 37.
"Really, it is not." VIII, 49.
The Rear Porches of an Apartment Building. VII, 292.
The Reconciliation. VIII, 125.
Recuerdo. VII, 283.
Red Jacket. III, 113.
The Red Wheelbarrow. VII, 146.
Reese, Lizette Wordsworth. VI, 84-90.
"Reg wished me to go with him to the field." VII, 273.
Remarks on the Bright and the Dark Side...William Thompson. I, 158.
Reminiscence. V, 257.
The Removal. X, 170.
"Reptilian green the wrinkled throat." VIII, 193.
The Rescue. X, 86.
The Residual Years. IX, 91.
The Return. V, 246.
Reuben Bright. VI, 154.
"Reviewing me without undue elation." VIII, 230.
Rexroth, Kenneth. IX, 1-8
Reznikoff, Charles. VIII, 151-158.
Rhapsody on a Windy Night. VIII, 72.
The Rhodora. IV, 21.
Rhotruda. IV, 282.

"The rhyme of the poet." IV, 35.
Rich, Adrienne. X, 181-192.
Richard Cory. VI, 153.
Ridge, Lola. VII, 26-31.
Riley, James Whitcomb. V, 284-298.
"The ring is on my hand." IV, 193.
The Ring Of. X, 17.
Riprap. X, 205.
"Rise from the dells where ye first were born." III, 120.
The River-Merchant's Wife: A Letter. VII, 198.
The River of Bees. X, 173.
River Roads. VII, 82.
The Road Not Taken. VII, 51.
Robin Redbreast. IV, 12.
The Robin's My Criterion for Tune. V, 207.
Robinson. IX, 157.
"Robinson at cards at the Algonquin." IX, 156.
Robinson, Edwin Arlington. VI, 150-192.
Rock Me to Sleep. V, 238.
Roethke, Theodore. IX, 9-34.
Romance. IV, 184.
"Romancer, far more coy than that coy." IV, 8.
Romantic Letter. IX, 65.
Roots and Branches. IX, 273.
Rosalie. III, 25.
"Roses and butterflies snared on a fan." V, 249.
"Round de meadows am a ringing." IV, 297.
A Route of Evanescence. V, 211.
"Row after row with strict impunity." VIII, 187.
"The royal feast was done; the King." V, 264.
Rukeyser, Muriel. IX, 125-133.
Rule Britannia. VII, 164.
The Ruling Passion, sels. II, 175.
"The russet leaves of the sycamore." VI, 148.
Rutherford McDowell. VII, 10.

"The sad and solemn night." III, 193.
"The sad great gifts the austere Muses bring." VI, 72.
Saffin, John. I, 61-64.
The Sage Lectured Brilliantly. VI, 218.
The Sail of Ulysses. VIII, 28.
"Sail, Monarchs, rising and falling." IX, 273.
Saint Cecilia's Day, 1941. IX, 38.
Sandburg, Carl. VII, 73-92.
"Sandra and that boy that's going to get her..." X, 221.
Sangster, Margaret Elizabeth. VI, 19-21.
Santayana, George. VI, 103-114.
Sarajevo. VII, 161.
"Satan/the envious." VII, 165.
Saturday Night. VIII, 204.
Saturday Night in the Parthenon. IX, 82.
"Say not of Beauty she is good." VII, 179.

The Scarlet Woman. VII, 256.
Scenes from the Life of the Peppertrees. X, 45.
Schizophrenic Kiss. X, 289.
Schwartz, Delmore. IX, 96-114.
The Science of the Night. VIII, 228.
"Science! true daughter of Old Time thou art!" IV, 185.
Scottsboro, Too, Is Worth Its Song. VIII, 220.
Scrapbooks. X, 273.
Sea-Birds. V, 237.
Sea Gods. VII, 240.
The Sea Gypsy. VI, 119.
The Seafarer. VII, 194.
Seawall, Samuel. I, 150-151.
"See how the black ship cleaves the main." II, 160.
"See! I give myself to you, Beloved!" VII, 33.
"See, see, bluff winter quits the town." III, 7.
"Seeds in a dry pod, tick, tick, tick." VII, 5.
Seer. IX, 62.
"Señora, it is true the Greeks are dead." VIII, 129.
"Sephora held her to her heart." III, 253.
"September 1957 summoned by my vision-agent." X, 203.
"September twenty-second, Sir: today." IX, 247.
A Serenade. III, 271.
The Serenade. III, 243.
Sestina from the Home Gardener. X, 256.
Sestina: Altaforte. VII, 191.
Seth Compton. VII, 8.
Shadow-Evidence. V, 234.
The Shadow Dance. V, 250.
Shadows. IX, 279.
"The shadows lay along Broadway." IV, 50.
Shake, Mulleary, and Go-ethe. V, 307.
"Shall we win at love or shall we lose." X, 121.
The Shape of the Fire. IX, 24.
Shapiro, Karl. IX, 134-154.
Shaw, John. III, 11-14.
She Came and Went. IV, 265.
"She comes—the spirit of the dance!" IV, 221.
"She drew back; he was calm." VII, 70.
"She grew up in bedeviled southern wilderness." IX, 118.
"She in whose lipservice." X, 43.
"She limps with halting painful pace." VII, 134.
"She sang beyond the genius of the sea." VIII, 19.
"She sat beside her lover, and her hand." III, 236.
"She sees her image in the glass." V, 250.
She Was a Beauty. V, 306.
"Shedding out petty pruderies." VII, 131.
A Shelf Is a Ledge. X, 295.
Sherman. VI, 35.
Sherman, Frank Dempster. V, 313-316.
Shiloh. V, 56.
Shine, Perishing Republic. VIII, 44.
"A shiny arm from/the hoary firmamemt." X, 288.

"Shot-off/arms and legs." VII, 162.
"Should I get married? Should I be good?" X, 194.
Should the Wide World Roll Away. VI, 197.
"Should you ask me whence these stories?" IV, 113.
The Shrine. VII, 242.
"Shun radiant Love and bar him out." VI, 82.
"Shut fast again in beauty's sheath." VI, 102
"Shuttle-cock and battle-dore." VII, 129.
Siegfried. IX, 167.
A Sigh. VI, 18.
Sigourney, Lydia (Huntley). III, 117-141.
Silence. VII, 23.
Sill, Edward Rowland. V, 263-270.
"A silver Lucifer." VII, 125.
Simms, William Gilmore. III, 273-278.
"Simon my son, son of my Nuptiall knott." I, 62.
The Simple Cobler of Aggawam in America, sels. I, 2.
Simplicity. II, 5.
Simpson, Louis. 52-62.
The Sin of Hamlet. IX, 102.
"Since every quill is silent to Relate." I, 143.
"Since of no creature living the last breath." VII, 287.
Sing with Your Body. X, 309.
The Singers in a Cloud. VI, 275.
The Sins of Kalamazoo. VII, 83.
Sir Gawaine and the Green Knight. VIII, 193.
The Sisters. VI, 38.
Siwashing It Out Once in Siuslaw Forest. X, 216.
Six O'Clock. IX, 193.
"Six street-ends come together here." VII, 80.
The Skeleton in Armor. IV, 56.
"The skies they were ashen and sober." IV, 202.
"Skimming lightly, wheeling still." V, 56.
Skipper Ireson's Ride. V, 4.
The Sky Is Low, the Clouds Are Mean. V, 200.
"A sky that has never known sun, moon or stars." VII, 292.
"The sky/Is that beautiful old parchment." VII, 159.
A Slant of Sun. VI, 226.
The Slave's Dream. IV, 61.
The Slave. VII, 114.
"Sleep softly...eagle/forgotten...under the stone." VII, 98.
"Sleep sweetly in your humble graves." V, 173.
The Sleeper. III, 156.
The Sleepers. V, 145.
Slow but Sure. VII, 162.
"Slowly the black earth gains upon the yellow." VI, 112.
"The sluggish smoke curls up from some deep dell." IV, 244.
Smoke. IV, 237.
Smoke in Winter. IV, 244.
"A smoky rain riddles the ocean plains." IX, 288.
Snapshots of a Daughter-in-Law. X, 186.
Snodgrass, W.D. X, 128-142.
"Snow falling and night falling fast, oh, fast." VII, 67.

Snow-bound. V, 14.
Snow-Flakes. V, 235.
The Snow-Storm. IV, 21.
"Snowmelt pond warm granite." X, 214.
Snyder, Gary. X, 204-218.
"So fallen! so lost! the light withdrawn." V, 2.
"So love is dead that has been quick so long!" V, 252.
"So much comes to mind." X, 303.
"So much depends/upon/a red wheel." VII, 146.
"So much I have forgotten in ten years." VII, 272.
"So what said the others and the sun went down." VIII, 23.
"So you have swept me back." VII, 245.
"So youre playing." X, 265.
Socrates' Ghost Must Haunt Me Now. IX, 107.
"Softly now the light of day." IV, 11.
"Softly the moonlight." III, 243.
Solar Myth. VIII, 132.
"Soldier boys." VII, 161.
"A soldier of the Cromwell stamp." V, 258.
The Soldier's Visit to His Family. III, 145.
"Solemn he paced upon that schooner's..." III, 262.
Solipsism. VI, 108.
"Some say the world will end in fire." VII, 64.
"Some time now past in the Autumnal Tide." I, 39.
Some Trees. X, 148.
"Somebody loses whenever somebody wins." VII, 82.
"Someone has fallen to the earth." IX, 79.
"Something that woke me out of sleep." IX, 94.
"Sometimes when my eyes are red." X, 100.
Sometimes, When Winding Slow. IV, 280.
Song. III, 270.
Song. X, 93.
The Song of Hiawatha, sels. IV, 113.
Song of Myself. V, 84.
Song of Slaves in the Desert. V, 9.
Song of the Stars. III, 194.
A Song of the Wave. VI, 235.
Song, fr. The Marriage of Guenevere. VI, 116.
Song, to the Gods, Is Sweetest Sacrifice. V, 247.
The Songs of Maximus. X, 12.
Songs to a Woman. VII, 293.
Sonnet—To Science. IV, 185.
Sonnet from 'One Person'. VII, 182.
"Soon as the sun forsook the eastern main." II, 134.
"Soon will the lonesome cricket by the stone." VI, 54.
"Sorrow is my own yard." VII, 142.
Sorrow Is the only Faithful One. IX, 198.
The Sot-Weed Factor, sels. I, 170.
The Soul Selects Her Own Society. V, 212.
Sourwood Mountain. IV, 311.
The Sower. VI, 54.
"Space is too full. Did nothing happen here?" VIII, 135.
"The spacious Noon enfolds me with its peace." V, 253.

"Spades take up leaves." VII, 58.
Sparkling and Bright. IV, 47.
The Sparrow. VII, 154.
"Spawn of fantasies." VII, 127.
"Speak! speak! thou fearful guest." IV, 56.
The Speaking Tree. IX, 132.
Speech to a Crowd. VIII, 126.
The Speeding of the King's Spite. V, 286.
Spenser's Ireland. VIII, 60.
The Spider and the Ghost of the Fly. VII, 106.
A Spirit Sped. VI, 223.
"Spirit that breathest through my lattice..." III, 223.
Spofford, Harriet Elizabeth. VI, 14-18.
The Spoon River Anthology, sels. VII, 2.
The Spooniad. VII, 13.
Sprague, Charles. IV, 1-6.
Spring. III, 248.
Spring and All. VII, 143.
Spring in Carolina. V, 180.
Spring in New Hampshire. VII, 273.
Spring Night. VII, 169.
A Spring Night in Shokoku-ji. X, 216.
"Spring, with that nameless pathos in the air." V, 180.
"Squeak the fife, and beat the drum." III, 2.
St. Malachy. IX, 226.
"Stand from my shadow where it goes." X, 179.
"Stand! the ground's your own, my braves." III, 8.
Stansbury, Joseph. II, 72-76.
Starbuck, George. X, 219-227.
The Stars. V, 232.
The Stars Are Hidden. VIII, 152.
"The state with the prettiest name." IX, 53.
Statue and Birds. VIII, 161.
Stedman, Clarence Edmund. IV, 1-13.
Steere, Richard. I, 128-149.
A Stein Song. VI, 125.
"Stephen Smith, University of Iowa sophomore burned." X, 220.
Steps. X, 115
Sterling George. VI, 145-149.
"Sternly my eyebrows meet as murmuring" IX, 37.
Stevens, Wallace. VIII, 9-35.
Stickney, Trumbull. VI, 239-269.
"Still as/On windless nights." VI, 278.
"Still was the night, Serene and Bright." I, 70.
Still, Citizen Sparrow. IX, 294.
"Stirring porchpots up with green-fingered witchcra." X, 222.
Stone Reality Meditation. X, 33.
Stonewall Jackson. V, 37.
Stopping by Woods on a Snowy Evening. VII, 64.
A Story About Chicken Soup. X, 53.
"The stranger in my gates—lo! that am I." VI, 148.
"Stranger, if thou hast learned a truth which needs." III, 180.
The Stranger. X, 190.

Stray Animals. X, 286.
A Street in Bronzeville. IX, 258.
"Strengthened to live, strengthened to die for." VIII, 62.
The Strife Between the Poet and Ambition. IX, 221.
"A striped blouse in a clearing by Bazille." IX, 296.
"Stronger for stress and strain." V, 41.
Strontium 90 Is Slowly Falling Out. IX, 67.
A Strut for Roethke. IX, 187.
"The students, lost in raucousness." IX, 231.
The Subverted Flower. VII, 70.
Subway Wind. VII, 280.
Suicide. VII, 163.
Summer Rain. IV, 235.
"Summer. Sunset. Someone is playing." IX, 166.
Summertime and the Living... IX, 124.
"The sun rises." X, 157.
"The sun shines bright in the old Kentucky home." IV, 295.
"The sun sought thy dim bed and brought forth light." VII, 277.
"The sun that brief December day." V, 14.
"The sun woke me this morning loud." X, 119.
Sunday Morning. VIII, 10.
Sunlight Is Imagination. IX, 289.
A Sunny Day. VIII, 154.
"Suppose it is nothing but the hive." VII, 11.
Supposing That I Should. VI, 205.
"Surely that moan is not the thing." X, 170.
Susanna and the Elders. VI, 278.
The Swamp Fox. III, 274.
Sweet Betsy from Pike. IV, 302.
"Sweet Robin, I have heard them say." IV, 12.
Sweet Sixteen Lines. X, 266.
"Sweetly (my Dearest) I left thee asleep." I, 63.
"Swift across the palace floor." V, 245.
"Swift o'er the sunny grass." V, 234.
Swing Low, Sweet Chariot. IV, 319.
"Switzerland! my country! 'tis to thee" III, 151.
A Sword in a Cloud of Light. IX, 6.
The Synagogue. IX, 142.

"T'was mercy brought me from my Pagan land." II, 133.
Tabb, John Bannister. VI, 36-40.
Taggard, Genevieve. VIII, 131-139.
"Take him away, he's as dead as they die." VIII, 198.
"Take this kiss upon the brow." IV, 215.
Taliesin, sels. VI, 121.
Tall Stately Plants with Spikes and Forks of Gold. IV, 281.
"Tall, sombre, grim, against the morning sky." V, 222.
Tamerlane. IV, 164.
Tasting the Earth. VII, 119.
Tate, Allen. VIII, 184-190.
Tate, James. X, 282-289.
"Tawny are the leaves turned but they still hold." VIII, 107.

Taylor, Bayard. IV, 288-293.
Taylor, Edward. I, 96-115.
"Teach me the secret of thy loveliness." VI, 128.
Tears. VI, 87.
Teasdale, Sara. VII, 167-177.
Tell Brave Deeds of War. VI, 199.
"Tell her I love." VIII, 165.
"Tell me not, in mournful numbers." IV, 54.
"Tell me, my patient friends—awaiters of messages." VIII, 126.
"Tell me/ Was Venus more beautiful." VII, 33.
The Telltale. V, 240.
Ten Definitions of Poetry. VII, 76.
Ten Dreamers in a Motel. IX, 71.
"Tender, semi/articulate flickers." X, 79.
The Tennis Court Oath. X, 150.
"Terrible streets, the manichee hell of twilight." IX, 286.
Thanatopsis. III, 174.
"Thank heaven! the crisis." IV, 210.
A Thankful Acknowledgment of God's Providence. I, 5.
"Their faces do not change at their mouths." X, 252.
"Their time past, pulled down." VII, 151.
"Theris was a language within ours, a loge." X, 107.
Theme for English B. VIII, 210.
"Then sang Kalypso yet another song." VI, 240.
Theocritus. V, 244.
Theory of Flight. IX, 130.
"There are birds larger than us, I know that." X, 283.
"There are harps that complain...presence of night." III, 170.
"There are hermit souls that live withdrawn." V, 310.
"There are many monsters that a glassen surface." X, 110.
"There are miracles that happen." X, 310.
"There are no handles upon a language." VII, 78.
"There are no stars to-night." VIII, 168.
"There are too many waterfalls here..." IX, 58.
There Came Whisperings. VI, 212.
"There comes Emerson first, whose rich words..." IV, 266.
"There comes Poe, with his raven, like Barnaby..." IV, 276.
There Exists the Eternal Fact of Conflict. VI, 233.
There Has to Be a Jail for Ladies. IX, 227.
"There in his room, whene'er the moon looks in." VI, 92.
"There is a great amount of poetry in unconscious." VIII, 50.
"There is a place that some men know." VIII, 187.
"There is a sweetness in woman's decay." III, 241.
"There is a singer everyone has heard." VII, 52.
"There is an evening twilight of the heart." III, 110.
"There is Bryant, as quiet, as cool, and...dignified." IV, 268.
"There is Hawthorne, with genius so shrinking..." IV, 272.
"There is no dearer lover of lost hours." V, 187.
There Is Such Power Even in Smallest Things. VI, 50.
"There is the star bloom of the moss." IX, 202.
"There is Whittier, whose swelling and vehement..." IV, 270.
"There was an open grave,—and many an eye." III, 124.
"There once dwelt in Olympus some notable oddities." III, 265.

There Was a Child Went Forth. V, 63.
There Was a Crimson Clash of War. VI, 198.
There Was a Man and Woman. VI, 220.
There Was a Man Who Lived a Life of Fire. VI, 221.
"There was an infidel who." IX, 283.
"There was never a sound beside the wood but one." VII, 47.
There Was One. VI, 207.
There Was Set Before Me. VI, 203.
"There was such speed in her little body." VIII, 99.
There Was, Before Me. VI, 201.
There Were Many Who Went. VI, 199.
"There will be rose and rhododendron." VII, 284.
There Will Come Soft Rains. VII, 174.
"There's a fierce gray bird—with a sharpen'd beak." III, 143.
"There's beauty in the deep." III, 263.
"There's something in a noble boy." IV, 49.
"These are amazing: each." X, 148.
"These are my murmur-laden shells that keep." VI, 257.
"These autumn gardens, russet, gray and brown." VI, 262.
"These dried-out paint brushes which fell..." X, 256.
"These men were kings, albeit they were black." VIII, 219.
These Strewn Thoughts by the Mountain Pathway Sprung. VI, 105.
"They all looked dead with tingling ears." IX, 38.
"They brought me ambrotypes." VII, 10.
They Clapped. X, 270.
They Found Him Sitting in a Chair. VIII, 164.
"They lean over the path." IX, 13.
They lived Enamoured of the Lovely Moon. VI, 257.
"They say there is no hope." VII, 240.
"They set the slave free, striking off his chains." VII, 114.
"They tell me, Liberty! that in thy name." IV, 44.
"They wait all day unseen by us unfelt." V, 232.
"They went after him with a long stick." IX, 217.
"They will never die on that battlefield." X, 198.
"They've got a bran new organ, Sue." V, 274.
"Thine eyes shall see the light of distant skies." III, 224.
Things to Do Around a Lookout. X, 207.
Think as I Think. VI, 213.
"Think you I am not fiend and savage too?" VII, 276.
The Third World. X, 31.
Thirteen Ways of Looking at a Blackbird. VIII, 14.
"This bronze doth keep the very form and mould." VI, 34.
This Day Is Not Like That Day. IX, 208.
"This day writhes with what? The lecturer." VIII, 26.
"This ends: entering the show of silence." IX, 77.
"This I beheld, or dreamed it in a dream." V, 270.
This Is My Letter to the World. V, 212.
"This is the forest primeval. The murmuring pines..." IV, 63.
"This is the song of the wave! The mighty/one!" VI, 235.
"This is the black sea-brute bulling through wave..." X, 175.
"This is the world we wanted." X, 280.
"This is the beauty of being alone." X, 286.
"This loud morning." X, 31.

"This lovely flower fell to seed." VIII, 214.
"This morning of the small snow." X, 13.
"This old piano with a sweeter treble." IX, 36.
This Quiet Dust Was Gentleman and Ladies V, 197.
"This sparrow/who comes to sit at my window." VII, 154.
This Very Hour. VI, 90.
"This world is gradually becoming a place." IX, 190.
This World Is Not Conclusion. V, 204.
"This world was not." V, 300.
Thoreau. IV, 9.
Thoreau, Henry David. IV, 232-245.
"Those rivers run from that land." X, 93.
Thou Art Not Lovelier Than Lilacs, No. VII, 282.
"Thou ill-form'd offspring of my feeble brain." I, 39.
"Thou lookest up with meek, confiding eye." IV, 231.
"Thou sorrow, venom Elfe." I, 113.
"Thou unrelenting Past!" III, 221.
"Thou wast that all to me, love." IV, 192.
"Thou who wouldst see the lovely and the wild." III, 207.
"Thou, Sibyl rapt! whose sympathetic soul." IV, 8.
"Though gifts like thine the fates gave not." V, 255.
"Though I am native to this frozen zone." V, 257.
"Though I am little as all little things." VII, 115.
"Though loath to grieve." IV, 37.
"Though the Clerk of Weather insist." V, 53.
"The thoughts are strange that crowd into my brain." III, 260.
"Thrash away, you'll hev to rattle." IV, 257.
"Three A.M., the night is absolutely still." IX, 6.
Three Little Birds. VI, 194.
Three Quatrains. VI, 153.
"Thrice happy race! how blest were freedom's heirs." II, 130.
"Through the crowded street returning..." VI, 80.
"Thus briefly sketched the sacred Rights of Man." II, 115.
"Thy trivial harp will never please." IV, 32.
"Thy various works, imperial queen, we see." II, 135.
Time. X, 90.
Time in the Rock, sels. VII, 270.
"Time like the repetitions of a child's piano." VIII, 125.
"Time present and time past." VIII, 91.
"Time was when America hallowed the morn." II, 18.
"The times come round again." VIII, 192.
"The times wherein old Pompion was a Saint." I, 117.
Timrod, Henry. V, 164-182.
"Tiny green birds skate over the surface of the room." IX, 82.
Tired. VII, 255.
"[Tis Braul I Cudgel,] Ranters, Quakers *Braul.*" I, 7.
"To arms, brave countrymen!..." II, 22.
"To be able to see every side of every question." VII, 8.
"To him who in the love of Nature holds." III, 174.
"To hurt the Negro and avoid the Jew." IX, 137.
"To loosen with all ten fingers held wide & limber." IX, 14.
"To me, one silly task is like another." VIII, 161.
"To show the lab'ring bosom's deep intent." II, 137.

"To the sea shell's spiral round." V, 255.
"To what new fates, my country, far." VI, 120.
To-Night. V, 249.
To—. III, 105.
To a Dog's Memory. VI, 100.
To a Friend. III, 230.
To a Military Rifle. VIII, 192.
To a Recruiting Sergeant. IV, 257.
To a Robin. II, 171.
To a Waterfowl. III, 176.
To a Wind-Flower. VI, 128.
To a Young Man. VI, 52.
To an Author. II, 111.
To Cole, the Painter... III, 224.
To Delmore Schwartz. IX, 249.
To Elsie. VII, 144.
To Fancy. II, 171.
To Hafiz. V, 255.
To Helen I. IV, 187.
To Helen II. IV, 218.
To John Ashbery. X, 127
To Miss Ten Eyck. II, 128.
To My Mother. IV, 214.
To One in Paradise. IV, 192.
To Russia. VI, 29.
To S.M., a Young African Painter. II, 137.
To Seneca Lake. III, 240.
To Shelley. VI, 37.
To Sleep. IV, 224.
To the Americans of the United States. II, 117.
To the Dandelion. IV, 256.
To the Goddess of Liberty. VI, 146.
To the Holy Spirit. VIII, 195.
To the Memory of the Brave Americans. II, 98.
To the Moon. III, 126.
To the Rev'd Mr. Jno. Sparhawk on the Birth of His Son... I, 151.
To the White Fiends. VII, 276.
To W.P. VI, 106.
To Waken an Old Lady. VII, 141.
To Whistler, American. VII, 193.
"Toil on! toil on! ye ephemeral train." III, 119.
Tompson, Benjamin. I, 116-127.
"Too green the springing April grass." VII, 273.
The Torn Hat. IV, 49.
Torrence, Frederic Ridgely. VI, 270-275.
Tourist Death. VIII, 128.
Tourists. IX, 69.
"Towards the Noel that morte saison." VII, 190.
Tower of Babel. IX, 222.
The Town Ecologue. III, 7.
Tract. VII, 149.
Tradition, Thou Art for Suckling Children. VI, 212.
Transient Barracks. IX, 166.

Transplanting. IX, 15.
The Trees in the Garden. VI, 229.
"The trees rise from the darkness of the world." IX, 163.
Troop Train. IX, 139.
A True Account of Talking to the Sun at Fire Island. X, 119.
Trumbull, John. II, 28-71.
Trust. VI, 88.
Truth, Said a Traveller. VI, 204.
Try Tropic. VIII, 137.
Tuckerman, Frederick Goddard. IV, 278-287.
The Tuft of Flowers. VII, 47.
"Turning it over, considering, like a madman." IX, 188.
"'Twas sunset's hallow'd time—and such an eve" III, 28.
"'Twas the night before Christmas, when" III, 35.
"Twelve o'clock." VIII, 72.
"Twenty men crossing a bridge." VIII, 17.
Twenty Million. VII, 161.
Twilight. III, 110.
"'Twill soon be sunrise. Down the valley waiting" VI, 259.
"Twirling your blue skirts, traveling the sward." VIII, 100.
Two British Airmen. IX, 220.
The Two Comets. III, 265.
Two Epitaphs. VI, 101.
Two in August. VIII, 106.
Two or Three Angels. VI, 206.
"Two roads diverged in a yellow wood." VII, 51.
"Two that could not have lived their single lives." VIII, 106.
Two Tramps in Mud Time. VII, 65.
Two Ways. VII, 300.
"Two white heads the grasses cover." VI, 101.
Tyler, Royall, III, 1-18.
"Type of the antique Rome! Rich reliquary." IV, 190.

Uccello. X, 198.
Ulamlume. IV, 202.
The Ultimate Poem Is Abstract. VIII, 26.
Under a Keeping Spring. IX, 93.
"Under damp layers of pine needle." X, 213.
Under the Green Ledge. IX, 78.
"Under the lamp your hands do not seem red." X, 135.
Unfriendly Witness. X, 224.
"Unhappy dreamer, who outwinged in flight." VI, 104.
University. IX, 137.
The Unknown Dead. V, 177.
Unmanifest Destiny. VI, 120.
Unseen Spirits. IV, 50.
Untermeyer, Louis. VII, 219-224.
Unto My Books So Good to Turn. V, 198.
Unwind My Riddle. VI, 231.
"Up and down he goes." VII, 159.
"Up the reputable walks of old established trees." X, 132.
"Up with thy banners! Out with all thy strength." III, 166.

Upon a Spider Catching a Fly. I, 113.
"Upon the Earth there are so many Treasures." I, 129.
Upon the Much-To Be Lamented Desease of...John Cotton. I, 35.
Upon the Road of My Life. VI, 219.
An Upper Chamber in a Darkened House. IV, 281.
An Urban Convalescence. X, 108.

V-Letter. IX, 144.
A Valentine. IV, 201.
Van Doren, Mark. VIII, 146-150.
Vanishing Patriot. VII, 162.
Vapor Trail Reflected in the Frog Pond. X, 158.
Vendor's Song. VI, 277.
The Ventian Blind. IX, 162.
Venus Transiens. VII, 33.
The Vernal Age. II, 83.
Verses to the Shearwater. II, 163.
Very, Jones. IV, 229-231.
The Vestal Lady on Brattle. X, 199.
Vicksburg. V, 223.
Victor and Vanquished. VI, 80.
Views to See Clayton From. IX, 65.
The Village Atheist. VII, 12.
Villanelle: The Psychological Hour. VII, 199.
Villonaud for This Yule. VII, 190.
Virgilia. VI, 66.
The Vision of Columbus, sels. II, 141.
Vision of Rotterdam. X, 203.
A Vision of the Alps. III, 127.
A Visit from St. Nicholas. III, 35.
A Visitor in Marl. V, 206.
The Voice. VII, 173.
Votive Song. III, 272.
Voyages. VIII, 177.
The Voyages. X, 295.
"The vultures hover wheel and hover." IX, 121.

"Wade/through black jade." VIII, 48.
"Wakeful, vagrant, restless thing." II, 78.
Wakowski, Diane. X, 253-262.
Wales Visitation. X, 97.
A Walk in Late Summer. IX, 30.
Walker, Alice. X, 290-293.
Walking in the Sky. VI, 219.
"Walking to the museum." X, 223.
"Wallowing in this bloody sty." IX, 243.
Walt Whitman. VI, 76.
Walt Whitman at Bear Mountain. X, 54.
The Wander-Lovers. VI, 117.
"Wandering oversea dreamer." VII, 86.
The War Against the Trees. VIII, 227.

Ward, Nathaniel. I, 1-3.
The Warning. VI, 279.
Warren's Address to the American Soldiers... III, 68.
Warren, Mercy. II, 4-9
Warren, Robert Penn. VIII, 232-237.
The Waste Land. VIII, 74.
"Watching hands transplanting." IX, 15.
Water. X, 207.
Water Walker. IX, 283.
"The Water-Lily." VI, 37.
Waterchew! X, 202.
"The waves forever move." VI, 38.
"Way down upon de Swanee ribber." IV, 298.
The Way to Arcady. V, 303.
The Wayfarer. VI, 226.
"We are but two—the others sleep." IV, 2.
"We are children of the sun." VII, 253.
"We are here, in another provisional city." X, 302.
"We are large with pity, slow and awkward." IX, 204.
"We are the hollow men." VIII, 87.
"We are things of dry hours & the involuntary plan." IX, 258.
"We are waiting in separate rooms." IX, 211.
"We break the glass, whose sacred wine." III, 270.
"We couldn't even keep the furnace lit!" IX, 249.
"We follow where the Swamp Fox guides." III, 274.
"We love with great difficulty." X, 309.
"We make our meek adjustments." VIII, 169.
"We might have coupled." VII, 130.
We Needs Must Be Divided in the Tomb. VI, 106.
"We poor Agawams." I, 2.
"We stood up before day." VIII, 116.
"We took it to the woods, we two." V, 233.
"We were very tired, we were very merry." VII, 283.
"We'd rather have the iceberg than the ship." IX, 49.
"We've our business to attend day's duties." IX, 278.
The Weary Blues. VIII, 203.
Weaver, John V.A. VII, 297-300.
Wedding-Ring. X, 46.
"Weehawken! In thy mountain scenery yet." III, 111.
Weekhawken. III, 111.
"Weep not, weep not." VIII, 6.
Weiss, Theodore. IX, 230-237.
"Welcome me, if you will." X, 123.
"Well, as you say, we live for small horizons." VII, 262.
Westport. X, 166.
Westward Ho! VI, 26.
"Westward, hit a low note, for a roarer lost." IX, 187.
What Are Years? VIII, 59.
What Do I Know of the Old Lore? IX, 273.
"What does not change/is the will to change." X, 3.
"What god will choose me from this labouring nation." VI, 109.
"What good is life without music." X, 287.
"What great yoked brutes with briskers low." VI, 28.

"What had you been thinking about." X, 150.
"What I am trying to say is this." IX, 214.
"What is Africa to me." VIII, 215.
"What is it now with me." X, 149.
"What is our innocence." VIII, 59.
"What is there saddening in the Autumn..." III, 264.
"What is this, behind this veil, is it ugly...?" X, 234.
"What love is this of thine, that cannot bee." I, 99.
"What means these dreams, and hideous forms..." II, 93.
What Mr. Robinson Thinks. IV, 262.
What My Lips Have Kissed, and Where, and Why. VII, 286.
"What shall her silence keep." VI, 129.
"What strength! what strife! what rude unrest!" VI, 26.
"What wholly blameless fun." IX, 288.
"What's the brightness of a brow?" VI, 17.
"What's this A dish for fat lips." IX, 24.
"Whatever it is, it must have." X, 53.
Wheatley, Phillis. II, 132-139.
"When a mere/Serb shot." VII, 161.
"When Abraham Lincoln was shoveled into the tombs..." VII, 79.
"When Ah was young Ah use' to wait." IV, 313.
"When Alexander Pope strolled in the city." VIII, 185.
"When beechen buds begin to swell." III, 178.
"When breezes are soft and skies are fair." III, 198.
"When Christmas-Eve is ended." VI, 7.
"When elemental conflicts rage." I, 190.
"When Faction, in league with the treacherous Gaul." II, 74.
"When first thou on me, Lord..." I, 97.
"When first this canvas felt Giogrione's hand." VI, 258.
"When Freedom, from her mountain height." III, 227.
When Good Queen Elizabeth Governed the Realm. II, 73.
"When I am dead and over me bright April." VII, 170.
"When I am feeling depressed and anxious sullen." X, 126.
"When I am the sky." X, 43.
"When I consider Life and its few years." VI, 87.
"When I died, the circulating library." VII, 8.
When I Heard at the Close of the Day. V, 69.
When I Heard the Learned Astronomer. V, 63.
"When I was a child." X, 127.
"When I was about ten." X, 299.
When Lilacs Last in the Dooryard Bloom'd. V, 154.
"When Nature had made all her birds." IV, 226.
"When night believes itself alone." IX, 292.
When on the Marge of Evening. VI, 99.
"When psalms surprise me with their music." IX, 225.
When She Comes Home. V, 285.
"When spring to woods and wastes around." III, 177.
"When sun, light handed, sows this Indian water." IX, 224.
"When the flowers turn to husks." X, 157.
"When the forests have been destroyed..." X, 169.
When the Frost Is on the Punkin. V, 297.
"When the Norn Mother saw the Whirlwind Hour." VI, 58.
"When the radiant morn of creation broke." III, 177.

"When the stars pursue their solemn flight." VI, 17.
When the Sultan Goes to Ispahan. V, 256.
"When the tree of love is budding first." III, 106.
"When the world turns completely upside down." VII, 182.
"When we see/the houses again." X, 170.
"When Yankees, skilled in martial rule." II, 59.
"When youth was lord of my unchallenged fate." V, 183.
"When, to the common rest that crowns our days." III, 181.
Whence with morn's first blush of light." II, 163.
"Whence, O fragrant form of light." VI, 37.
"Whenever a snow-flake leaves the sky." V, 235.
"Whenever Richard Cory went down town." VI, 153.
"Where are Elmer, Herman, Bert, Tom and Charley." VII, 2.
"Where are we going? where are we going." V, 9.
"Where is/the physic." VII, 166.
Where Knock Is Open Wide. IX, 27.
"Where the pheasant roosts at night." II, 83.
Where the Rainbow Ends. IX, 248.
"Where the wings of a sunny Dome expand." V, 44.
"Where the wind/year round out of the gap." X, 174.
"Where were the greenhouses going." IX, 14.
"While I recline." V, 164.
"Where my hair was still cut straight across..." VII, 198.
While the Musician Played. V, 291.
"While this America settles in the mold...vulgarity." VIII, 44.
"Whirl up, sea." VII, 239.
"The whiskey on your breath." IX, 17.
"A whisper woke the air." IV, 221.
"White fog lifting & falling on mountain-brow." X, 97.
"A white sheet on the tail-gate of a truck." IX, 146.
White Symphony. VII, 232.
"Whither, 'midst falling dew." III, 176.
Whitman, Walt. V, 60-163.
Whittier. IV, 270.
Whittier, John Greenleaf. V, 1-34.
"Who are these people at the bridge to meet me?..." X, 236.
"Who can make a delicate adventure." VII, 292.
"Who has ever stopped to think of the divinity of." X, 243.
"Who has robb'd the ocean cave." III, 14.
Who Is That A-Walking in the Corn? VII, 251.
"Who nearer Nature's life would truly come." IV, 9.
"Who tamed your lawless Tartar blood?" VI, 29.
"Whole-towns shut down." X, 215.
"Whose furthest footsteps never strayed." VI, 124.
"Whose woods these are I think I know." VII, 64.
Why Do You Strive for Greatness, Fool? VI, 216.
"Why do you talk so much." X, 160.
"Why do you/complain." VII, 163.
"'Why do/You thus devise.'" VI, 278.
"Why has our poetry eschewed." VII, 221.
Why I Am Not a Painter. X, 118.
"Why make your lodging here in this spent lane." VI, 90.
"Why seraphim like lutanists arranged." VIII, 21.

"Why should this Negro insolently stride." VII, 179.
The Widow's Lament in Springtime. VII, 142.
Widows. VII, 21.
Wigglesworth, Michael. I, 69-92.
Wilbur, Richard. IX, 282-298.
"Wild Carthage held her, Rome." VI, 89.
Wild Cherry. VI, 90.
The Wild Honeysuckle. II, 108.
Wild May. VII, 274.
Wild Peaches. VII, 182.
"Poet, will you, like other men." VII, 294.
Williams, Roger. I, 26-33.
Williams, William Carlos. VII, 136-157.
Willis, Nathaniel Parker. IV, 48-50.
Wilson, John. I, 6-8.
"The wind shakes the mists." VII, 226.
"The wind stuffs the scum of the white street." VII, 131.
The Wind-Flower. IV, 231.
The Winged Worshippers. IV, 3.
"Winked too much and were afraid of snakes..." VIII, 51.
"The winters close. Springs open, no child stirs." IX, 178.
Winters, Yvor. VIII, 191-196.
The Witch of Coos. VII, 59.
With Child. VIII, 132.
With Eye and with Gesture. VI, 218.
"With eyes hand-arched he looks into." VI, 128.
"With its baby rivers and little towns..." VIII, 52.
"With Joy erst while, (when knotty doubts arose)." I, 35.
With Wild Flowers to a Sick Friend. III, 120.
"Within a delicate grey ruin." X, 199.
"Within the Casket of thy Coelick Breast." I, 62.
"Witness now this trust! the rain." VIII, 170.
"Wo worth the days! The days I spent." I, 153.
The Wolverine's Song. IV, 301.
"A woman in the shape of a monster." X, 185.
"The woman named Tomorrow." VII, 88.
Women. VIII, 160.
"Women have no wilderness in them." VIII, 160.
Wonder-working Providence of Sions Saviour in New-England. I, 25.
The Wood-Pile. VII, 49.
"The woods stretch wild to the mountain side." VI, 130.
Woodworth, Samuel. III, 41-44.
Woof of the Sun, Ethereal Gauze. IV, 245.
Words. X, 239.
World Breaking Apart. X, 281.
The World Is a Mighty Ogre. VII, 257.
"The world is bright before thee." III, 105.
The World is Not a Pleasant Place to Be. X,
The World. X, 87.
"Wrap up in a blanket in cold weather and just read." X, 200.
Writing for Nora. X, 301.
Writing in the Dark. X, 51.
Wylie, Elinor. VII, 178-185.

'Wynken, Blynken, and Nod one night." VI, 42.

"Ye Alps audacious, through the heavens that rise." II, 148.
"Ye elms that wave on Malvern Hill." V, 48.
"Ye hard fisted, log cabin, Wolverine boys." IV, 301.
"Ye young debaters over the doctrine." VII, 12.
"The years have gone. It is spring." IX, 2.
The Yellow Violet. III, 178.
"Yes, faint was my applause and cold my praise." III, 230.
Yes, I Have a Thousand Tongues. VI, 195.
"Yes, there is yet one way to where she is." VI, 153.
"Yes, when the toilsome day is gone." III, 39.
Yet Vain, Perhaps the Fruits. IV, 282.
"You also, our first great." VII, 193.
"You are a friend then, as I make it out." VI, 172.
"You are like startled song-wings against my heart." VII, 293.
"You bet it would've made a tender movie!" X, 266.
"You do not do, you do not do." X, 230.
"You look/in your glass." VII, 164.
"You said, that October." X, 217.
You Say You Are Holy. VI, 215.
"You sing, you." X, 15.
"You speak. You say: Today's character is not." VIII, 33.
"You that know the way." X, 176.
"You were angry and manly to shatter the sleep..." IX, 140.
You Were Wearing. X, 76.
"You would think the fury of the aerial bombardment." VIII, 224.
"You'd scarce expect one of my age." III, 10.
You, Andrew Marvell. VIII, 122.
"You, once a belle in Shreveport." X, 186.
"A young editor wants me to write on Kabbalah..." IX, 273.
The Young Housewife. VII, 140.
Young, Al. X, 263-267.
"Your face did not rot." X, 289.
"Your hand in mine, we walk out." IX, 6.
"Your heart is a music-box, dearest." IV, 223.
"Your leaves bound up compact and fair." II, 111.
"Your mind and you are our Sargasso Sea." VII, 193.
"Your thighs are appletrees." VII, 138.
Youth. VI, 237.
A Youth in Apparel That Glittered. VI, 204.
"Youth is the time when hearts are large." V, 46.

"Zeus lies in Ceres' bosom." VII, 213.
Zizi's Lament. X, 187.
Zophiel, sels. III, 253.

ACKNOWLEDGMENTS

Permission to reprint copyrighted poems is
gratefully acknowledged to the following:

ATHENEUM PUBLISHERS, INC., for "The Asians Dying" and "The River of Bees" from *The Lice* by W.S.
Merwin. Copyright © 1967 by W.S. Merwin. "Leviathan" from *Green with Beasts* (1956) in *The First Four
Books of Poems* by W.S. Merwin. Copyright © 1975 by W.S. Merwin. "Fog-Horn" and "The Drunk in the
Furnace" from *The Drunk in the Furnace* by W.S. Merwin. Copyright © 1960 by W.S. Merwin. "Lemuel's
Blessing" from *The Moving Target* by W.S. Merwin. Copyright © 1963 by W.S. Merwin. "The Removal"
and "Footprints of the Glacier" from *The Carrier of Ladders* by W.S. Merwin. Copyright © 1970 by W.S.
Merwin. "Blind William's Song" from *A Mask for Janus* in *The First Four Books of Poems* by W.S.
Merwin. Copyright © 1975 by W.S. Merwin. Copyright © 1952 by Yale University Press; copyright renewed
© 1980 by W.S. Merwin. "Last Words" from *The Fire Screen* by James Merrill. Copyright © 1969 by James
Merrill. "The Octopus" from *The Country of a Thousand Years of Peace* by James Merrill. Copyright 1951,
1952, 1953, 1954, © 1957, 1958, 1970; copyright renewed © 1979, 1980, 1981, 1982 by James Merrill. "An
Urban Convalescence" from *Water Street* (1962) in *From the First Nine: Poems 1946-1976* by James Merrill.
Copyright © 1982 by James Merrill. "The Broken Home" and "The Mad Scene" from *Night and Days* (1966)
in *From the First Nine: Poems 1946-1976* by James Merrill. Copyright © 1982 by James Merrill. "The
Peacock" from *First Poems* (1951) in *From the First Nine: Poems 1946-1976* by James Merrill. Copyright ©
1982 by James Merrill.
BOA EDITIONS, LTD., for "Magda Goebbels" from *The Fuhrer Bunker: A Cycle of Poems in Progress* by W.D.
Snodgrass. Copyright © 1977 by W.D. Snodgrass.
GEORGE BORCHARDT INC. and JOHN ASHBERY, for "The Instruction Manual"; "Some Trees" and
"A Boy" from *Some Trees* by John Ashbery. Copyright © 1956 by John Ashbery. "Endless Variation" by
John Ashbery (first appeared in *Brooklyn Review*). Copyright © 1984 by John Ashbery.
CITY LIGHTS BOOKS, for "The Mad Yak"; "Vision of Rotterdam"; "Zizi's Lament"; "Uccello"; "But I Do Not
Need Kindness" and "Hello" from *Gasoline* by Gregory Corso. Copyright © 1955, 1958 by Gregory Corso.
"The Vestal Lady on Brattle" from *The Vestal Lady on Brattle and Other Poems* by Gregory Corso.
Copyright © 1955, 1958 by Gregory Corso. "Steps" and "Poem (Lana Turner Has Collapsed!)" from *Lunch
Poems* by Frank O'Hara. Copyright © 1964 by Frank O'Hara.
DOUBLEDAY & COMPANY, INC., for "Patriotic Poem"; "From a Girl in a Mental Institution"; "Belly Dancer"
and "Picture of a Girl Drawn in Black and White" from *Trilogy* by Diane Wakoski. Copyright © 1962, 1966,
1967 by Diane Wakoski. "Janie Crawford," copyright © 1964 by *Aphra*. vol. 5, no. 3; "Now That the Book Is
Finished," copyright © 1979 by Alice Walker; "Facing the Way" first appeared in *Freedom Ways*. vol. 15, no.
4 and "Good Night, Willie Lee, I'll See You in the Morning" first appeared in *Iowa Review*, copyright © 1975
by Alice Walker. All poems from GOOD NIGHT, WILLIE LEE, I'LL SEE YOU IN THE MORNING by
Alice Walker.
THE ECCO PRESS, for "Gretel in Darkness" from *The House on Marshland* by Louise Glück, published by The
Ecco Press in 1975. Copyright © 1971, 1972, 1973, 1974, 1975, by Louise Glück. "The Garden"; "Portrait"
and "World Breaking Apart" from *Descending Figure* by Louise Glück, published by The Ecco Press in
1980. Copyright © 1976, 1977, 1978, 1979, 1980 by Louise Glück. "The Lost Pilot" from *The Lost Pilot* by
James Tate. Copyright © 1978 by James Tate. Published by the Ecco Press in 1982.
ESTATE OF CHARLES OLSON, for "The Kingfishers"; "The Ring Of"; "A Newly Discovered 'Homeric' Hymn"
and "The Moon Is the Number 18". Copyright © 1960, 1970 by Charles Olson.
LAWRENCE FERLINGHETTI, for "He" by Lawrence Ferlinghetti. Copyright © by Lawrence Ferlinghetti.
GROVE PRESS, for "Les Etiquettes Jaunes" from *Meditations in an Emergency* by Frank O'Hara.
HARPER & ROW, PUBLISHERS, INC., for "The Gourd Dancer" and "Krasnopresnenskaya Station" Copyright
© 1976 by N. Scott Momaday. "The Delight Song of Tsoai-Talee" copyright © 1975 by N. Scott Momaday.
From *The Gourd Dancer* by N. Scott Momaday. "My Sad Self" copyright © 1958 by Allen Ginsberg. "Ode
to Failure" copyright © 1982 by Allen Ginsberg. "Wales Visitation" copyright © 1968 by Allen Ginsberg.
From *The Collected Poems of Allen Ginsberg 1947-1980*. "Daddy"; "A Birthday Present" and "The Bee
Meeting" copyright © 1963 by Ted Hughes. "Nick and the Candlestick" copyright © 1966 by Ted Hughes.
"Words" copyright © 1965 by Ted Hughes. From *The Collected Poems of Sylvia Plath* edited by Ted
Hughes.

HOUGHTON MIFFLIN COMPANY, for "In the Fields of Summer"; "Cells Breathe in the Emptiness"; "For Robert Frost"; "The Homecoming of Emma Lazarus" from *Flower Herding on Mount Monadnock* by Galway Kinnell. Copyright © 1964 by Galway Kinnell. "The Bear"; "Vapor Trail Reflected in the Frog Pond" from Body Rags by Galway Kinnell. Copyright © 1967 by Galway Kinnell. "Westport" from *What a Kingdom It Was* by Galway Kinnell. Copyright © 1969 by Galway Kinnell. "The Comfort of Darkness" from *The Avenue Bearing the Initial of Christ into the New World* by Galway Kinnell. Copyright © 1953, 1954, 1955, 1959, 1960, 1961, 1963, 1964, 1970, 1971, 1974 by Galway Kinnell. "Physical Universe" from *The Best Hour of the Night* by Louis Simpson. Copyright © 1983 by Louis Simpson. Reprinted by permission of Ticknor & Fields, a Houghton Mifflin Company.

MARK JARMAN, for "Lullaby for Amy" and "Writing for Nora" from *North Sea* by Mark Jarman. Copyright © by Mark Jarman. "Greensleeves" from *The Rote Walker* by Mark Jarman. Copyright © by Mark Jarman.

ALFRED A. KNOPF, INC., for "The Colossus" from *The Colossus and Other Poems* by Sylvia Plath. Copyright © 1961 by Sylvia Plath. "Mhtis Ou Tis"; "At the Park Dance" from *Heart's Needle* by W.D. Snodgrass. Copyright © 1959 by W.D. Snodgrass. "Autobiographia Literaria"; "Ode: Salute to the French Negro Poets"; "Why I Am Not a Painter"; "A True Account of Talking to the Sun at Fire Island"; "Hotel Transylvanie"; "For James Dean"; "Poem" ("A la recherche d'Gertrude Stein"); "To John Ashbery" from *The Collected Poems of Frank O'Hara* edited by Donald Allen. Copyright © 1956, 1958, 1959, 1960, 1967, 1968, 1971 by Maureen Gransville-Smith, Administratrix of the Estate of Frank O'Hara. "April Inventory" and "The Campus on the Hill" from *Heart's Needle* by W.D. Snodgrass. Copyright © 1957, 1958 by W.D. Snodgrass.

KENNETH KOCH, for "Mending Sump"; "Fresh Air" and "You Were Wearing". Copyright © 1962 by Kenneth Koch.

LITTLE, BROWN AND COMPANY, in association with THE ATLANTIC MONTHLY PRESS, for "Of Late" from *White Paper: Poems* by George Starbuck. Copyright © 1966 by George Starbuck. Originally appeared in *Poetry Magazine*.

LOUISIANA STATE UNIVERSITY PRESS, for "Birthday Poem" and "One West Coast" from *The Blues Don't Change* by Al Young. Copyright © 1965, 1966, 1967, 1968, 1969, 1970, 1971, 1972, 1973, 1974, 1975, 1976, 1977, 1978, 1979, 1980, 1981, and 1982 by Al Young.

JAMES MERRILL, for "Foliage of Vision" and "The Parnassians" by James Merrill. Copyright © by James Merrill.

JANICE MIRIKITANI, for "Breaking Silence"; copyright © by Janice Mirikitani. "Sing with Your Body" from *Awake in the River*, Isthmus Press. Copyright © 1978 by Janice Mirikitani.

WILLIAM MORROW & COMPANY, INC., for "Guerrilla Handbook"; "Ka'Ba"; "Political Poem"; "In Memory of Radio"; "Beautiful Black Women"; "Preface to a Twenty Volume Suicide Note"; "An Agony. As Now" and "Goodbye" from *Selected Poetry of Amiri Baraki/LeRoi Jones*. Copyright © 1961, 1969, 1979 by Amiri Baraka. "They Clapped"; "The World Is Not A Pleasant Place To Be" and "Scrapbooks" from *My House* by Nikki Giovanni. Copyright © 1972 by Nikki Giovanni. "Knoxville, Tennessee"; "The Funeral of Martin Luther King Jr." and "Nikki Rosa" from *Black Feeling, Black Talk, Black Judgement* by Nikki Giovanni. Copyright © 1968, 1970 by Nikki Giovanni. "Kidnap Poem" from *The Women and the Men*. Copyright © 1975 by Nikki Giovanni.

THE NATION, NATION ASSOCIATES INC., for "The Third World" by Lawrence Ferlinghetti.

NEW DIRECTIONS PUBLISHING CORPORATION, for "Marriage" and "Waterchew" from *The Happy Birthday of Death* by Gregory Corso. Copyright © 1960 by New Directions Publishing Corporation. "Constantly Risking Absurdity"; "The Penny Candy Store Beyond the El" and "I Am Waiting" from *A Coney Island of the Mind* by Lawrence Ferlinghetti. Copyright © 1958 by Lawrence Ferlinghetti. "Stone Reality Meditation"; "An Elegy to Dispel Gloom" and "Night Light" from *Endless Life* by Lawrence Ferlinghetti. Copyright © 1973, 1981 by Lawrence Ferlinghetti. "Monet's Lilies Shuddering" from *Who Are We Now* by Lawrence Ferlinghetti. Copyright © 1975 by Lawrence Ferlinghetti. "Rain Spirit Passing" and "Writing in the Dark" from *Candles in Babylon* by Denise Levertov. Copyright © 1982 by Denise Levertov. "The Old Adam"; "Come into Animal Presence" and "Crystal Night" (111) from *Poems 1960-1967* by Denise Levertov. Copyright © 1961, 1964 by Denise Levertov Goodman. "Wedding Ring" from *Life in the Forest* by Denise Levertov. Copyright © 1978 by Denise Levertov. "The Hands"; "The Goddess"; "Scenes from the Life of the Peppertrees" and "Pleasures" from *Collected Earlier Poems: 1940-1960* by Denise Levertov. Copyright © 1957, 1958, 1959 by Denise Levertov Goodman. "Cancion" from *The Freeing of the Dust* by Denise Levertov. Copyright © 1975 by Denise Levertov. "Four Poems for Robin" from *The Back Country* by Gary Snyder. Copyright © 1968 by Gary Snyder. "Logging"-14, 15; "Hunting"-3,4 and "Burning"-17 from *Myths and Texts* by Gary Snyder. Copyright © 1960 by Gary Snyder. "Affluence" and "Bedrock" from *Turtle Island* by Gary Snyder. Copyright © 1974 by Gary Snyder.

W.W. NORTON & COMPANY, INC., for "Snapshots of a Daughter-in-law"; "Orion"; "Planetarium"; "Prospective Immigrants Please Note"; "The Stranger" and "Diving into the Wreck" from *Adrienne Rich's*

Poetry, selected and edited by Barbara Charlesworth Gelpi and Albert Gelpi. Copyright © 1975 by W.W. Norton & Company, Inc.

GREGORY ORR, for "Making Beasts" and "Gathering the Bones Together" by Gregory Orr. Copyright © by Gregory Orr.

RANDOM HOUSE, INC., for specified lines 1-119 of "In Bed" from *Day and Nights* by Kenneth Koch. Copyright © 1982 by Kenneth Koch.

W.D. SNODGRASS, for "Old Apple Trees"; "Inquest"; "After Experience Taught Me" and "Monet: Les Nympheas" by W.D. Snodgrass. Copyright © by W.D. Snodgrass.

GARY SNYDER, for "Milton by Firelight" from *Cold Mountain Poems* by Gary Snyder. Copyright © by Gary Snyder. "Riprap" and "The Late Snow & Lumber Strike of the Summer of Fifty Four" from *Riprap* by Gary Snyder. Copyright © by Gary Snyder. "Things To Do Around a Lookout" and "Water" by Gary Snyder. Copyright © by Gary Snyder.

JAMES TATE, for "The Eagle Exterminating Company"; "Pity Ascending the Fog"; "Stray Animals"; "Read the Great Poets" and "Letting Him Go." Copyright © by James Tate.

UNIVERSITY OF CALIFORNIA PRESS, for "For You"; "For My Mother: Genevieve Jules Creeley"; "The Name"; "Kore"; "The Language"; "The Rescue"; "A Gift of Great Value"; "The World"; "Fire"; "Time"; "Just Friends"; "For Fear" and "Song" from *The Collected Poems of Robert Creeley, 1945-1975*. Copyright © 1983 by The Regents of the University of California. "I, Maximus of Gloucester, to You"; "The Songs of Maximus"; "Maximus to Himself" and "Cole's Island" from *The Maximus Poems* by Charles Olson. Copyright © 1982 by the Regents of the University of California.

UNIVERSITY OF PITTSBURGH PRESS, for "Poem for the Young White Man Who Asked How I, an Intelligent, Well-Read Person Could Believe in the War Between Races" from *Emplumada* by Lorna Dee Cervantes. Copyright © 1981 by Lorna Dee Cervantes.

VIKING PENGUIN INC., for "Fear of Death" from *Self-Portrait in a Convex Mirror* by John Ashbery. Copyright © 1974 by John Ashbery. Originally published in *The New Yorker*.

DIANE WAKOSKI, for "Sestina from the Home Gardener" and "An Apology" from *Inside the Blood Factory* by Diane Wakoski. Copyright © by Diane Wakoski.

FRANKLIN WATTS, INC., for "Chocolates" from *Caviare at the Funeral* by Louis Simpson. Copyright © 1980 by Louis Simpson.

YALE UNIVERSITY PRESS, for "Cora Punctuated with Strawberries"; "Outbreak of Spring"; "On First Looking in on Blodgett's Keats's 'Chapman's Homer'"; "Bone Thoughts on a Dry Day"; "Unfriendly Witness" and "Communication to the City Fathers of Boston" from *Bone Thoughts* by George Starbuck. Copyright © 1960 by George Starbuck.

AL YOUNG, for "Sweet Sixteen Lines" copyright © 1984 by Al Young. "Identities" copyright © 1971 by Al Young.

WESLEYAN UNIVERSITY PRESS, for "The Tennis Court Oath" from *The Tennis Court Oath* by John Ashbery. Copyright © 1962 by John Ashbery. "Schizophrenic Kiss" from *Viper Jazz* by James Tate. Copyright © 1973 by James Tate. "Walt Whitman at Bear Mountain"; "American Poetry"; "A Story About Chicken Soup" and "My Father in the Night Commanding No" from *At the End of the Open Road*. Copyright © 1960, 1963 by Louis Simpson. "My Father in the Night Commanding No" first appeared in *The New Yorker*. "Hot Night on Water Street" from *A Dream of Governors* by Louis Simpson. Copyright © 1957 by Louis Simpson. "The Voyages" and "A Shelf Is a Ledge" from *We Must Make a Kingdom of It* by Gregory Orr. Copyright © 1986 by Gregory Orr.